Psychology for Police Officers

Psychology for Police Officers

Ray Bull, Bob Bustin, Phil Evans and Denis Gahagan

JOHN WILEY & SONS

Chichester · New York · Brisbane · Toronto · Singapore

Library of Congress Cataloging in Publication Data:
Main entry under title:

Psychology for police officers.
  1. Police psychology. I. Bull, Ray.
HV7936.P75P79 1983   363.2'01'9   83-6806

ISBN 0 471 90194 6

British Library Cataloguing in Publication Data:

Psychology for police officers.
  1. Police psychology
  I. Bull, Ray
  363.2   HV7935.5

ISBN 0 471 90194 6

Typeset by MHL Typesetting Ltd., Coventry
Printed at the Pitman Press Ltd., Bath, Avon

Liberty is always dangerous, but it is the safest thing we have.

Harry Emerson Fosdick, *Liberty*.

Contents

Preface

In recent years I have become more and more of the opinion that the discipline of psychology has a lot to offer to the police officer in the great variety of tasks which he or she is required to carry out. This view has been supported by the feedback I have received from police officers who have attended one of our three-day residential psychology courses here at North East London Polytechnic. In the design of these courses (called 'Psychology for Police Officers') and the subsequent compilation of this book, we four psychologists gathered advice from police officers of all ranks concerning which aspects of human behaviour they wished to be advised about. The results of this fairly wide-ranging 'market research' are the chapters of this book. Each of the authors had a major responsibility for one or more chapters, he being a recognized expert on those topics. The resultant differences in style for the various chapters are the result of a decision we made to ensure that the book is readable and does not require any specified minimum of academic qualifications on the part of the reader.

Many people, including police officers, have only a vague idea of what psychology is and what psychologists do. The usual misconceptions concerning psychology are that it deals only with mental illness and child rearing, and that psychologists can read your mind or analyse you in some way. In fact, the vast majority of psychologists are engaged in work designed to further our understanding of the behaviour of *normal* people.

I am aware that some police officers and some individuals in the legal profession are indifferent or hostile towards psychology. If you know of any such people I hope that, due to reading this book, you will be able to modify a little their views. One can understand why some people say that psychology is of no use, or that it creates more problems than it solves. Each of us rightly believes that we possess a great deal of common sense concerning our understanding of human behaviour. We come into contact with people every day of our lives and we seem to interact successfully with them, and even understand them quite often. This intuitive knowledge that we have acquired, though frequently useful, may not always be a firm foundation upon which to base decisions. By their *scientific* study of human behaviour psychologists attempt to increase our understanding of why people do what they do, and what may be done to change things (if change is desirable).

In recent years I have become convinced that modern psychology has quite a lot to say that may be relevant to policing. In this book the relevance of some of the points being made will be obvious to you, but in other cases the relevance may be a little more indirect. The points of apparently more indirect relevance may permit you to see certain things partly in a new light and certain problems from a new angle.

In compiling this book we have taken from the vast breadth and depth that goes to make up the discipline of psychology those topics which we believe relevant to policing. In doing this we have kept in mind that police officers hold a variety of posts of responsibility in different forces, and that in the future they will move on to new forms of responsibility. We are also aware that the amount of formal study readers have already undertaken of human behaviour and of psychology in particular varies from a great deal to very little.

We four authors of this book are psychologists who believe that psychology should and can be applied to real life. Many readers will be practising police officers with much experience of real-life police work. I hope, in fact I'm sure, that we can work together towards a greater understanding of the problems which face us.

RAY BULL
NORTH EAST LONDON POLYTECHNIC, 1983.

Acknowledgements

Permission to reproduce the following material is gratefully acknowledged:

Figure 1.5, Canadian Psychological Association and B.R. Bugelski;
Figure 1.6, G.H. Fisher; Figures 1.9, 1.11, 1.12, 1.13, R.L. Gregory;
Figures 7.5, 7.6, 7.7, 7.8, J. Wiley and Sons; Table 7.1, Academic Press and
R. Schuler.

CHAPTER 1

The Senses and Memory

One of the major reasons why I am so interested in making psychology available to professional groups (such as the police) is that since 1971 I have conducted psychological research of an applied or real-world nature. Some psychologists prefer to remain in their laboratories testing theories (which is an important aspect of any science), whereas I prefer to use my psychological knowledge and skills to influence and improve present real-life organizations and practices. In 1971 I began my research on improving the effectiveness of daily operational briefings and by way of introduction to what psychology has to offer you on the powers and limitations of the senses and of memory, I shall describe some aspects of this work. The first force in which I began this work was in the south-west of England. The Police Scientific Development Branch of the Home Office wanted to investigate whether the daily, traditional, face-to-face, operational briefings could be superseded by closed circuit television briefings broadcast from a central studio to several police stations in a fairly large city. The aspect of daily briefing I am talking about concerns those items of information directed to all the officers on a parade.

Remembering daily briefings

If the effectiveness of such briefings were improved then, at first sight, one might expect this to bring greater success in the finding of criminals, missing persons, and property, etc. However, on further reflection, it might be too optimistic to expect the effect of a change of briefing style to be conclusively demonstrated in this way, since the quality of briefing is only one factor among many, and frequently the successful actions taken by officers in the course of duty are by their very nature unforeseen. Consequently an evaluation of a briefing system which concentrated on this type of information would not only be insensitive, it would also provide little data, since individual action as a result of briefing is infrequent (Reid and Bull, 1973). A feature of briefing is that many officers are presented with the same information and from the individual's point of view the likelihood of being able to act on the information is low. (However, from the force's point of view, informing several hundred officers may be an effective way of apprehending a wanted person, for example.) While action as a result of briefing is infrequent, it is possible to broadly assess the effects of a briefing in terms of the amount of its content which can be remembered. If information could be shown to be more memorable when presented by a new method than by the old, then the new method would be judged to be the better one. The underlying assumption would be that action depends on memory. Broadly speaking this is undeniable. Consequently, in the context of my research, briefing effectiveness was gauged by how memorable the information was.

However, the recall of relevant information in the course of duty when the appropriate circumstances arise may not be perfectly related to the scores given by any particular test of recall. Some slight degree of caution may be necessary in interpreting any indirect measure of briefing effectiveness such as recall, but it would be difficult to reject the commonsense assumption that the man who can on request recall what he has been told, is in a better position to act on the information than one who cannot do so.

In the south-west I conducted a number of experiments concerning memory (e.g. Bull and Reid, 1975). In one of my first memory studies I tested how much officers could remember of the information presented in traditional briefings. On average they could remember sixteen facts from the briefing they had received that day, eight facts from yesterday's briefing and four facts from the day before yesterday's briefing. (A typical briefing would in total contain over one hundred facts.) This amount of recall was fairly consistent from police station to police station, and from month to month.

After some police stations had been running closed circuit television briefings for several months I again tested how much officers would remember of their daily briefings. (I should point out that the officers whose memories were tested had no prior warning of the memory tests.) On average with TV briefings twenty-three facts were remembered from that day's briefing. This improvement over the effectiveness of traditional, face-to-face briefing may have been due to what is commonly referred to by psychologists as the 'honeymoon' effect. That is, any new method of doing something is *at first* interesting or exciting, but after a while its appeal may wane. With this in mind I tested the effectiveness of TV briefing after many months' experience of it had occurred. The results of this second testing of the effectiveness of TV briefing was that, on average, officers remembered thirty-eight facts from today's briefing, twenty from yesterday's briefing and nine from the day before yesterday's. From these data it can readily be concluded that TV briefings led to significantly more information being remembered. What are the possible explanations of this finding?

One possible explanation is that if the TV briefings presented or contained more facts than the traditional ones, then perhaps more was remembered because more was provided. However, this was not the case. If anything the TV briefings took less time to present than the traditional ones (this having the additional benefit of permitting the men to go out on patrol sooner). As a psychologist I was aware (as was my colleage Professor R.L. Reid) that man is what we refer to as 'a limited information processor' and that, as with any machine or process, overload can occur. Because of this I had a hunch which might explain the greater recall after TV briefings. Psychologists who study memory have consistently found experimental evidence to support the common sense notion that sometimes you can give a person too much information too quickly. Now, psychology is often accused of merely finding out what common sense already could tell us. This is a naive criticism. It can be of immense value (for example, to decision making) to know that what common sense suggests is, in fact, supported by the findings of scientific investigations. Furthermore, one person's common sense is often not the same as another's. In the context of police briefing I thought that perhaps the traditional, face-to-face briefings were considerably less memorable than the TV style of briefing because they contained *too much* information. This, in fact, turned out to be the case and in our final report to the Home Office we concluded that TV briefings were more memorable not due to any effect of the TV as such (i.e. to the medium of TV), but to the fact that (almost by chance) their scripts contained *fewer* items of information. I conducted an experiment in which the scripts made up for TV briefings were, in fact, presented in the traditional face-to-face style. Recall of the information was much improved. Thus our main conclusion was that for daily operational briefings to be more effective they should contain less information than is commonly the practice.

I conducted further experiments to find the optimum number of items of information to be contained in a briefing. (By 'item of information' I mean, for example, a telex message or a description of a wanted or missing person.) Those of you with some knowledge of psychology may have heard of the phrase 'the magic number seven' (following the work of G.A. Miller). Miller's work showed that most people can remember approximately seven different things (or 'chunks of information') from a list of items which they are required to recall. It came as no surprise when I found seven to be the optimum number of items to be contained in a briefing. Giving more than seven items resulted in less information (in absolute terms) being remembered. Traditional briefings characteristically contained many items, and informal discussions with officers who presented briefings revealed that they presented so many items because they considered that the officers on parade should be aware of every item that may possibly be relevant to them. The officers in charge of parades want to avoid being accused of inadequately briefing their men. Thus the suggestion that the number of items of information that consitute a briefing should be reduced has met with some opposition, although it is widely agreed that shorter briefings would be of benefit by enabling officers to leave a station more quickly. Officers in charge of parades do, however, generally admit that they have always edited the briefing material available to them by omitting irrelevant and unimportant items from their briefing. In order to implement the new system, all that is required is a more severe form of editing.

The results of the research I have briefly described to you led a force in the north of England to attempt to improve the effectiveness of their daily operational briefings without the use of TV. The force asked me to conduct experiments to see if having a maximum allowable number of seven items per briefing led to more effective briefings.

This force's decision to reduce the amount of information contained in their daily operational briefings did lead to thirty per cent more information being recalled. Following this, a force in the Midlands has adopted the recommendation of having no more than seven items per briefing, and has added to this a practice developed in the northern force of highlighting or accentuating certain parts of each item of information in the hope of making it more memorable. (Some examples of this are provided in table 1.1.) Whether this practice leads to

Table 1.1 Making briefing items more memorable: some real-life examples

DECEPTIVE CREW
The following described are wanted for attempted criminal deception of the Midland Bank, Eardley Road. (1) White male, 5'9" slim build, CREW CUT HAIR, ruddy complexion, wearing a black zip-up leather jacket. (2) White male, 5'10", stocky build, DARK CREW CUT HAIR, wearing a black leather zip-up jacket. Both youths aged 19/20 yrs and have a local accent. Any info to D.C. Brown, Ash Lane.

FLASHER IN FULL BLOOM
At 21.55 hrs October 2nd, at The Green, London Road, the following described man was seen flashing, and you will like this, White male, 45, 5'10" tall, slim build, thin hair receding at the front, dark suit, a light coloured shirt, and...flower patterned underpants. I do not know how you will be able to see these to assist identification. Any info to Steve Phillips, Riverside.

PINTA PINCHER
An unusually heavy spate of milk thefts, they have even taken whole crates from schools. Anywhere in the city centre seems to be at risk. Look for one or more well developed thieves.

PEERAGE AT PERIL
There have been several break-ins at shops in the 'DUKES' chain. Good quality men's clothing has been taken each time, usually bearing the firm's own 'Lord Charles' tag. Someone obviously has a market for this stuff so further attempts are likely. A list of premises at risk is on the Collator's notice board.

greater remembering has not been experimentally tested in the police setting, but other research by psychologists does suggest that it may be effective (provided it is not too 'gimmicky').

I would like to turn to what psychology has to say about the senses and memory in general. For something to be remembered by a person, that person in some way must have sensed or perceived the thing which later will be recalled or recognized. I will describe to you some psychological research on memory and forgetting, and finish this chapter with some further references to the senses and perception.

Failure to sense or perceive something can be caused by many factors. Perhaps the thing (or'stimulus' as we refer to it in psychology) was not of sufficient strength to be sensed or perhaps the person's sense organs were damaged. In this chapter I am not proposing to discuss the fairly simple limitations of perception such as colour blindness or visual acuity. These are matters which can be left to the physiologist. Instead I wish to discuss the more central psychological processes which go on not in the eye nor in the ear, but in the brain. The eye sends messages towards the brain, which are usually literal representations of what it is focused on. It is the brain which (with its inbuilt limitations) interprets these messages, and such limitations and processes of interpretation are of great interest to psychologists and they are also of relevance and value to policing.

Forgetting

No matter in what way memory performance is assessed all the methods of testing show that memory is rarely perfect. The reasons why we forget have been a major focus of a great deal of psychological research over the decades. Until recently most of this research took place in laboratories and it consistently found that with the lapse of time the amount remembered (as shown in figure 1.1) decreased rapidly at first and then gradually tapered off. Recent research on memory in real-life situations (e.g. eyewitness memory which will be discussed in a later chapter) suggests that such a 'curve of forgetting' may not readily apply to all memory situations. Nevertheless, some degree of forgetting over time almost always occurs. One of the oldest explanations for this is what is referred to as 'the passive decay theory', which simply suggests that with the passing of time memories simply fade away due to chemical or metabolic processes which break down the memory trace. (The breaking down or fading away

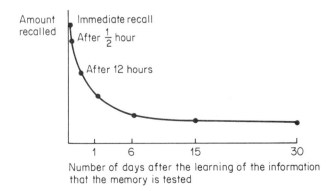

Figure 1.1 A graph of the typical forgetting curve derived from laboratory experiments

of your garden's grass cuttings is somewhat analogous to this hypothesized process.) Although this theory seems plausible enough there is no real evidence to support it and many memories do not fade away with disuse (e.g. if you have learnt to swim, even though you do not go swimming for several years, when you return to the water you haven't forgotten how to swim). Furthermore, often people do subsequently remember things that they could not remember when they tried to do so sometime earlier.

Another theory, this time one which has received much experimental support, is called 'the interference theory' of forgetting. This explanation of forgetting is not concerned with the fading away of memory, but instead it gives a central role to the happenings either before the initial input (or storing) of the memory or between it and the later attempt at remembering (as shown in figure 1.2).

Retroactive interference	=	Learn 'A', then learn 'B', then tested on 'A', but 'B' interferes
Proactive interference	=	Learn 'B', then learn 'A', then tested on 'A', but 'B' interferes

Figure 1.2 The effects of interference

The more similar two separate things are, the more they will be confused or interfere with each other in the memory process. Here is an example from the context of eyewitness memory. An armed robbery took place at a railway station ticket office and later the ticket seller attended an identification parade. He confidently picked out from the parade a man whom he thought had been involved in the robbery. For reasons I do not need to go into here the man he picked out could not have been associated with the crime, *but* he did sometimes buy tickets at the station from the ticket seller. The ticket seller's memory of this man (caused by the man's ticket buying) had interfered with his memory of the robbery. When questioned the ticket collector said that he had picked out the man largely 'because his face looked familiar'. The more two things are alike the more they will interfere or be confused with each other in the memory process. You may remember the names of two people (called X and Y) that you met for the first time today and you may also remember their faces, but it is quite possible that if you ever meet again you'll put name X to face Y and vice versa. Everything we try to remember bears some similarity to other things that we have learned either previously or subsequently. Laboratory based research on this phenomenon (for example with the learning of lists of unrelated words) has shown it to sometimes have a powerful effect on forgetting. How much it operates in real life is open to debate, but I would like to suggest that (if you do not already do so) you bear it in mind, especially when giving instructions to the public or to other officers, or in training.

Another explanation of forgetting concerns what is called 'systematic distortion of the memory trace'. This theory states that although some memories may, in some way, be lost forever, it is quite likely that many memory errors are due to distortion. That is, when something is remembered it is frequently not an exact replica of the original information but a distorted or modified form. This can easily be shown in many ways. If people are given some shapes to remember and if these are line drawings *somewhat* resembling a common object, then at recall the people will tend to draw the common object and not the original shape. You may initially feel that this phenomenon has little to do with police work, but you should be aware that it will be present whenever the police or the public are required to remember something. Further, this phenomenon has its greatest effect on memory for things or actions seen only imperfectly. Eyewitness memory often falls into this category. For example, suppose a woman saw a man leaning over a baby in a pram outside a shop. The man was smoking a cigarette. The next day the woman reads in the paper that a baby outside a shop received some burns on the face. She attempts to recall the man's actions and checks her recall against her imagination of how the man *would* have behaved in order to burn the baby. At this moment she correctly recalls that she saw nothing to suggest that the man she saw burnt the baby. A few days later she hears from a friend that the police are asking anyone who was near the shop at the time of the incident to come forward. The woman goes to the police station and is asked to describe what she saw. When she now attempts to access her memory she retrieves from it an amended or distorted form of the original memory (i.e. her earlier imagining of how the man *would* have behaved in order to burn the baby) and describes the actions of the man as being commensurate with burning the baby. When asked by the police why she did not intervene and stop the man, she cannot explain. Some days or weeks later she is questioned about the incident. Her memory of the incident has now been further distorted by the perfectly correct question (from the police point of view) of why she did not stop the man. The police question may have further distorted her memory into now remembering that

(1) not only was the man smoking and leaning over the pram; but also
(2) he was behaving suspiciously; and further
(3) she saw him burn the baby.

In court this witness could well testify under oath that she saw the man burn the baby. She would do this in all honesty since she is unaware that her memory of the initial incident has been unwittingly systematically distorted. No-one planned this distortion and no-one can be blamed for it. It is just a fact of life that such things occur all the time in memory.

A memory process somewhat similar to that of 'systematic distortion' is referred to as 'confabulation'. This process is concerned with the way we fill in gaps in our memory to make our recall of something (e.g. a sequence of events) logical and meaningful. These memory gaps may have been due to the fact that we did not in the first place perceive all parts of the sequence of events, or due to the possibility that parts of the overall memory have been lost. When such gaps occur they are often filled in unconsciously with false information which is, however, relevant logically (i.e. which is based on our past experience). Several examples of this will be given in the chapter entitled 'Summing up or assessing people' but a fairly simple experiment is relevant here.

In a series of experiments conducted in our psychology department by Clive Hollin some evidence has been found to support the idea that witnesses often infer the presence of one physical feature from their recall of the observed person's possession of another. A person entered a lecture to search for a briefcase and after walking around the room the lecturer asked him to leave. In the first of such incidents the 'target' person was *blond*, with *green* eyes and a *fair* complexion. The eyewitnesses description of the target person were very accurate for hair colour, ninety-three per cent of the witnesses reported that the hair was blond. However, of this ninety-three per cent almost half described the person as having *blue* eyes, whereas only seven per cent correctly said green. (Fourteen per cent incorrectly reported other colours and the remainder did not mention eye colour at all.) Of those who reported blond hair three-quarters correctly reported the target person as having a fair complexion. Thus the proportion of the observers which indicated that the target person had blond hair, a fair complexion and *blue* eyes was thirty-six per cent. In the second incident, with a different audience, the target person had *dark* hair, *grey* eyes and a *light* complexion. All the observers in this part of the study described correctly the target person's hair colour. However, over half of them incorrectly reported the eye colour as being *brown* and none of them correctly reported it as being grey. Forty-four per cent correctly reported a fair complexion whereas fifty-six per cent reported the target person as having a *dark* complexion. Thus the proportion of the observers who reported that the target person had dark hair, *brown* eyes and a *dark* complexion was forty-four per cent. These effects of blond hair incorrectly implying blue eyes, and dark hair suggesting brown eyes and a dark complexion indicates that witnesses fill in gaps in their recall by employing stereotypes or known population norms. Sometimes such confabulation will be correct but on some occasions it will lead to inaccurate remembering. Further, the people attempting to recall the information are usually unaware that confabulation has occurred.

A further explanation of forgetting is called 'retrieval failure'. (Before I describe this explanation we should note that the theories described here are not incompatible with one another. All of them may be relevant to certain aspects of forgetting.) Retrieval failure is concerned not with the possibility that memories decay or are lost for ever, but with the possibility that they become inaccessible. This approach argues that the information is still in memory but that we cannot access it or get it out. The well known 'tip of the tongue' phenomenon is an example of this, as is research on hypnosis. It has been shown that under hypnosis people can *sometimes* accurately recall things which they could not recall when in their normal waking state. However, a great deal of memory confabulation and distortion often occurs under hypnosis (Gibson, 1982) and this procedure must be treated with the *greatest caution* by the police.

The final explanation of forgetting that I wish to mention is that commonly referred to as 'motivated forgetting'. This approach argues that we purposely make our memory of unpleasant or undesirable things inaccessible to ourselves. That is, we purposely make our retrieval of such information difficult or impossible. As you may know, Freud put forward this rather strange sounding idea. Modern memory psychologists tend not to accept Freud's rather untestable explanation of such phenomena. Instead they point out that at the time of the initial incident and/or at the time of attempted recall the person attempting recall is usually in an anxious, aroused or tense state. Experimental psychologists have repeatedly shown that such states lead to poor input to memory and very inefficient retrieval from memory. Thus the fact that people are sometimes unable to recall accurately incidents that were personally stressful is easily explained.

Before I leave the topic of forgetting there is one more factor that I wish to mention. So far I have discussed the forgetting of things that once were in memory. There exists at least one other reason why people sometimes are unable to remember things and this explanation is concerned with the fact that much of what we experience never gets put into memory in the first place.

Input limitations

Many people assume that if something is seen by the eyes or heard by the ears then this information will automatically be put into memory by the brain. They believe that the eyes act like a camera putting into memory an accurate film of the event, and that the ears act like a tape recorder. Such assumptions are in fact incorrect. The eyes are not like a camera, nor are the ears like a tape recorder. The brain, which puts things into memory, has what is called a 'limited processing capacity'. This means that information can only be put into memory at a certain rate. If the information which one wants to remember arrives at the eyes or ears at too fast a rate then the brain simply will not be able to put it all into memory, and some will be lost forever. A useful analogy is that of pouring water from a large bowl into a bottle (i.e. memory) with a funnel placed on the top of the bottle. If the water is poured fairly slowly from the bowl into the funnel then all the water will go into the bottle (so long as there is not more water than the bottle can hold). If, however, the water is quickly poured into the funnel, the funnel will overflow and some water will not get into the bottle. Memory works in a similar way. If the rate of presentation of information is too fast then some of this information will not even have the chance to enter memory, let alone to be forgotten.

Psychologists' experiments have convincingly shown that the processing limitation which the brain has for putting information into memory is a major reason why people do not remember things or cannot act upon information they have been given. This limitation of the brain is one reason why, for example, road signs on motorways need to be a minimum distance apart. It takes the brain a second or so to process the information which the eyes have read and this processing goes on even after the road sign has been passed. Consequently, if the next sign has to be read before the brain has completed the processing of the previous one, then the information on these two signs will not be fully processed and therefore cannot be fully acted upon.

The senses and perception

I now wish to focus on psychological knowledge concerning the senses and perception. Before something can be put into memory it has to be sensed and psychologists have conducted much research concerning the powers and limitations of perception.

The process of the perception of objects, of actions or of people is made up of a number of stages. First, an object or event has to provide sufficient stimulation to activate the possible perceiver's sense organs. However, if this stimulation is not sufficient to activate the sense organs the person will not perceive the object or event. That is to say there is a 'threshold' of stimulation below which a sense organ will not respond. In order to stand any chance of being perceived, the stimulation provided by an object, event or person must exceed the perceiver's sensory threshold. Psychologists have found that the amount of stimulation required to exceed such thresholds varies quite a lot from person to person. It also varies within a person as a function of their mood and where their attention is focused.

Selective attention

Even if the amount of stimulation exceeds the threshold the object or event may still not be perceived. Whether perception occurs also depends upon where the perceiver has focused his attention. Psychologists have shown that the concept of attention has two interrelated yet somewhat distinct parts. First, there exists what one may for simplicity's sake refer to as 'external' attention. This is concerned with whether, for example, the perceiver's eyes were open or closed or where he was looking. If an event occurred outside a perceiver's field of vision then he would not see it, even though it was strong enough to exceed his sensory threshold if he had been looking towards it. In addition to this rather obvious 'external' aspect of attention there exists what I shall refer to as 'internal' attention (see figure 1.3). This aspect of attention I referred to earlier when I said that man can be viewed as a 'limited information processor'. If a variety of sense organs are stimulated at a level above threshold then many messages are passed on by the sense organs to the brain. If several complex messages arrive during the same time period then, quite frequently, the brain cannot cope. You will have experienced this yourself. A common example is to imagine yourself driving along unfamiliar roads when you are late for a party. You are having an argument with your companion in the car and there's a lot of traffic about. In such a situation it is commonly found that we cannot cope. The typical ways of dealing with this information overload are either to tell your companion to shut up, or to stop the car. Crashing the car is another alternative which, fortunately,

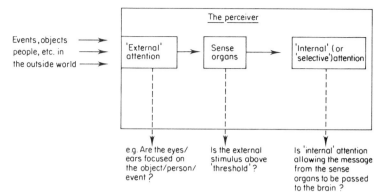

Figure 1.3 The role of attention

most people avoid. When we are receiving a variety of information from different sources we devote our 'internal' selection to some or perhaps one of these sources and ignore or block out the others. This phenomenon is referred to as 'selective attention' and its operation explains how we can fail to perceive (and therefore fail to remember) objects, events, or people even though they provided sufficient stimulation to activate (even strongly) our sense organs. By the use of selective attention we can protect the information processing parts of our brain from overload and/or the receiving of too many complex messages. Selective attention blocks out or filters the incoming information and this is usually done by attention being devoted to the most crucial source of information, other sources being filtered out. This explains how an eyewitness, say a rape victim, cannot remember what the rapist said to her whilst she was focusing all her attention on possible means of escape. Though his words activated the sense organs (i.e. her ears), the messages from the sense organs to the brain were filtered out by the selective filter before they had a chance to be put into memory. She cannot remember what he said because, at the level of memory and her brain, she never heard him.

To which of the many sources of possible external information our selective attention is drawn depends on many things. It depends upon expectancy (i.e. what we expect to happen) and our past experience, as well as on what we judge to be the most important source of information. It is a fact that different people will selectively attend to different parts of the same set of events or people. (Chapter 3 discusses this point more fully).

Before I leave the concept of selective attention I would like to mention one further source of information to which a person can selectively attend. This is not an external source of stimulation but an internal one concerning a person's own thoughts. You will all have experienced this phenomenon of concentrating so much on your own thoughts that you failed to notice external events. Driving a car can serve here again as a useful example. Those of you who drive to work regularly will have had the experience of suddenly realizing that for the last few minutes you have been so bound up in your own thoughts as you proceeded along your familiar route that you have not been concentrating fully on the road and all its dangers. Nevertheless you have arrived at your destination safely even though you cannot remember, for example, whether the last traffic lights were red or green. The fact that you have arrived safely shows that you must have responded adequately to the needs of the road conditions, yet at the time of so responding you were 'unaware' that you were doing so and you now cannot remember anything about those adequate responses. The concept of 'selective attention' is fascinating and illustrates how we decide what ('internally') to attend to and the effects that this can have.

Set and expectancy

What we decide to attend to is often based on what we expect to happen. Another psychological aspect of perception that may be of interest to you is that referred to as 'set'. The operation of this concept of 'set' can, I hope, be easily demonstrated (see figure 1.4). In a very simple experiment one can have two groups of people (A and B) and each person's task is to say out loud the word that is shown to them briefly by flashing it upon a screen. The first word that the people in group A are shown is the word 'Cup', and their responses show that they successfully recognize this. The first word that the people in group B are shown is 'Wood'. The second word shown to group A is 'Tea', and the second to group B is 'Dry'. The third thing that is shown on the screen is the same for both groups and in reality it is 'Γot'. The people in group A call out 'Pot' and those in group B call out 'Rot'. Why should this be? This phenomenon is explained by saying that the subjects saw what they expected, or were 'set' to see. If questioned afterwards about the first letter in the last 'word' that they were shown, the subjects recall nothing about the incompleteness of its first letter. Even when the experimenter says things like, 'some of the letters in some of the words may not have been clearly printed. Did you see any of these?', the observers say 'no'.

	Group A	Group B
First word	CUP	WOOD
Second word	TEA	DRY
Third word	ΓOT	

Figure 1.4 The operation of 'set'

A theory in psychology that has been used to explain this kind of phenomenon is called 'signal detection theory'. I shall not go into detail about this complex theory, but one of its components should be mentioned. The aspect of signal detection theory which is very relevant to people seeing only what they expect to see is called 'the criterion'. This concept suggests that in order to decide if something is present or is happening, the perceiver 'decides' (not usually in a conscious way) how much information or stimulation energy will need to occur before he will decide that something is present. When something is expected the amount of information from the outside world necessary to confirm this is low. However, if something is unexpected (that is, the perceiver has a high criterion for its occurrence) then the stimulation from it will need to be quite strong before the person realizes that it is occurring. Figure 1.5 will serve to illustrate what I am saying. The larger drawing in the upper half of the figure can be seen either as the face of a bespectacled man who is looking to your left, or as a rat with its head facing the same way. One can easily influence which of these two alternatives a perceiver will experience seeing. This can be done by showing either a series of faces or a series of animals prior to the displaying of the ambiguous 'rat—man' picture. This illustrates how easy it is

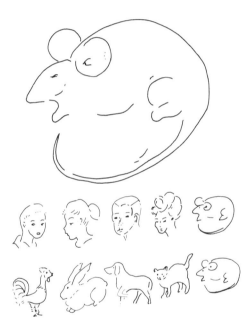

Figure 1.5 The rat—man figure and a series of drawings which create set or expectancy Reproduced with permission from Bugelski (1961). Copyright (1961) Canadian Psychological Association

for people to see what they expect to see. Figure 1.6 presents a similar illustration of this effect. As one looks across the upper row of diagrams one sees the first diagram as representing a face and, in fact, all four diagrams in this row are seen as faces. If one then looks across the lower row one sees the first diagram as representing a female figure and, in fact, all four diagrams as female figures, even though the last diagram in the lower row is identical to the one above it. Figure 1.7 is a well known illustration of the effects of expectancy in

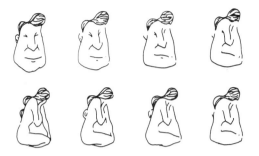

Figure 1.6 Nasty man or nice lady? Reproduced by permission of A.H. Fisher

Figure 1.7 Old woman or young lady?

which can be seen either an old woman or a young lady. The fact that after a while most observers can see both of these things in the same drawing, *but only one at a time*, argues that the brain is selecting which sensory input to attend to.

When shown figure 1.8 many people cannot immediately perceive what is there. (Be sure to look at figure 1.8 before reading any further.) But when they are given the clue 'dog' or 'spotted dog' many immediately experience seeing a dog. Initially they perceived the picture as a meaningless collection of black shapes but when provided with the 'set' of 'dog', although the input to their eyes does *not* change (and that is an important point), they now see something that was not 'there' before.

Illusions

Some illusions are examples of how sensory input and memory interact to lead people to see (or hear) what is not there. An illusion is different from a delusion. When someone experiences a delusion they are 'perceiving' something that no-one else with them (say in the same room) is perceiving (e.g. if you now perceive someone walking into the room through the wall). An illusion is a trick on perception that all perceivers can see—as in figure 1.9. In this illusion most

Figure 1.8 What do you see here?

Figure 1.9 Which of the two rolls of carpet on the road is the larger? Reproduced by permission of R.L. Gregory

people see the upper of the two horizontal white bars as being longer than the lower one. In reality, of course, they are of equal length. One explanation of this illusion says that we make the judgement that the light and dark shadings of grey in this picture represent a dual carriageway and that we are standing, say, on a bridge over the road. If we see the two white bars as lying on the ground, then because we know that such a road has a fairly constant width, then the upper white bar must necessarily be longer than the lower white bar. Hence the illusion, and I hope you have grasped how very dependent it is on our use of past experience and what we 'expect' to be the case. Suppose I now ask you to imagine that you are not standing on the bridge over the dual carriageway, but are seated in a coach which has stopped on the bridge. You are looking out of the coach window, and stuck on the coach window are two strips of white tape. What happens to the illusions now? For most observers the two white bars now look equal when they adopt this changed point of view.

Figures 1.10 and 1.11 are further examples of illusions. Some of these have an 'expectancy' explanation and others can be explained by recourse to the physiology of our visual system. In figure 1.10 the two inner circles are, in reality, of equal size and in figure 1.11 there are no triangles. In figures 1.12 and 1.13 there is no bulge nor depression.

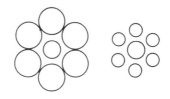

Figure 1.10 Is one of the inner circles larger
than the other inner circle?

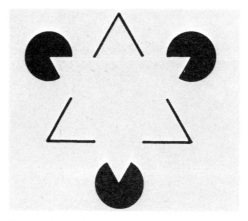

Figure 1.11 How many triangles are there?
Reproduced by permission of R.L. Gregory

Figure 1.12 Is there a bulge? Reproduced by permission of
R.L. Gregory

Figure 1.13 Is there a depression? Reproduced by permission of
R.L. Gregory

Such illusory effects do not apply only to the static pictures. People with different expectancies can 'perceive' the same series of events differently. A while ago in the United States a film of a football match was shown to people who supported one or other of the two teams involved. The observer's task was to count up the number of fouls committed by each of the two teams. These observers 'saw' their team as committing fewer fouls than the other team. Which set of observers was correct, those supporting team A or those supporting team B? Furthermore, supporters judged the fouls committed by their own team as mostly being 'mild' ones, whereas they judged the fouls committed by the opposing team as mostly being 'flagrant'. This study revealed a strong tendency for the supporters to see their own team as the victims, and the other team as the aggressors. Each perceiver's view of the game was 'real' to him but who is correct?

Let us now turn to a real-life court case in which perceptual expectancy played a major role. Some years ago in North America a hunting party of five men went out one day to shoot deer. Whilst driving around the area in which they expected to see deer their car broke down. Two of the men volunteered to get help and they set off across country. After a few minutes one of these two men decided that both of them need not go for help and that he would instead scout around for deer. The men who had stayed with the car were not aware that one of their colleagues who had set off for help was now, in fact, moving around some way away from them. Suddenly one of the men with the car said, 'Look over there! That's a deer isn't it?' One of his colleagues said, 'Looks like it'. With that the first man raised his rifle and shot at the object. It half fell and let out a cry. Then it got to its feet again and began to run. A second man shot at it and then the third man did and it fell to the floor dead. Excitedly the three men ran the few hundred yards over to their kill. As they ran up to it they realized that it was not a deer but was their friend!

Later, in court one of the 'murderers' said that, 'In my thoughts and in my eyes, it was a deer'. A policeman testified that when he had observed, from where the men had shot their friend, a similarly dressed man in the 'murder' spot, he had clearly seen him as a man and nothing like a deer. Expectations have strange effects on our perceptions and it is important to realize that we, as the perceivers, are usually unaware of these effects upon us.

Police accuracy

A recent police recruitment advertisement made the following claims: 'You develop on the beat the ability to observe and remember. To make the seemingly unimportant stick. You will be taught to be observant and to develop a quick eye for detail.' While this may be true, is it possible, because of the difficult job most policemen have and because of what society expects of them, that police officers can perceive things differently from the ways in which other people perceive them? In Cambridge two psychologists showed films of ongoing events in a shopping street. These films lasted for one, two or four hours and they contained a number of deliberately staged thefts. These were shown to twenty-four policemen and one hundred and fifty-six civilians. The observers' task was to watch for certain people and certain kinds of action—theft, normal exchange of goods, and general antisocial behaviour. The crucial finding was that the police officers judged many quite innocent events as being thefts much more so than did the civilians. In accurate detections of people and actions, there was no difference between civilians and the police. (All similar experiments in Britain and in the USA have come to the same conclusions.)

The understandable tendency of the police to recall or perceive things not actually present is found in other research. Many studies have shown that what better recall policemen have is seriously impugned by a 'confabulation factor' (i.e. the filling in of gaps, or the imputation of intentions not actually present). One study showed how the police view events in different ways from non-policemen. A researcher presented eleven scenes to a number of policemen and to an equal number of the general public, and the observers were asked to recall details of the scenes and possible intentions. There was no difference between the two groups in recalling objective detail, but the police reported significantly more 'criminal episodes'. A man walking round a corner carrying a can was interpreted by the non-police observers as having run out of petrol. The police mostly saw him as an arsonist. In another study observers (including both police and civilians) were shown a forty-two-second film in which a man approached a pram, pulled down its protective net, and then walked off. As he was walking away, a woman appeared out of a house. Statements about what was observed in the film were taken both immediately and one week later. It was found that the police noted and remembered more detail, but were prone to special types of error—especially where actions were concerned. The police remembered more correct details about dress and appearance, and they recalled twice as many incorrect facts—details that were not there, events that never happened. With the actions depicted in the scene, the civilians merely reported what was there—without imputation of suspicious intent. The police, on the other hand, 'saw' more than actually happened. One in five of the policemen said that they saw the man put his hand into the pram and take the baby out! Many said they saw the woman running towards the man with a look of worry on her face. A vital supplementary finding was that while the police were better at remembering details initially (up to one minute) they made many more errors than the non-police one week later. The public remembered less initially but forgot less over time. The information presented in this chapter should go a long way towards explaining these findings.

One explanation of forgetting which still has value is that it is caused by one event 'interfering' with another stored event, especially where the events are highly similar. The more that is stored, of a similar nature, the greater will interference be, and therefore the greater the forgetting. The policeman, by the very nature of his job, is asked to selectively perceive and store many similar events for future potential usefulness; the civilian is not. Thus policemen will forget more information of a specific type, over a given length of time, than a civilian would. This is very understandable and should not be taken as a criticism of the police. Police officers are as human as anybody else and consequently they suffer to some extent from the limitations of perception and memory that affect us all. I hope that one benefit of this book will be for you to better understand human behaviour as it applies to both civilians and police.

Suggested further reading

Clifford, B.R., and Bull, R. (1978). *The Psychology of Person Identification,* Routledge and Kegan Paul, London.
Gruneberg, M., Morris, P., and Sykes, R. (1979). *Practical Aspects of Memory*, Academic Press, London.
Radford, J.K., and Govier, E. (1980). *A Textbook of Psychology*, Sheldon Press, London.

CHAPTER 2

Witness Memory

In the last few years psychologists have been contributing more and more to the understanding of criminal and legal processes. In 1978 the British Psychological Society formed a Division of Criminological and Legal Psychology and there are now over one hundred members in this Division of psychologists who actively apply their knowledge in these areas. 1978 also saw the first of the Social Science Research Council's 'Psychology and Law' conferences, which are now held regularly at Oxford University. With this recent upsurge of collaborative work between psychologists, the legal world, and the police, has come growth in several areas of research. One of these topics is that of person identification. However, police officers seem to have a poor understanding of this topic. A recent survey conducted by a Canadian psychologist (Yarmey and Tressillian Jones, 1982) revealed that many officers had little idea of the effects of most factors upon eyewitness accuracy.

In 1974 in response to general disquiet, the UK Home Secretary appointed Lord Devlin to chair a committee to examine the law and procedure on criminal identification. This committee's report was published in 1976 and I was then critical of the committee's apparent ignorance of the existing psychological research on the topic (Bull and Clifford, 1976). This ignorance may have been more the fault of psychologists than of the committee since no collection of psychologists' work in this area was then available. It was partly in order to rectify this situation that Brian Clifford and I wrote our book (Clifford and Bull, 1978). The Devlin Report called for exploration, of a research nature, into 'establishing ways in which the insights of psychology could be brought to bear on the conduct of identification parades and the practice of the courts in all matters relating to evidence of identification'. In recent years the status of identification evidence has been called into question. Indeed, one of the recommendations in the Devlin Report was that judge and jury pay attention to the possible weaknesses of identification evidence. Some people went so far as to claim, 'There is certainly a persuasive argument that the human memory for faces is so fallible that evidence of identification is virtually worthless. It seems likely that most people are quite incapable of remembering a face' (Cole and Pringle, 1974). However, such claims have been based on little more than anecdotal evidence. What was obviously needed in this area was a scientific assessment of witnesses' identification powers. Even though Lord Gardiner said that, 'Most wrong convictions were on the matter of identification' this should not be taken to mean that all, or even the majority, of identification evidence is of little value. Psychological research has shown that witnesses' identification performance can range from total accuracy to total inaccuracy depending upon a multitude of factors. Unfortunately, there is by no means always a positive relationship between how confident a witness feels in his or her identification and the real accuracy of this identification.

The concept of identification as used by the legal profession is naive. It seems to imply that perceiving and remembering is a simple, single process. Many lawyers appear to assume, given suitable viewing conditions and no mental abnormality of the witness, that failure to recall of recognize the culprit should not occur. Yet, as has been shown in the previous chapter, psychologists have for decades known that quite often people not only fail to see and hear everything presented to their senses, they also 'see' and 'hear' things which did not occur. Further, people frequently fail to remember things which happen to them, but do 'remember' things which did not, in fact, occur. The eye is not like a camera, nor the ear like a tape recorder. Far from being a single, simple process, person identification in the criminal setting needs to be thought of as taking place in three stages. The first stage involves witnessing the incident and this involves perception and all its vagaries. The second stage involves either recounting the person's appearance to the police, trying to construct a photofit or attempting to aid a police artist in creating a likeness of the criminal, each of these procedures involving memory and its inherent fallibilities. The third stage sees memory and perception operating in tandem when the witness either tries to locate the criminal in a photo album or tries to match his current perceptions of the members of an identification parade to his stored image of the criminal. It is important to stress that error can creep in at any and all of these stages. This is not to say that all identification evidence is of little value. However, claims for its fallibility were being widely publicized in the media in the mid-1970s. In contrast to the rather extreme claim that all eyewitness testimony is worthless, psychologists (who are often accused of creating more problems than they solve) have repeatedly shown that sometimes witnesses do accurately remember important things. They have, however, demonstrated (and this needs to be stressed) that the recall a witness provides is rarely entirely accurate.

Thus, not only is it wrong to view perception and memory as all or none processes but it must be noted that other factors such as the witness's own beliefs about criminal behaviour may also affect testimony. For example, it is very likely that as some identification parades witnesses pick out the person who most resembles their expectancy of what that type of ciminal would look like even when they cannot remember any details of the true culprit. Many policemen have claimed (some even in print) that they can pick out a criminal 'by his face'. Is this likely? It may or may not be, but there is no doubt that errors will frequently occur.

The area of criminal identification that most psychologists have been researching is that concerning identification by means of the culprit's face. Research in laboratories using photographs shows that members of the public have an exceedingly high ability to correctly pick out dozens of faces even months after they originally saw them. However, research using life-like situations (simulated criminal episodes 'out in the street' so to speak) shows that facial identification by witnesses is much poorer in such circumstances. Psychologists have shown how the stress of a criminal episode and the inability of a witness both to concentrate on self-preservation and on remembering details of the culprit, can reduce testimony accuracy.

Psychologists have also recently been researching aspects of the culprit other than his face which may be important for identification. A crime seldom takes place without the culprit speaking. Just how good is memory for a person's voice? You may be able to recognize your friend on the telephone but how likely is it that the victim of a crime (e.g. rape) will be able to recognize this 'stranger' when she hears him again? Psychologists are now able to say something of value on this point, and nobody else ever has (see Bull and Clifford, 1983).

Apart from how accurately the witness keeps details of the culprit in his memory, there is the problem of how best to get out from his memory store this information. The way in which a witness is asked to reproduce details of the criminal can be as important as the psychological processes involved in either his initial perception of the criminal or in his maintaining the memory of this perception. Whether visual means (e.g. photo-fit, searching through a photo album) or verbal means (e.g. asking the witness to give a verbal description) are used there are important psychological factors to be borne in mind. Simply asking a witness to recall as much as possible in his own words will usually produce much information but some of it will be wrong and some important points will be omitted. A questionnaire can be used but it is a fact that the nature of the questions can produce biased answers.

Psychologists are also examining the efficiency of identification parades. It is well known that eyewitnesses frequently fail to pick out the true criminal (who is later found guilty on other grounds, or confesses) and that they pick out a non-suspect who could not possibly have committed the crime. Critics of present police procedures have naively taken these errors as evidence that identification parades are useless. I do not share this view. Errors are made at identification parades only in part because of the procedures used, and the main cause of the errors may well be the witness himself.

Though psychologists are now able to make a meaningful contribution to the study of criminal identification processes and procedures, there still remains much to be done. One thing which has to be achieved is the drawing to the attention of the police and lawyers exactly what psychologists are doing. In this chapter I shall attempt to show that psychology can make and is making a practical contribution to the understanding of eyewitness memory. Contrary to common belief, and to what the 1976 Devlin Committee thought to be the case, psychologists are able to offer advice and explanations on this topic. However, until fairly recently psychologists had failed to make widely known their knowledge in this area.

The view which the layman or the juror holds of a witness's ability to report accurately the details of an observed event or to identify an observed criminal differs markedly from that of experimental psychologists. While Marshall (1969) believes that 'The life of the courts, the trial process, is based upon the fiction that witnesses see and hear correctly and so testify', and while the legal concept of testimony or identification seems to imply that perception and memory are single, simple processes, experimental memory research argues that such cognitive processes are characterized by inbuilt structural and processing limitations. As a result of these structural and functional short-comings sense data is held to be fallible, recall to be idiosyncratic and memory to be inherently unreliable (Clifford and Bull, 1978).

When a person is asked to identify someone after seeing him briefly, he or she is being asked to do something that the normal human is not equipped to do. Human memory and perception are selective, generative, decision-making processes: to view them as copying processes is both wrong and dangerous. Additionally many aspects of eyewitness behaviour are inexplicable unless we take into account what the person is, what he is trying to do and the ways his beliefs, values, and motivations act not only at the time of perception but also during the period of storage and especially at the time of recall.

From this it follows that many of the implicit assumptions of non-psychologists concerning testimony may be wrong. Specifically, all witnesses will not be equally accurate or inaccurate and secondly, we cannot decouple memory from other cognitive sub systems, such as language, or from more socially based processes such as stereotyping.

Eyewitness limitations

Memory errors are of two types: errors of omission and errors of commission. The first type of error, generally speaking, stems from inherent limitations in processing structure and capacity, the latter from the fact that memory is reconstructive rather than literal. To take information processing limitations first, a great deal of evidence is available that man exhibits selective attention. This strongly suggests that in real life we should be careful of equating duration of exposure to a crime with probability of accurate identification of perpetrator, because in such situations victims or potential witnesses may be focusing all their attention on aspects of the situation relevant to escape rather than on stimuli useful for later identification. Over and above inappropriate selection, emotion also is known to have a disruptive effect upon attention and perception. Perception also is limited, not so much in terms of actual registra-tion, but rather in the conversion of these sensory inputs into more durable memories. Perception is also limited by being selective. The way we perceive things depends on our past experience and the ways we have learnt (by our hobbies, jobs, outlook on life) to see things. The limitations and selectivity found in attentional and perceptual processes are also found in memory. It was noted in the previous chapter that memory is known to be fallible due to such factors as passive decay, systematic distortion of the memory traces, interference between traces (such that similar memories cannot be distinguished), confabulation, retrieval failure, and displacement of existing memories by incoming material. (Additionally, physical trauma, drug abuse and senility are other causes of forgetting.) While all these psychological factors have some validity no one theory explains all the facts of eyewitness testimony and in addition few if any of the theories explain the errors of commission found in testimony. Processes of distortion are crucial features of human memory in general and eyewitness testimony in particular. Fortunately, recent research has begun to investigate this distortion process.

While a somewhat sterile debate has developed around the issue of whether memory errors occur at input or at output, the facts of distortion are not at issue, and the main explanatory mechanism—inference drawing—has been shown to be a robust effect (Clifford and Bull, 1978). Thus, there is little reason to doubt that such processes also go on in eyewitness testimony, and there is a good deal of evidence that they do. The important point to grasp in terms of assessing eyewitness accuracy is that it is almost impossible for witnesses to differentiate between their factual memories and their inferential memories. However, there seems to be a paradox between what I have just said and what visual memory data suggest. If we address the question 'How good is witness memory?' by making recourse to laboratory-based face photograph research we would have to estimate witness accuracy as somewhere around eighty per cent. Thus recognition rates with visual material can be phenomenally high. In addition, there is an apparent absence of a delay effect with face photographs at lags of twenty minutes to thirty-five days. However, the paradox is more apparent than real. The estimate of just how good face memory can be varies with the methodology employed. Face photograph research lacks ecological validity and realism. Thus when we ask how good witness memory can be, and use event, or mock-crime methodology, we find accuracy to be a great deal lower.

Which people are accurate eyewitnesses?

Can psychology provide any guidelines concerning what kind of person is likely to be the more accurate witness? Age has consistently been shown to be an important factor in testimony, with both earlier research and more modern research suggesting that children are poorer witnesses than adults. There is, however, some suggestion of a peak age beyond which adult memory does not improve and may deteriorate (Clifford and Bull, 1978).

Sex difference in witness memory was one of the first variables to be examined in testimony research and from the onset conflicting evidence was produced. It now seems that females can often be more accurate witnesses than males, except when the witnessing involves a lot of stress.

Personality may be a witness factor which may relate to eyewitness accuracy. However, only a small number of personality dimensions have been studied and few, if any, of these bear any relationship to eyewitness accuracy. The last difference we will look at is that of race. The generally accepted finding is that one race has difficulty remembering and identifying faces of another race. Explanations of this finding fall under three main headings: the 'inherently more difficult' hypothesis; the 'differential experience or familiarity' hypothesis; and the 'attitudinal component' hypothesis. While overall no one theory has overwhelming support, and all hypotheses have some truth, the applied point is that eyewitness memory is not simply a function of intact sense organs. Testimony will be of doubtful validity if the race of the witness and the suspect differ (Clifford and Bull, 1978).

The effects of language

Evidence has been accumulated which suggests that language can 'bewitch' eyewitness memory for seen people and events, and that law enforcement agents must be careful not only that they ask the right questions, but that they ask the right questions in the right way. I will now focus on the use of language by the witness in the form of labels and the use of language by those who are concerned to elicit an identification or the recall of a description.

The basic question is, does language in any way influence memory for visual material? Figure 2.1 shows that subjects given the pictures in the central column to remember, reproduced the pictures sometime later in a way which was distorted by the label the experimenter gave to the pictures. We seem to dissect and interpret nature along lines laid down by our native languages. Work with multi-dimensional scaling shows that subjects can readily ascribe adjectives (labels) to seen faces. The important question is whether such labelling aids memory for faces? McKelvie (1976) investigated the effects of labelling on the encoding and recognition of schematic faces. He presented easy-to-label and hard-to-label schematic faces and he found that giving a label to a hard-to-label face produced better recognition than merely observing the hard-to-label face, and when sufficient care was taken experimentally, labels also aided recognition of easy-to-label faces. Thus labelling faces might improve later recognition, at least with schematic faces. McKelvie showed that labels have their main effect by focusing attention on specific facial features during viewing, and that the labels may be stored along with the visual trace to be used at output.

In crime episodes it may be a single, stereotypic, verbal labelling response which is stored with a poorly perceived and therefore poorly registered face. In 1973 there was an incident in which two men stole seven thousand dollars from a Canadian supermarket. The only description of the criminals that the female cashier was able to provide was that one of them 'was rather good-looking'.

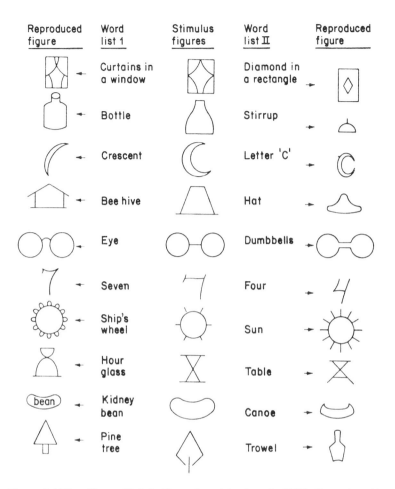

Reproduced figure	Word list 1	Stimulus figures	Word list II	Reproduced figure
	Curtains in a window		Diamond in a rectangle	
	Bottle		Stirrup	
	Crescent		Letter 'C'	
	Bee hive		Hat	
	Eye		Dumbbells	
	Seven		Four	
	Ship's wheel		Sun	
	Hour glass		Table	
	Kidney bean		Canoe	
	Pine tree		Trowel	

Figure 2.1 The effects of labels (from Carmichael *et al.*, 1932). Reproduced by permission of the American Psychological Association

Witnesses usually have to give descriptions of seen criminals before they are actually asked to recognize or identify them. Now it would seem that if a witness says, 'Was rather attractive' then she will remember this description and feel committed to it. At recognition she will try to pick out the person who best fits this publicly given description. Thus what we have is a visual sighting, a verbal labelling and then a later visual recognition based on the remembered verbal label. The label can be the same but the two visualized people can be different. The composition of an identification parade predisposes witnesses to this type of error.

The effects of the questions asked

If it can be accepted, with qualification, that subject-generated verbal input can affect, either positively or negatively, accuracy of recognition then it ought to follow that linguistic input from outsiders could also affect memory for seen events and people. The input from outsiders is usually in the form of questions. The interesting possibility then becomes whether such questions will influence memory for the event. One psychologist asked people who had just seen a sports film the simple question, 'How tall was the basketball player?' or 'How short was the basketball player?' Observers asked the former question gave an answer whose average was seventy-nine inches, while the second group gave an answer whose average was sixty-nine inches. This shows rather clearly that the changing of one word in a question can have a large effect on the answer given.

Loftus had a hundred students view a short film sequence depicting a multi-car accident (Loftus and Palmer, 1974). Immediately after viewing the film the subjects were given a twenty-two item questionnaire which contained six critical questions, three referring to items present in the film, and three referring to items not present. For half the subjects all the six critical questions began with the words, 'Did you see a.....?', for the remainder of the subjects all the questions began with, 'Did you see the.....?' *The* presupposes the presence of something, *A* does not. *The* questions produced a greater number of perceptions of non-present items than did *A* questions.

In 1974 Loftus presented a video film of a car crash and asked viewers questions about it (Loftus and Palmer, 1974). The questions used were shown to influence the numerical estimate of speed of the colliding cars. The questions were identical except for the verb. All the questions were in the following form: 'What speed were the cars going when they _____ (into) each other?' The gap was filled by different verbs for different subjects. The verbs used were 'contacted', 'hit', 'collided', 'smashed'. The numerical estimates of speed increased significantly with the increased 'violence' of the verb (from 31 m.p.h. to 41 m.p.h.).

These studies serve to show that the form and wording of an outsider's question can bias the way in which subjects access their stored visual memory. Can it also be shown that the type of question may actually alter the storage of memory traces? Loftus' basic paradigm is to present a video film, then ask a series of questions and then, at a later date, ask another series of questions and compare answers to the second set of questions given by groups of subjects given different initial questions. The crucial manipulation is the first questionnaire which contains presuppositional type questions. The rationale is that if the subjects treat the first set of questions as new information then they will introduce this into their already stored memories, and so change this initial memory.

In one study a ten-item questionnaire was administered. The first question asked about the speed of the car in one of two ways: either,

1 (a) 'How fast was the car going when it ran (past) the stop sign?'

or,

1 (b) 'How fast was the car going when it turned right?'

The last question was identical for all subjects:

10 'Did you see a stop sign for the car?'

Subjects responded to question (10) by circling Yes or No. Fifty-three per cent of the group who received question 1 (a) said they had seen a stop sign, while thirty-five per cent of those subjects who had been given question 1 (b) answered 'yes', they had seen a stop sign. Loftus argues that it could be the case that the persons who answered 'yes' had seen the stop sign and stored it, and question 1 (a) merely served to strengthen this storage. Alternatively, it could be argued that the person did not see the stop sign and thus had no stored memory of it, but when the question 1 (a) was asked the subject reconstructed the scene as it must have been, and thus stored a stop sign as a memory trace. Thus when he answered question (10) he was reading off from a stored memory trace which was not the product of a visualization or perception, but was rather the outcome of a verbal input (the question which involved a stop sign). The way to sort out these two possible alternatives is to use presuppositional questions which refer to something *not* present in the film. This was done by Loftus in the study which varied the verb used in the question about the speed of the cars. These questions were used as 'priming' or 'distorting' questions, because one week later the subjects were brought back and, among other questions were asked: 'Did you see any broken glass?' The number of sightings of broken glass increased with the vigour of the verbs used one week earlier. No broken glass appeared in the film! The subjects could not have had an initial memory of broken glass because none appeared in the film. This shows clearly the role of inferential processes in human memory because there is more chance of broken glass occurring as the severity of the car collisions increase. Loftus has found that when subjects are exposed to either consistent, misleading, or irrelevant information, the misleading information produced less accurate responding. Loftus concluded that, 'information to which a witness is exposed after an event is integrated into the witness's memory of the event'.

This research clearly shows the subtle influences at work in the processes of person and event identification. It seems beyond doubt that the use of presuppositional questions can affect remembering. Presuppositional questions are all too easy to ask if one is dealing with a question of fact about which you have some theory—precisely the position which may characterize the police interrogation of witness and suspect.

Another important area is the overall style of questioning: whether it is better to allow people to freely construct their own accounts (narrative reports) or for a list of questions to be produced which they have to respond to (interrogative reports). Research has concluded that narrative reports are more accurate but less wide ranging. Generally speaking an interrogative report produces greater range but less accuracy. The proportion of inaccurate items is something like a tenth for narrative reports and a quarter for interrogative. Why should this be so? In free report the subjects may report only what he remembers and is sure of, while under interrogative report he will be asked questions about which he has no relevant memory, but because he is being asked by an authority figure an answer is likely to be given; also, by the very fact of being asked a question the implication is that he ought to know the answer, and is considered capable of giving it. When an answer has been given, however uncertainly and haltingly, it becomes a 'fact' and the witness leaves all doubts behind and accepts his output as the outcome of genuine recall, and this is especially the case if the inter-rogator seems pleased with the answer, and goes on to ask further, consecutive or follow-up questions. Such effects occur most frequently with difficult-to-remember material.

Current uses of eyewitness memory

I wish now to consider current uses of eyewitness memory. There are a number of ways in which witness memory plays a role in real life. Three major areas are:

(1) the giving of verbal descriptions by the witness;
(2) the witness's construction of photo-fit resemblances;
(3) the witness's performance at identification parades.

The first of these has already been mentioned.

Ellis and Davies recently conducted a comprehensive study of the efficiency of the photo-fit system of reconstructing faces. They found that there was no effect on reconstruction accuracy of either the delay interval between seeing a face and later trying to reconstruct it nor of the initial face inspection times. They also found that subjects 'who made a special effort to remember the face' performed no better than those not so instructed, and that reconstructing a photo-fit did not affect witnesses's subsequent recognition accuracy. Addi-tionally, the individual differences of sex, imagery, field dependence and the witnesses's confidence in their reconstruction all failed to relate meaningfully to accuracy of photo-fit reconstruction. They did find white subjects to reconstruct more accurately white faces than black faces. However, the main conclusion which these psychologists arrived at was that the photo-fit aid to eyewitness memory was, in fact, a very insensitive instrument which frequently led to poor resemblances being constructed. These researchers have also investigated the effectiveness of identity parades (Shepherd, *et al.*, 1982). Again they found no effect of delays of up to three months (although a delay of twelve months led to chance levels of performance).

The validity of identification parades has been much discussed recently and a UK government committee of inquiry was set up. This Devlin Committee recognized that the differences between visual and verbal processes that were discussed earlier are relevant to criminal identification when it noted that, 'recognition depends upon the human ability to memorise a face, even when it cannot be described with any accuracy'. As Devlin put it, the problem in legal settings at the moment is that, 'Evidence of recognition if accepted, proves identity, it can be attacked as false or mistaken, but if the attack fails it is enough by itself to constitute proof'. The Committee suggested that if a witness could be no surer of identification than that the suspect resembled the wanted person then such evidence is not as strong as that of recognition. This distinction has some merit but it glosses over the problem that there is little evidence than an eyewitness's confidence in his visual identification is of any use when judging the true accuracy of the identification. Devlin noted that, 'Psychological studies of the processes of memory and recall underline the need to approach evidence of eyewitness identification with great caution'.

The relationship between accuracy and confidence

One important topic of great relevance to the legal system is the relationship between the eyewitness's objective correctness and his subjective confidence in this correctness. It seems intuitively plausible that a person is more likely to be correct if he or she is certain of being correct. But is this intuition correct? It would seem to be true in general memory research but in eyewitness testimony research the issue seems much less clear. One or two studies of visual eyewitnessing have found a positive relationship between accuracy of testimony and witnesses' confidence. However, other studies have either found no relationship, or a *negative* relationship between confidence and accuracy (i.e. the more confident the witness the *less* the accuracy) (Deffenbacher, 1980). In the light of this visual identification research, one psychologist concluded that 'witness confidence is not a reliable predictor of either recognition or recall accuracy across eyewitness and task variables'. Other researchers have shown that non-psychologists believe the relationship between accuracy and confidence to be strong and that people rely heavily on confidence to determine the credibility of an eyewitness.

The first requirement for a satisfactory appraisal of identification parades is to get clear just how accurate eyewitnesses are, and how their behaviour can be assessed. In the absence of any information from actual cases we have to rely on experimental estimates, because at real identification parades the guilt or innocence of the suspect is not generally known. However, by the use of controlled experimentation the variables present in real-life situations can be partially separated out to isolate the most relevant ones and their effect upon accuracy determined. Estimates of identification accuracy vary—but the estimations are uniformly low.

As far back as 1929 the Royal Commission on Police Powers and Procedures noted that some witnesses, 'may unconsciously tend to identify the person who most resembled their recollection of the culprit disregarding, apparently the alternative that he may not be present at all'. Since recognition and identification are *always* the result of an *approximate match* between initial memory and subsequent perceptions of an individual and since a witness may be cognizant of the possibility that the culprit's appearance may have changed somewhat since initial perception, there is value in Dent and Gray's (1975) point that, 'whether or not the witness decides to identify someone depends not only on how closely that person resembles his memory of the criminal, but also on how close he thinks the resemblance ought to be before he makes a positive identification'. It is precisely here that social psychological factors such as stereotypes can have a profound effect (see the following chapter).

Patterson (1978) has examined the effects of purposely changing aspects of an individual's appearance between initial perception and subsequent attempts at recognition (a change which any intelligent criminal might make). She found that the disguise of adding or removing a wig, or a beard, or both, significantly reduced recognition performance compared with the case in which no change of appearance occured. Further, she noted that changing the method by which the targets were presented (photo *vs* film) from initial viewing to later recognition caused a similar significant decrease in performance. Patterson pointed out that witnesses often see a criminal in the way portrayed in her film, yet they are often required by the police to try to pick that person out from photographs. Thus, an identification parade which required all the participants to be seen to be moving might prove to be an improvement. I am of the opinion that the present identification parades should be replaced by a system in which each person who would have been a member of a traditional parade enters in turn a room where the witness is present (together with one or more police officers). Thus the witness would see the people one at a time and each would leave before the next enters. The witness would not be told how many people are available for viewing and a court could note if the witness needed a second run through this sort of 'parade'. If such a system were adopted (and here research is needed) it would prevent non-suspects from unwittingly conveying to the witness who the real suspect was and it would provide information on how readily the witness made his choice. Furthermore, since the witness would not know how many people were going to be in this 'parade' it might reduce the number of occasions upon which the witness picks out the 'best resemblance' as in a traditional parade. Also, since the 'parading' people would be seen walking this would help overcome the problem of present line-ups in which the witness is almost always asked to identify a static person, who may originally have been seen moving at the time of the crime.

I now wish to turn to a topic which is being widely discussed in connection with the gathering of information from witnesses.

Hypnosis

Another method of gaining information from witnesses which has been studied by psychologists is the use of hypnosis. In California in the summer of 1977 a coach with twenty-six children on board completely disappeared. It was kidnapped by three men who used vans to transport the children from the abandoned coach to an underground hideout. The kidnappers went away and the coach driver and children managed to get out of their underground prison. When he was interviewed by the police the coach driver could remember little about the vans used by the three criminals to transport the children from the bus to the underground hideout. However, under hypnosis he provided a vital clue—the last five letters and digits of one of the van's number plate. In another case in the USA a patrolman who witnessed the death of a sixty-nine year old man in a hit-and-run incident could not remember the number of the car. Under hypnosis he recalled four of the six numbers. In a case in Britain the police were anxious to trace a man who had been seen walking along a platform by a woman who had discovered a body on a train. This man could have been the murderer but the woman was unable to furnish an adequate description. The woman was put under hypnosis and she provided a thousand word description of the person she had seen. The man was traced, and found to be innocent. His presence on the platform had been purely coincidental but by eliminating him a great saving in police man-hours was achieved. It is often forgotten that eyewitness testimony operates not only to identify suspects but also to eliminate them.

While a great many safeguards have to be inaugurated, both ethical and scientific (Gibson, 1982), none the less the use of hypnosis as a means of probing eyewitness testimony should be rigorously investigated. The reason why hypnosis may aid witnesses' attempts at recall may not be shrouded in mystery. Much psychological research shows that people often recall things more fully when they are relaxed compared to when they are tense. Hypnosis may be effective simply by enabling the subject to relax, something which present witness interrogation practices and locations may prevent. However, there are problems with hypnosis. First, not all people are capable of being hypnotized. Secondly, at the present time information gained via hypnosis cannot legally be used as evidence in most courts, though information gained from people under hypnosis may enable acceptable forms of evidence to be obtained. Thirdly, although it is acceptable for witnesses to by hypnotized, the hypnotizing of suspects may not be ethical. Finally, there is the problem of suggestion. I have already mentioned earlier how certain forms of questioning can alter people's memory. When under hypnosis witnesses may be even more susceptible to such influences. In one study people were shown a film of a road accident and later given a questionnaire concerning their recall of the accident. The questionnaire purposely contained some misleading questions of the sort I referred to earlier. Some time later all the witnesses were interviewed concerning their memory of the accident. During this phase of the study some of the witnesses were placed under hypnosis. It was found that those witnesses questioned whilst under hypnosis gave testimony that was more distorted by the earlier misleading questions on the questionnaire than were the non-hypnotized witnesses.

Though hypnosis has been used mostly to aid witnesses' recall of visual aspects of the crime it could also be used when attempting to discover other details of the event such as aspects of the criminal's voice. It is to voice identification that I now wish to turn.

Voice identification using machines

Though the police and judicial procedures for the recognition of persons by the way they speak are not as firmly laid down as they are for visual identification, the topic of identification by voice is one which has received quite a lot of attention from those wishing to develop electrical hardware for the purpose of identifying people. Some success has been claimed for voice identification by spectrographic analysis and given the possibility that the number of meaningful ways in which voices may differ may be less than the number of ways in which faces differ then such advances are not surprising. Whereas at the moment mechanized recognition of people using visual cues is still in its infancy, recognition by voice appears to have advanced a little further and may act as a guide for the development of visual systems and for their possible acceptance in legal settings.

Recognition by spectrographic voice analysis is based upon an electronic scanning of a speech sample which produces a visible amplitude/frequency/ time display. This spectrogram can then be compared with other spectrograms to see if a match can be made. This matching is usually done not by the spectrographic machinery but by means of visual comparison of the spectrograms by a human, though mechanized systems of matching are being developed. The sound patterns represented on the spectrogram are the product of the energy displayed during speech and they are determined by the interplay between the individual's vocal mechanism (i.e. mouth cavity, soft palate, nasal and pharyngeal cavities, the vocal folds, etc.) and the coupling and placement of his articulators (i.e. the tongue, lips, jaw, etc.). The validity of this technique as a means of identification rests on the assumption that the sound patterns produced in speech are unique to the individual and that the spectrogram accurately and sufficiently displays this uniqueness. Kersta (1962) was one of the first advocates of spectrographic voice analysis, claiming that voiceprint identification is closely analogous to fingerprint identification and that it is a more reliable method than handwriting comparisons.

In 1969 the Technical Committee on Speech Communication of the Acoustical Society of America asked some of its members to scientifically examine speaker identification by speech spectrograms. Their report concluded that the differences between identification by voice spectrograms and identification by fingerprints seemed to exceed the similarities and it was stated that, 'we doubt that the reliability of voice identification can ever match that of fingerprint identification'. Hall (1974) compares the reliability of fingerprints and voiceprints and concludes that, 'it is not valid to compare fingerprints with voiceprints'.

Kersta formulated the theory of invariant speech which holds that the spectral patterns of the same words spoken by two different people are more dissimilar than two such patterns resulting from the same person. He provided evidence that, at least to some extent, this theory is supportable. Trained spectrogram examiners were able, with minimal error, to select from a small set of spectrograms those two which were most alike, knowing that a match existed somewhere in the set. Kersta's early experiments were criticized on the grounds that the number of spectrograms provided to the examiners for their search for a match was small and that the examiners were told that a match did exist. In a later experiment Kersta enlarged the samples and he also developed an automated system of voice identification. This automated system counted the amplitude levels portrayed by the contour spectrogram at ten different locations on the spectrogram and a numerical code was devised for each voice sample. Fairly low error rates in identification were produced by this system if it was provided with speech samples five words in length or longer and these were due mainly to:

(1) the same word from the same speaker not always giving rise to the same code, and

(2) the same code resulting from two different people uttering the same word.

One of the questions that has only infrequently been asked of spectrographic voice identification is whether it is any better than simple human identification by ear. It would seem rather a waste of time and money if this were not the case. One group of researchers found error rates of over twenty per cent for speaker identification employing spectrograms, but the persons who matched the spectrograms in this study were not extensively trained in the art as Kersta claims they should be. (It was noted that as the study proceeded the examiners' efficiency increased.) These examiners were required both to identify speakers by visually comparing spectrograms and also to identify speakers by simply listening to the tape recordings on which the spectrograms were made. It was found that the identification performance accuracy from aural comparisons was far higher than that resulting from the visual comparison of spectrograms (ninety-four *vs* seventy-nine per cent at the end of the study), and that the time taken to arrive at the identifications was less for the aural input. Overall not only did the aural tests lead to better performance at the beginning of the study they also were the ones which derived the greatest improvement with practice. Further, for the aural information the length of utterance required for identification was shorter than that required by the spectrographic comparisons. The researchers concluded that 'differences between spectrograms of different talkers were much less apparent than the heard differences in the aural tests', and that, 'Authentication of voices is much poorer on a visual basis than on an aural basis'. This suggests that spectrographic voice analysis may certainly be no better than comparing the same voices by ear. Hecker (1971) stated that: 'whether future visual tests will provide lower error scores than future aural tests is debatable....The question about the perceptual bases of speaker recognition and their acoustical correlates remains largely unsolved.'

Many people have been sceptical about the claims made by the proponents of the accuracy of spectrographic voice identification and until a few years ago evidence based on such procedures was ascribed little status. However, a study by Tosi *et al* (1972) does lend some support to Kersta's view.

Prior to the appearance of Tosi's results a number of courts in the USA had held spectrographic voice identification evidence as inadmissible because it was believed that the technique's reliability had not been sufficiently demonstrated. Subsequent to the appearance of Tosi's results the technique was deemed admissible by several courts but not without some discussion of the weaknesses of Tosi's study. Though Tosi *et al.* had employed a larger sample of speakers than had previous investigators, doubts were raised concerning whether his data contained as much interspeaker and intraspeaker variability as any other possible group of speakers. It was believed that although the study appeared to be methodologically sound it just did not go far enough. Further, since the matching of the spectrograms was performed by eye it was held to be a purely subjective comparison which involved less scientific quantification than the polygraphic 'lie-detector' tests, the admissibility of which is still being debated, and there are a number of parallels between the judicial status of these two techniques.

Further problems for spectrographic voice analysis are the facts that no two examples of phonetically identical utterances from the same speaker are ever exactly alike and that different speakers can produce very similar spectrograms. Thus any match between two voice spectrograms can never be exact but can only involve a probability of having come from the same speaker and thus error is introduced. This question of probability is one which has always been a problem in legal settings. A person's face seen twice *never* provides the same visual input to the observer. No two fingerprints from the same finger are ever identical. Even your house has changed shape since you last saw it. Over and above these changes in the stimuli being perceived are the changes in physical viewing position of the observer, his mood, and expectancies. The important question is whether the error inherent in any recognition technique is acceptable or not. A further criticism of Tosi's study was that none of his spectrograms came from subjects under psychological stress. Such stress may well be present in a criminal investigation and it may have a significant effect upon speech production.

Edwards (1973) points out that the earliest judicial situations in which voiceprint evidence was admitted were those involving:

(1) the determination of probable cause, a point in criminal proceedings where 'incompetent' evidence can traditionally be used (e.g. the issuing of an arrest warrant); or
(2) the use of voiceprint information in a secondary role in the process of proof.

Greene (1975) draws attention to the fact that in Tosi's study the greatest type of error involved the spectrogram examiners failing to make a match when in fact one existed. He takes this to mean that the use of spectrograms will more often result in the guilty going free than in an innocent person being accused, and he points out that this technique has resulted in the elimination of far more criminal suspects than have been positively identified.

Block (1975) provides interesting anecdotal accounts of many legal trials in which the admissibility of voiceprint evidence played a part and in which scientists from various backgrounds argued either for or against its validity. Whether such evidence was finally admitted was a function of many factors including the nature of any other evidence, the type of crime, the expert witnesses and the US state in which the court was located. At the present time such evidence is still not widely accepted and the current status was well summed up by one Judge McGuire who concluded that, 'the voiceprint process requires substantial additional research before it is accepted by the scientific community, let alone admissible by the legal community'.

To sum up, spectrographic voice analysis, just like any other sort of evidence, can never conclusively prove guilt. However, it can sometimes be used to establish a high likelihood of guilt. Such an act requires not merely that two spectrograms (the perpetrator's and the suspect's) be deemed to have come from the same person when only these (or a few others more) are compared by an expert. What needs to be established is that one, or preferably more, experts can reliably pick out from a large number (say, in excess of thirty) of spectrograms from different but similarly spoken people the one which best matches the sample provided by the perpetrator.

At present not all courts agree on the admissibility of spectrographic voice identification evidence. Some deem it inadmissible whereas others view its shortcomings as insufficient to warrant ignoring it. Most seem to accept it in a way similar to their acceptance of visual identification evidence in that it is left to the court to note the possible weaknesses and unresolved questions that surround this technique. Both spectrographic voice analysis and polygraphic lie detection can be used not only by the prosecution buy also by the defence. The use of these techniques to exclude persons from suspicion receives less criticism than does their use to positively identify an individual.

Mechanized speech recognizers have had some success with a limited number of inputs from a small group of persons. If, for example, it was required that a door should open in the presence of a few specified persons then modern automated speech recognition systems are available which will respond to certain specified words spoken by these people if they have on previous occasions provided the machine with similar inputs for it to use in its matching task. It will respond to these people if they say the specified words in their usual manner. Martin (1974) presents evidence that in such situations ninety-nine per cent accuracy of response can be achieved but he is quick to point out that this kind of situation is far removed from one wherein a machine can respond to (or match) any words spoken by any person. In 1974 he stated that, 'No universal systems have been developed up to now that can perform for most users with an accuracy sufficient to be useful.' Thus, though voice recognition can be achieved by some machines for a very restricted sample, if a large sample of different voices were presented then today's machines would almost certainly be confused by them. Consequently, given the present level of development of voice recognition (or matching) machines there is little evidence that they could be of much use in person identification, especially since recognition is a different task from identification. However, since a substantial amount of research is taking place on this topic there may be some major developments in the next ten years, and any such developments will need to realize that a human identifies speech not only by the acoustic information upon which today's machines rely but also by the grammatical and contextual cues that are available.

Voice identification by human listeners

In 1976 the Devlin Committee, which reported to the UK Home Secretary its findings in respect of identification in criminal cases, stated that as far as they were concerned there had been no scientific research into the question of voice identification but that 'research should proceed as rapidly as possible into the practicality of voice parades ... or any other appropriate method'. Now while it is slightly inaccurate to say that no research has been conducted into voice identification it may be true to say that little directly relevant research has been conducted. In fact, despite the very long history of voice identification in legal cases, formal study and experimentation is a fairly recent development.

It was against the backdrop of research paucity and expressed government interest in the feasibility or otherwise of voice identification that at the North East London Polytechnic we undertook an extended experimental research programme into the nature and quality of voice recognition by human listeners (Bull and Clifford, 1983). This research was funded by the Home Office Research Unit.

At the present time there are three major types of investigative methodology within voice identification which have forensic potentiality. One approach is the investigation of the feasibility or otherwise of mechanized recognition (so called spectrographic analysis). A second approach is the detection of similarity or otherwise of two prepared speech samples by professional or academic, expert phoneticians. The third approach is experimental investigation of voice recognition by human, non-expert, listeners under a number of controlled conditions. Our research project fell squarely into the third type of investigation. It was felt that this approach to voice identification was to be encouraged for a number of reasons, chief amongst which is that voice identification in the absence of taping facilities is the most prevalent type of identification likely to be encountered by the police in everyday criminal detection.

Specifically we looked at the effect upon human voice identification accuracy of such factors as:

(1) the number of distractor (sound-alike but non-target) voices used when trying to identify a previously heard (target) voice in an 'identification parade' analog situation;
(2) the duration or quantity of speech sample initially heard;
(3) the delay between initially hearing a target voice and attempting identification of that voice;
(4) the disguising of a voice during initial hearing;

(5)   different methods of fixating a target voice for later identification;
(6)   telephone mediated *vs* non-telephone mediated to-be-identified voices;
(7)   instructions which could be taken to imply the presence or absence of a target voice in a recognition set;
(8)   blind listeners as witnesses;
(9)   age of listeners; and,
(10) sex of listeners.

In addition to these major concerns we also investigated the effects upon voice identification accuracy of the sex of the target voice and the relationship between a listener's objective correctness of identification and his subjective feelings of correctness in identification.

The general methodology was basically very simple. In all thirteen hundred listeners heard a taped voice (target) and were later asked to identify that voice among a variable number of other, fairly similar but non-target, taped (distractor) voices presented in a way analogous to a visual identification parade. The presentation of the target voice and subsequent identification constituted one trial. Most experiments involved six trials per subject. Unless otherwise specified, testing took place within one minute of hearing the target voice. This very short delay was designed to allow us to assess the maximum performance of witnesses in voice identification situations, there being little or no adequate evidence upon which to base an estimate. In most cases the specific experiments arose from problems commonly encountered in identification situations.

Much of our experimentation was motivated by Devlin's specific call for 'voice parade' research and thus several studies varied the 'parade' size while also looking at the effects of other factors. However, one group of studies addressed this problem directly. Specifically we sought to discover whether the number of 'distractor' voices used in an identification set influenced the accuracy of identification of a target voice placed within that set. We found that recognition accuracy was significantly better under a four distractor condition (sixty-four per cent), than under six and eight distractor conditions which did not differ between themselves (forty-eight and forty-nine per cent respectively). This latter finding suggested that identification performance did not decrease uniformally as parade size increased. To check this finding a second experiment was conducted and essentially identical results were found. Thus, actual parade size, once it reaches six distractors, does not seem to be an important consideration in identification accuracy.

Our next group of experiments were designed to test the intuitive belief that identification accuracy should increase as the size of the original speech sample heard increases. In the first experiment of this series listeners heard a target voice uttering either a one, two, or four sentence speech sample. In line with reviewed evidence we found no difference in recognition accuracy among these three speech sample size conditions (seventy-five, seventy-seven, and eighty-two per cent respectively). This suggested that hearing at least one sentence was sufficient to maximize identification performance. To test this a second experiment was conducted in which listeners heard either a one word or an eight word utterance and then attempted identification. This time there was a significant difference in identification performance with the eight word condition being better than the one word condition (fifty-one and thirty-seven per cent accuracy, respectively). However, even with a one word speech sample it should be noted that recognition accuracy was above chance level. A third experiment confirmed the first experiment's finding of no significant difference in performance following the hearing of a one or a two sentence speech sample. Thus it seems not to be the case that an extensive speech sample is required for accurate identification.

Another everyday criminal justice system problem that we built into our voice research was delay—the time gap between hearing a criminal and making an identification or proffering a description. In the first of our experiments in this area subjects tried to identify a target voice either ten minutes, forty minutes, one hundred minutes, or one hundred and forty minutes after hearing it. Generally speaking, increasing the delay interval slightly decreased identification performance (from fifty-six to forty-four per cent). In a second experiment, listeners attempted identification of a target voice after either ten minutes, twenty-four hours, seven days, or fourteen days had elapsed. Surprisingly no simple relationship was found to exist between accuracy and lag at these longer delays (forty-five, twenty-seven, twenty-three, and forty-five per cent respectively). A replication study using the same delay intervals but a new set of subjects produced the same non-linear pattern of results, but this time with a suggestion of a delay effect between ten minutes and fourteen days (forty-one and twenty-one per cent respectively). Taking all these studies together it seems that recognition performance is poorer with delays in excess of ten minutes but for delays greater than this, performance does not necessarily become progressively poorer.

Another problem which police have to contend with in terms of evidence is disguise—an obvious ploy for the criminal—whether visual or vocal. We looked at the effect of such voice disguise by having subjects try to identify a voice, which had initially been disguised (in any way the speaker chose), within voice parades of five, seven or nine non-disguised voices. Identification accuracy was clearly, but not totally, impaired by disguise, and further, it decreased progressively with increase in voice parade size, dropping from thirty-six per cent accuracy with four distractors through twenty-six per cent accuracy with six, to seventeen per cent with eight distractors. Thus voice disguise must be treated as a serious complication in the evaluation of the feasibility of voice identification.

The effect of the telephone, which plays a large part in many real-life cases, was investigated when we presented target voices either taped naturally or taped over the phone, and tested both types of presented voice via naturally taped or phone-taped voice parades. The results showed that the best identification performance resulted from the taped-voice/taped-parade condition (mean of 3.6

out of a possible 6), while all conditions which involved the phone (at presentation or test) were similar but lower (2.6 out of a possible 6). This finding suggests that while phone-mediated voices reduce identification accuracy somewhat, it neither suggests ruling out such voices in identification nor that comparability of listening conditions is necessary.

Both the Royal Commission on Police Powers and Procedures (1929) and, more recently, the new guidelines for the conduct of identification parades show an awareness of the crtitical importance of the wording used when a witness is introduced to either photographs or an ID parade for identification purposes. The wording must be such as to suggest that the actual perpetrator of the crime in question may not be present. This problem exercised us also, and we looked at it directly in one experiment by presenting some parade tapes which *never* contained the target voice ('open' tapes), and some tapes which always *did* contain the target voice ('closed' tapes). Half the listeners were told that the target voice 'would always be present' ('closed' instructions) while the other half were told that the target voice 'may be present' ('open' instructions). The major finding was that most subjects (eighty-seven and a half per cent) strongly believed that a target voice was present even when it was not *and* they had been given the instructions which suggested that it may *not* be present. This tends to offer support to the generally held belief that witnesses come to identification situations with a 'set' to select someone ('set' was explained in the previous chapter).

In another study we compared the voice recognition performance of sighted listeners with that of blind listeners (Bull *et al.*, 1983). The rationale for this was the common belief that deficits in one modality may occasion augmentation in others. If blind subjects were found to be better than sighted subjects this could suggest a possible auditory training component in voice identification. In the event we did find that blind subjects performed better than sighted subjects although performance was not directly related to degree of blindness and there were large individual differences within the blind groups. On average blind listeners performed about twenty-five per cent better than sighted listeners.

Common knowledge and extant research suggests that courts and jurors rely heavily upon the credibility of a witness which in turn stems from the confidence a witness communicates. But what is the actual relationship between subjective feelings of correctness and objective correctness? With eyewitnesses the relationship seems frequently to be either non-existent or in fact reversed. However, in our voice research we consistently observed a positive and significant relationship between confidence and accuracy. This was found in the studies which looked at delay, levels of processing, speech sample duration, telephone and 'open' and 'closed' tapes. Thus in voice identification there may be better grounds for believing in the witness who espouses certainty.

In terms of the most fundamental question we addressed—how good is the lay person at voice identification under very favourable conditions—collapsing the highest estimate in each experiment across thirteen such experiments we arrived at a figure of sixty-eight per cent accuracy. The range varied markedly, however, depending upon specific conditions, from a high of eighty-six per cent to a low of nil correct identification.

Conclusion

If society wishes to convict persons who commit crimes, and in some cases the *only* evidence against them is that of identification, then identification parades as presently conducted (or preferably modified in line with the suggestions which I have made (Clifford and Bull, 1978) are perhaps the most efficient way of achieving this, although they are very error prone. It is worth stressing that no type of conviction can ever be certain. As Samuel Butler said, 'Life is the art of drawing sufficient conclusions from insufficient data'. I believe that the Devlin Committee's recommendations to the UK Home Secretary are about right and I will finish this chapter with them. I hope that you, because of this book, will see why I, as a psychologist, broadly agree with them.

> 'We do, however, wish to ensure that in ordinary cases prosecutions are not brought on eyewitness evidence only and that, if brought, they will fail. We think they ought to fail, since in our opinion it is only in exceptional cases that identification evidence is by itself sufficiently reliable to exclude a reasonable doubt about guilt. We recommend that the trial judge should be required by statute,
> a. to direct the jury that it is not safe to convict upon eyewitness evidence unless the circumstances of the identification are exceptional or the eyewitness evidence is supported by substantial evidence of another sort; and
> b . to indicate to the jury the circumstances, if any, which they might regard as exceptional and the evidence, if any, which they might regard as supporting the identification; and
> c . if he is unable to indicate either such circumstances or such evidence, to direct the jury to return a verdict of not guilty'.

(Devlin Report, 1976, pp. 149 – 150)

The Devlin recommendation is, in a sense, a combination. It recommends that the trial judge give a special instruction to the jury, but in addition, it recommends that convictions based solely upon eyewitness testimony not be allowed unless the testimony is exceptional.

Suggested further reading

Clifford, B.R., and Bull, R. (1978). *The Psychology of Person Identification*, Routledge and Kegan Paul, London.

Loftus, E.F. (1979). *Eyewitness Testimony*, Harvard University Press, Boston.

Wells, G.L., and Loftus, E.F. (1983). *Eyewitness Testimony: Psychological Perspectives*, Cambridge University Press, New York.

Yarmey, A.D. (1979). *The Psychology of Eyewitness Testimony*, The Free Press, New York.

CHAPTER 3

Summing Up or Assessing People

For centuries man has tried to decide what sets him apart from other animals. We have asked ourselves: 'What are the abilities which we possess that animals do not have?' To provide an adequate answer to such a question is not as easy as initially it may seem. We could say that man possesses language. However, many non-human species do possess some measure of language skill. We could say, as has been said for centuries, that man is different from animals because man believes in God. However, not all human beings or human societies believe in a God. We could say that man is the only species to have a self-concept (that is, the awareness of oneself as a person). However, how could it be proved that non-humans do not have a self-concept? For me, one thing that to a considerable degree sets man apart from other species is his ability to *predict* either the likely consequences of his own actions before he actually commits himself to behaving in a certain way, or how someone else will behave. This ability to predict how someone else will behave is of great importance in human society. When we meet someone (a friend or a stranger) we wish our interaction with that person to be successful. ('Successful' encompasses anything from striking up a friendship with a 'nice' stranger to avoiding or getting away from a 'nasty' one.) We therefore want to predict what the other person is thinking and how the other person is likely to behave.

What I wish to cover in this chapter is how we sum up or assess people, and I want to consider when this is of use and when it leads to errors being made. If a person is smartly dressed and well mannered would you be less suspicious of him than of someone who is scruffily dressed or of abnormal appearance or manner? In the United States a policeman was shot dead by a smartly dressed, well mannered individual whom the officer neglected to search when arresting him. In their observational study of police officers' street contacts with juveniles Piliavin and Briar (1964) found the officers' behaviour and decisions to be greatly influenced by the juveniles' physical appearance (e.g. clothing and grooming). These researchers made the point that the police may behave in this way because their experiences have suggested to them that juveniles with certain physical appearances should be treated harshly. However, they went on to argue that such discriminating policing may result in self-fulfilling consequences in the sense that since certain juveniles are treated poorly by the police they in turn come to have little respect for the police and therefore behave accordingly. This is a hypothesis worthy of further investigation.

The predisposition to treat someone favourably because something about them is assessed positively by you is commonly known as 'the halo effect' and it is caused by a process psychologists refer to as stereotyping. In this chapter I shall attempt to illustrate the extent to which people's expectancies concerning how certain types of individuals behave can influence their perception and judgements of these individuals. Though many research studies in this area have found that observers frequently agree upon the attributes they assign to people solely on the basis of their appearance, the validity or truth of these observations often has little strength. Some of the first psychologists to study the way in which a person's outward appearance might be related to his behaviour claimed that there is a relationship between body build and personality. However, there exists little good scientific evidence to support such claims.

Criminals' appearance

In the USA a psychologist selected from the files of the Nebraska State Penitentiary the case records of twenty criminals, deliberately avoiding seeing the photographs of the criminals until this selection had been made. Since he was going to ask people to indicate which crime the particular individual had committed by looking at a portrait photograph of a criminal, the psychologist wisely wanted to avoid selecting criminals whose photographs matched his own stereotype. (Thus this researcher avoided the possibility of a biased selection of photographs about which observers might agree solely because the experimenter had specially selected the photographs in the first place.) These photographs were shown one at a time to a large audience who were required to say which of four crimes they thought each photographed individual had committed. The observers were correct more often than was accountable by chance factors alone but they were by no means overwhelmingly so.

In 1962 a German researcher obtained photographs of seven hundred and thirty convicted criminals which he then divided into sixteen categories depending upon the type of crime which had been committed. From each of these sixteen groups of photographs a composite portraiture was made and these facial portraits were shown to a large number of people who were required to pick out from a list of crimes the crime they thought related to the portrait. It was found that most people could do this and quite a few actually chose the correct crime for many of the portraits.

Modern criminologists do not believe that criminals belong to a single physical or psychological type, but do the general public? Casting directors of cinema and TV films frequently select actors to play parts for which they look 'right'. A study of stereotypes in fiction found that villains tended to be dark and swarthy whereas heroes tended to be blond. One wonders to what extent these same prejudices apply today and to what degree they should really be termed prejudices in the sense that this word implies prejudgements being made which have no validity. Could it be that in real life most heroes are blond? Nobody has really examined this question.

Recently Shoemaker *et al.* (1973) found evidence that we do have stereotypic notions about the appearance criminals have. They concluded that,

> 'on the basis of our findings it would be plausible to assume that stereotypic conceptions of what a particular suspect should look like could influence the selection of 'the one who did it' by an eyewitness of a crime, particularly when that eyewitness did not have a good, clear look at the offender'. (p. 432)

In this study fifty-four facial photographs of middle-aged, white males were shown to audiences of students who were asked to rate how likely the person was to have committed murder or robbery or treason. The twelve photographs which received the most extreme rankings were then shown to a second group of audiences and each audience rated the portrayed individual for his likelihood of having committed one of the crimes. Here significant differences were observed across photographs indicating the employment of stereotypes. Further audiences were given brief written accounts of ambiguously criminal incidents attached to which was one of the twelve photographs. The extent of attributed guilt was found to be significantly influenced by which of the photographs was attached. These results were obtained (with rather poor methodology) in artificial circumstances, but the processes which they claim to highlight are likely to be operative in the real world. In another psychologists's experiment observers briefly looked at a drawing of several people sitting or standing in a subway train. One of the people in this scene was black and a white man near to him was holding an open, cut-throat razor. When later asked to describe the scene, fifty per cent of the observers reported that the razor had been in the hand of the black man.

In the psychology department at NELP we conducted a study to see whether people do still share beliefs about which face fits which crime (Bull and Green, 1980). Since this study was planned to be an initial exploratory one for a possible planned programme of research, the facial photographs used were not of criminals but were of male friends of the researchers. Because people were going to be asked to match the photographs to certain types of crime (in order to see whether the general public do share common beliefs about criminal appearances) it was important that the photographed persons were all of a similar age so that age alone could not be used to pair a face to a crime. Each of the ten photographs used was of a male aged between twenty-seven and thirty-three years of age, each of the photographs having the same blank background. The amount of the photograph occupied by each face was similar and all the faces had (by design) a bland, expressionless look.

Each of forty-eight adult members of the public and of ten policemen were asked to say which of eleven listed crimes each of the ten faces had committed. These observers were allowed to allot more than one face to a particular crime. Each observer saw the faces in a different order and the order in which the lists of crimes was presented was also varied on a random schedule to avoid possible artificial bias. Of the non-police observers half were male, half female and within each of these two sub-groups one third were aged between eighteen and twenty-five years, one-third between twenty-five and thirty-five years, and the remainder were aged over thirty-five years.

Statistical analyses of the data revealed that for the crimes of arson, theft, rape, and burglary no face was chosen significantly more frequently than any other. However, for the crimes of 'mugging', robbery with violence, company fraud, soliciting, taking and driving away, illegal possession of drugs, and gross indecency, one of the faces was chosen much more frequently (and statistically significantly) than the others. Further, different faces were chosen for different crimes; that is, it is not the case that for every crime the observers merely chose repeatedly the same face.

The data were also analysed to see if the age or sex of the observers had played a part. No effects of age or sex of observer were found indicating that when there was agreement among the observers about a face fitting a particular crime this came equally from all ages and both sexes. The data gathered from the ten policemen who took part in this study is too small a sample to be analysed statistically in the same way as the data above. However, the conclusions to be drawn from the police data are similar to those from the general public. For the crimes for which the general public agreed upon a face, the police chose the same face to fit that crime (e.g. for the crime of gross indecency six of the ten policemen chose a particular face, as had the majority of the general public, the remaining four policemen each choosing a different face for this crime).

Validity

The question as to what extent physical appearances are valid indices of behavioural characteristics has been examined for many decades and was popular even before the advent of psychology as a scientific discipline. However, whether existing stereotypes are correct may be irrelevant to the role they can play in person recognition and description. It may not matter to what extent these biases, expectancies, and prejudices have any validity, what matters is if people believe that such relationships exist and if people base their judgements and reactions upon them.

Some years ago a psychologist gave a brief verbal personality account of two imaginary characters to a group of subjects. One of the characters was described as 'warmhearted and honest', the other 'ruthless and brutal'. The subjects were required to give some indication of the appearance they expected the characters to have by rating on seven-point scales each of thirty-two facial (and hair) characteristics. For twenty-five of these thirty-two features the ratings were found to be significantly different as a function of the personality accounts. It was noted that for the majority of those characteristics which differentiated between the two descriptions the 'warmhearted and honest' person was rated as being average (e.g. average width of nose) whereas the 'ruthless and brutal' individual was judged as having abnormal features (for example, the observers accorded to him either an extremely narrow nose or an extremely wide one). It seems that the observers in this study were employing a stereotype that I have frequently noticed in my research on the psychological significance of facial deformity, namely that the general public take abnormality of appearance to be indicative of abnormality of personality and likely behaviour. In his book entitled *Stigma*, Goffman (1963) notes that this term was orginated by the Greeks who burnt or cut signs into the body to signify that the bearer was a slave, a criminal, or a traitor. Goffman believes that today we often take abnormality of appearance to indicate not only that there is one thing abnormal about the person (e.g. the face) but that such people must therefore be *totally* abnormal (e.g. in personality, intelligence). Goffman suggested that society may frequently judge a person with a peculiar appearance to be bad or dangerous. Another psychologist showed photographs of persons, some with facial anomalies, to non-disfigured persons who were asked to describe the photographed individuals. One was of a man with narrow, deep-set eyes, a prominent nose, buck teeth, a small forehead, and lop ears. It was not mentioned that in fact he was of high intelligence and an executive in a large company. Descriptions of the man such as the following were often voiced: 'He looks like a maniac. He's a dope addict. He's mean and small. He is in a gang. He has a desire to kill.' The psychologist concluded that, 'facial features led respondents not only to impute to these patients personality traits considered socially unacceptable, but to assign to them roles and statuses on an inferior social level'. For our present purposes the studies cited above indicate that people will both deduce behavioural and attitudinal propensities from a seen face and will also generate likely facial features from behavioural data.

Another psychologist using line drawings of faces observed that people acted in a fairly regular and statistically predictable way in attributing personality characteristics to the faces. He found, for example, that when the eyes were placed 'up' on the schematic face, such a face was regarded as significantly more trustworthy than the same face on which the eyes were placed lower. Similarly, another psychologist observed fairly high consistency across rates of schematic faces (which varied only in the vertical positioning of eyes, nose, mouth) for judgements of intelligence, happiness and likeableness. The existence of such effects may have implications for procedures like that of photo-fit. We might ask ourselves why so many photo-fit reconstructions produce unattractive or ugly faces?

What the studies mentioned in the above paragraph were unable to do was to decide whether such stereotypes have any validity. Many years ago a psychologist collected forty facial photographs of female students who were all inter acquainted. 'True' character judgements were obtained by the friends of each photographed individual completing a number of rating scales whilst looking at the photograph of the person. High inter judge agreement was found here. Next the photographs were rated by people who were unacquainted with the photographed individuals. Again high inter judge agreement was noted. However, when the 'true' and 'stranger' ratings were compared for each of the photographs the resulting correlations were very low (save for 'beauty' and 'intelligence'.) Thus though the strangers agreed upon their expectancies about the photographed individuals these were not the same as those held by people who knew the individuals concerned.

One does not know to what extent a very senior London police officer was aware of the research which had been conducted in this area but he advised policemen (Bull and Clifford, 1978) to observe in court persons in custody for the theft or unlawful taking of motor vehicles to 'see to which category they belong. This will help you to slant your mind to the general type of person you must watch for when patrolling.' It is certainly not possible to say that such advice is worthless but it may be that such advice can sometimes cause problems.

Facial attractiveness

An individual's facial attractiveness has an effect on how threatening other people judge that person to be. Psychologists have found that the more attractive a person's face the less threatening that individual is believed to be. I have found that the addition of one or two small scars to a face leads to that face being judged as more dishonest.

In their investigation of the photo-fit system of recalling faces some psychologists at the University of Aberdeen conducted several studies concerning the photo-fit reconstruction of a seen face. In one study all the reconstructors (housewives) were shown the same face but half of them were told it was the face of a murderer whereas the other half were told that it was of a lifeboat captain. The face was removed and the women were asked to construct a photo-fit of it. The next stage of this study involved presenting the constructed photo-fit faces to a new group of subjects who were required to describe these using some adjectives. It was found that the photo-fits of the face deemed to be of a lifeboat man were judged to be significantly more attractive and intelligent than the photo-fits of the same face when it was described as being of a murderer.

Physical attractiveness is a variable which is currently receiving much attention from psychologists (in the experimental sense!) and research suggests that we might not expect persons having certain appearances to be involved in crime and that we might not be inclined to pick them out in an identification parade or from memory.

A number of psychologists have suggested that low physical attractiveness contributes to careers of deviancy and in 1941 Monahan noted that,

'even social workers accustomed to dealing with all types often find it difficult to think of a normal, pretty girl as being guilty of a crime. Most people, for some inexplicable reason, think of crime in terms of abnormality of appearance and I must say that beautiful women are not often convicted.' (p. 121)

Several psychologists have studied the effects of defendants' attractiveness on 'juries'. Since it is not permitted to study jurors in real-life criminal cases, mock or pseudo 'jurors' are usually used. A Canadian psychologist examined the effect of physical appearance on judgements of guilt and severity of recommended punishment in a simulated jury task. As in many psychological experiments the people who took part in the experiment were students who may or may not behave in the same way as would other members of the population. Over one hundred people filled in a questionnaire and this survey revealed that (1) only twenty-one per cent believed that a defendant's character and previous history should not influence juror's decision, whereas (2) over ninety-three per cent believed that the defendant's physical appearance should *not* bias these decisions. A further sixty-six students received written details of an example of alleged cheating during an examination and they were required to rate how likely it was that the person mentioned had been cheating and the extent of punishment that should be given. Two-thirds of the 'jurors' also received a photograph of the defendant and these were also required as their last task to rate the defendant for physical attractiveness. For each of these 'jurors' the photograph was of an opposite sexed individual. If was found for female defendants that the more physically attractive individuals were judged to be significantly less guilty and to merit milder punishment than the unattractive female defendants. No effect of physical attractiveness was apparent for the male defendants. This difference could be due to the possibility that the physical attractiveness of male defendants does not play a role in such settings with female 'jurors', or to the possibility that the male defendants did not differ much in their level of physical attractiveness. This latter suggestion is supported by the attractiveness ratings. Whereas the female defendants did significantly differ in the attractiveness ratings they received, the male defendants did not. Whether the male defendants did not in reality differ much in attractiveness, or whether the allegation that they were cheats reduced the good-looking ones' attractiveness for the female jurors is not known. However, the male photographs which were used had been deemed to be significantly different in attractiveness in one of the psychologist's earlier studies.

Other psychologists' studies have found that the appearance of the defendant has a significant effect upon 'jurors'' decisions about the length of prison sentence that they thought should be given. The unattractive defendant is usually 'sentenced' more severely for a given crime than a defendant with an attractive character and appearance. In part of one study the character of the victim of the crime was also varied and it was found that the defendant tended to receive a more severe sentence if the victim was attractive. In another study the attractiveness of the (female) defendant again had an effect upon the sentence given. However, the effect of attractiveness interacted with the nature of the crime.

That is, as expected from previous findings, an attractive burglar received a less severe sentence than an unattractive burglar (six *vs.* nine years), but an attractive swindler received a stiffer sentence than an unattractive swindler. Interestingly, 'jurors' given no information about the defendant's beauty attributed significantly greater physical attractiveness to her as a swindler than as a burglar.

As stated above, these studies were not performed on real-life court cases. However, recently in Canada a study was based on real-life cases. In this study defendants' faces were rated for facial attractiveness and these judgements were then related to the true outcome of the many court cases involved. It was found that unattractive defendants were more likely to have been found guilty and to have received harsher real sentences than were attractive defendants. Thus what psychologists had earlier found in simulated settings seems to be the case in real life.

Now these studies have been mentioned not only to describe the effects of physical appearance on 'jurors'' decision making but also to act as examples of how, in general, we may judge, predict, and react to people on the basis of their appearance.

Many psychologists believe that good-looking people are seen as possessing more socially desirable traits than unattractive individuals. A Canadian researcher found that the attractiveness of the photograph on a child's report card had an effect upon judgements of misbehaviour. Female students were given written details of a child's misbehaviour together with a photograph which was supposed to be of the child. The description of the misdeed was always exactly the same and the only thing that varied was that some students saw a photograph of an attractive child and some saw a photograph of an unattractive child. It was found that the students suggested more lenient treatment for the attractive child. Those who saw a photograph of an attractive child said that the misbehaviour was likely to be only a temporary thing whereas those with a photograph of an unattractive individual frequently said that they believed it likely that the child was often naughty, was antisocial, and should be severely punished.

In the above study inexperienced students were employed as the assessors but in a similar study by two other psychologists experienced teachers were shown a nursery child's report card to which was attached a photograph. The teachers were asked to rate the child and it was found that although the report card always said exactly the same thing, the more attractive the child in the photograph (established by prior study) the more favourable were the teachers' evaluations of IQ, peer relationships, likely future educational accomplishments, and parents' attitudes towards school. Another study again used as subjects experienced teachers who were given a child's report card plus a photograph. The teachers were asked to say how likely it was that the child had been the naughty one in class and if so, what punishment should be given. As would be expected, the nature of the report card greatly influenced the teachers' decisions. If the report card was good then little punishment was advocated.

However, if the report card was bad the teachers who had the unattractive male photographs were more inclined to suggest harsher punishment. These three studies illustrate that the physical attractiveness stereotype may operate even in the world of young school-children. It is important to note here that we not only make inferences about individuals' likely antisocial behaviour by the way they look but that in behaving towards children in this way we may create in them certain predispositions which then result in the existence of some self-fulfilling prophecies. Physically attractive children may receive more positive attention and support when they are young and because of this they develop greater social skills and self-confidence. As a consequence they become attractive in more than just the physical sense and in adulthood such people may indeed be worth approaching and be more successful than physically unattractive individuals who have not developed such attributes. It seems likely to be a widely held stereotype that physically attractive individuals are not so inclined to do unpleasant or antisocial things.

Body build

Variations in body build have also been found to lead to stereotypic expectancies. One psychologist noted that with the face kept constant differences in stature led to significantly different judgements of personality. It has also been observed that differences in body build reliably have effects upon the judgements children make about individuals. As a child develops, the imposition of stereotypes will shape his behaviour and this might result in the stereotypes actually becoming valid (i.e. if a child looks 'naughty' and people act accordingly towards him might he therefore believe that this is his role in life?). Some studies have shown that it is possible to judge with some validity a person's occupation solely from their photograph. Other experimenters have looked at whether perceptual judgements of height would be affected by the status of the person being judged. It was hypothesized that as authority status increased there would be a related tendency by subjects to perceive the person as being taller. The results of one study showed this clearly to be the case since estimations of height were found to be directly related to authority status. However, this finding should be treated with some caution since the equally tall people being judged (fellow staff and students of the same college), varied along other dimensions besides authority status. Thus the systematic over- and underestimations could just as well be related to differences in body types, facial characteristics, etc. of the people being evaluated. Because of this criticism another experiment was conducted this time using only one stimulus person, who was unknown to the observers, and who for different groups of observers was given imaginary academic status. There were five conditions of status: student, laboratory demonstrator, lecturer, senior lecturer, and professor. The stimulus person was introduced to a class of students as one of the above persons. A different class of students was used for each of the five conditions. After the stimulus person had left the room, the subjects were asked to estimate his height to the nearest half-inch. The results showed a significant relationship between ascribed status and estimations of his height, the relationship being a tendency by subjects to estimate him as being taller in relation to an increase in status, the 'mean' estimations being; 5'9½" (student), 5'10" (laboratory demonstrator), 5'11" (lecturer), 5'11½" (senior lecturer), and 6'½" (professor), the stimulus person's actual height being 6'1"

Another study looked at the relationship between the accuracy of height estimations as a function of the sex and height of the observer, and the height of the person being judged. It was found that both males and female underestimate the height of tall people, and overestimate the height of short people. In general observers tend to guess toward some kind of average. A significant relationship between subjects' own height and their estimation of the stimulus persons' height was found in another study.

Recently George Ward and I conducted a study which was concerned with the effects of several variables on the estimation of height. First, it was designed to examine the hypothesis that as ascribed status increases there is a related tendency by observers to judge the person as being taller. Secondly, it considers how such an effect may be influenced by the variable of 'distance'. This variable is clearly important in an examination of perceptual distortion of size, for it may well be easier to estimate the size of someone who is only ten feet away, as opposed to fifty feet away. This point is particularly relevant in an experiment concerned with estimations of height, as (at close range) estimations can usually be made in relation to one's own height. However, should the person being evaluated be at such a distance as to make estimations more difficult, then other strategies may be employed which may involve stereotyping factors. Therefore it could be hypothesized that if the social status variable does have a direct effect on estimations of height, then the 'strength' of the effect may increase in relation to an increase in distance. Figure 3.1 presents the results

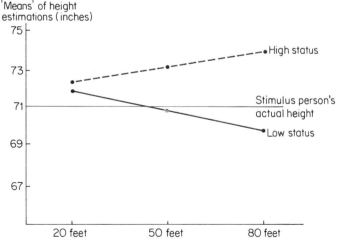

Figure 3.1 The effects of status and distance on height estimation

from our experiment. You will readily see that as the distance between the person whose height was being estimated and the people making these estimations increased, so the effects of ascribed status (professor *vs* student) increased. At a distance of eighty feet away, the stimulus person when described as 'a professor' was judged to be four inches taller than when he (i.e. the *same* stimulus person) was described as 'a student'.

Implications

The implication of several of the studies which I have cited is that observers' recall of individuals will be a function not only of what they actually perceived at the time of the relevant incident but also of what their stereotypic notions suggest to them. Furthermore, some researchers believe that stereotypes can have an influence not only on the nature of recall but also at the time of perception. More research is certainly needed on this point but it does seem likely that when the sighting of an individual is incomplete (or memory fades) the observer will add factors, and these probably will be a function of his stereotypes and expectancies. (This 'confabulation' was discussed in the previous chapter). The publication *Science and the Police* (from the British Association for the Advancement of Science) noted that there is a tendency to fill in gaps in remembrance, even of those parts of a happening where what actually occurred has been forgotten.

Several studies reveal that the general public (and the police) do form expectations about people based on their appearance. This being the case, we should ask what influences these expectations may have. Do they have an effect in the eyewitness testimony situation, or on the activities of the police, or both? Further, is it possible that children (and adults) with certain sorts of faces come to perform criminal acts because that is what society tells them it expects of them? Is it true that beautiful people are nice and ugly people nasty? If so, why should this be?

As Yarmey (1979) observes, understandably,

'the police are more likely to stop and question suspicious persons whenever certain social factors or environmental conditions exist. Officers are guided by their common sense, intuitive guesswork, and their schematic representations of 'criminal types' based upon experience in the field. The quality of police decision making can be improved by minimizing the conditions that lead to self-fulfilling prophecies.' (p. 19)

We should not however forget that,

'Although stereotypes can be midleading in that they ignore the wide variety of individual differences which exist among people, they are functional in some respects. Stereotypes are employed because they reduce the tremendous amount of information we have about others into more manageable units.' (Yarmey, 1979, p. 89)

(This need for manageable units of information was discussed in chapter 1 on the limitations of the series and memory.)

As suggested in chapter 1, the way a person perceives and remembers information can be strongly influenced by their own beliefs, expectations, and predispositions. Such biases also operate during the stereotyping process in that the way a person chooses to sum up or react to other people will be influenced by his initial views about them. Kirkham (1974), a former correction counsellor in the USA, professor of criminology, and part-time policeman noted that,

> 'I found that there was a world of difference between encountering individuals, as I had, in mental health or correctional settings, and facing them as the patrolman must: when they are violent, hysterical, desperate... Now, as a police officer, I began to encounter the offender for the first time as a very real menace to my personal safety and the security of our society. The felon was no longer a harmless figure sitting in blue denims across my prison desk, a 'victim' of society, to be treated with compassion and leniency. He became an armed robber fleeing from the scene of a crime: a crazed maniac threatening his family with a gun; someone who might become my killer crouched behind the wheel of a car on a dark street'. (p. 130)

This chapter will have succeeded if the strong possibility that stereotypic factors can play an important role in policing has been conveyed to the reader. However, most of the research cited in this chapter was conducted in rather non-life-like situations and ecologically valid research in life-like settings needs to be undertaken. Nevertheless, in all aspects of policing one has to compare the possible successes against the likely errors when deciding whether to sum up or assess people on the basis of their appearance.

Suggested further reading

Bull, R. (1979). 'The influences of stereotypes on person identification', in *Psychology, Law and Legal Processes* (Eds. D. Farrington, K. Hawkins, and S. Lloyd-Bostock), Macmillan, London.

Bull, R. (1983). 'Physical appearance and criminality', *Current Psychological Reviews*, **2**, 269–282.

Clifford, B.R., and Bull, R. (1978). *The Psychology of Person Identification*, Routledge and Kegan Paul, London.

CHAPTER 4

Settings and Situations : The Influence of Others on Individual Behaviour

In an earlier chapter, we reviewed some of the recent psychological research into impression formation and eyewitness testimony, showing how it directly relates to many aspects of police work. We saw how a police officer's observations of an incident and of the persons involved could easily and unwittingly be affected by such internal factors as the officer's own attitudes, expectations, needs, and current mood as well as by external factors peculiar to the setting in which the incident occurred. We also saw how the distortions produced may then be further compounded by additional factors which affect the storage and retrieval of information in memory. Thus, initial errors in perception of an event by a police officer together with subsequent errors of recall may readily find their way into reports written up sometime later back at the station or appear in evidence presented to court a long time after the incident. Finally, and equally important, we pointed out how a police officer may inadvertently elicit false testimony from others involved in or present at an incident simply by the manner in which questions are put to them.

However, susceptibility to error and bias through sources of influence of which we may be scarcely aware is not confined to the fields of 'eyewitness testimony' and 'impression formation'. In this chapter we will examine some of the social processes which psychologists have shown to have an important influence on individual action. We believe that an awareness and understanding of these processes will enable a police officer to function more effectively in the great variety of social settings and situations in which police intervention occurs. We assume that the reader has little formal knowledge of social processes and that the social psychological perspective is an unfamiliar one. Consequently, we thought it sensible to organise the chapter into two parts. In Part One we will introduce you to some of the key concepts and theoretical notions developed by social psychologists in their attempts to understand social life. This will inevitably be somewhat theoretical. However, we believe that, in order for you to be able to appreciate fully the significance of some of the major research findings which we will be dealing with in Part Two, it is important that you have some grasp of the theoretical underpinning of social psychological thinking.

Part one

One of the most cherished beliefs that people hold—and it is unlikely that either police officers or off-duty psychologists are any exception—is that they are the sole authors of their own actions. For most of the time we like to believe that we have arrived at decisions, made judgements, or engaged in actions solely on the basis of *our own* assessment of the situation. Normally, we like to see ourselves as acting completely independently of others, whether these others be friends and colleagues or the wider social world. Of course, there are circumstances, admittedly infrequent, when we do acknowledge other influences. For example, often when something has gone wrong, we find ourselves attributing our actions or inaction to some *physical* influence such as drink, excessive fatigue, or the onset of a bout of sickness. But it is rare for us to acknowledge *social* influence. In many circumstances, to admit that we have been influenced by others is somehow to admit that we are less than we should be. We often go to considerable lengths to deny to others—and even to deny to ourselves—that we have been influenced by others, whether through direct social pressure or, more commonly, through indirect, implied, or even imagined pressure. Yet, one of the major outcomes of social psychological thinking and research over the past few decades has been to demonstrate exactly how important social factors can be in determining how people behave.

Socialization

It is unlikely that you would want to disagree that the kind of home you were born into and the circle of close relatives and friends who surrounded you during childhood helped in no small way to shape the sort of person you've become. It is not surprising, therefore, that people often refer to childhood as the formative years.

Psychologists use the term 'socialization' to refer to the processes involved in our acquisition of knowledge about the world. This knowledge includes not just beliefs about the *physical* world and how to manipulate it, but also beliefs, attitudes, and values about the *social* world together with rules concerning what is and is not considered appropriate behaviour in any particular situation. We are not born with beliefs, attitudes, and values or with an awareness of the norms of social behaviour. Nor probably are we born with very much of what one might call a personality. All of these we acquire in the process of growing up. And growing up necessarily implies interaction with others. From the moment of birth, we are enveloped in an expanding *social* world, composed initially of immediate family, friends, and neighbours, and later of peers, teachers, and a host of others with whom we come into regular contact as we grow up. It is this *social* world, in which we are all enmeshed, which makes us what we eventually are and which continues to exert a profound influence over us for the duration of our lives.

In childhood, the continuous and pervasive influence that others have may be deliberate and direct, as, for example, when an adult encourages and praises a child's generosity in sharing a tube of 'Smarties'. On the other hand, it may be, and more often is, informal and unintended, as, for example, when a child observes its parents' selfish actions towards one another and unconsciously but inevitably internalizes this mode of behaviour, making of it a blueprint for its own future actions. Just as we might make use of an ordnance survey map to find our way about an unfamiliar *physical* environment, so will the young child use others' words and actions as a guide to how to get by in the *social* world.

The self

This process of *social comparison* with others begins very early in life. It is particularly evident in the development and maintenance of the self. Psychologists have found it useful when talking about the self to distinguish between three aspects : self-image, self-esteem, and self-ideal. Your *self-image* refers to the view that you have of yourself. It includes your awareness of your name, age, sex, occupation, previous biography, physical characteristics, more salient personality traits, your religious and political values and attitudes, your interests and hobbies—and indeed everything that you would say about yourself if asked to give as full a description of yourself as possible. Your self-image is what makes you feel uniquely who you are. Thus, to an admittedly unusual request, an account might begin as follows:

> 'I'm a fairly extravert, 26 year old police officer. I joined the Force after several years working in an office. I'm 5 feet 7 inches tall, have brown eyes and usually chestnut hair. I come from a large Catholic family and am the oldest of five girls. I've a boyfriend in the Force, but am not planning to get married just yet. I like driving and have my own car. I'd like to try my hand at grass-track racing. I hate canteen food, but like cold curry, tapioca pudding, and peanut butter sandwiches. I'm hopeless at adding up and can't seem to give up smoking. I can't stand pompous people, especially the station inspector....'

As you read this self-description, you probably found yourself evaluating this police officer, liking or disliking her, approving of some things about her but not of others. However, she also will have evaluated herself. She too will like or dislike parts of herself, will have some degree of positive or negative regard for her own worth. It is this evaluation of self which psychologists call *self-esteem*.

As we go through the ups and downs of our daily lives, we all of us experience fluctuations in self-esteem. It can even be temporarily affected by physical factors, as when we sometimes begin to entertain self-doubts after missing out on a night's sleep or when excessively hungry. However, over and above these temporary fluctuations, there seems also to be a more enduring aspect to self-esteem. We tend to evaluate ourselves in response to events in our lives in a fairly consistent manner. Self-esteem seems to be an important part of our character. It is also a characteristic on which people differ quite considerably. For example, people who are generally high in self-esteem are likely to feel attractive to others, confident in their own abilities and generally optimistic about their own future. On the other hand, those low in self-esteem probably perceive their lives so far as a failure, have little expectation that others will like them and will generally be pessimistic about their ability to cope successfully in the future. At a pathological level, the extremes of self-esteem are well illustrated by the mood swings of manic depressive patients, as they alternate between elated grandiosity and abject self-abasement. For most people, fortunately, feelings of self-regard are less liable to major fluctuations. They tend rather to form a fairly stable pattern of reaction which is of considerable interest to psychologists and which can be traced back in origin to early socialization.

Finally, there is *self-ideal*. This is the term used by psychologists to refer to the fact that all of us would like in one way or another to be better than we are. We might wish we were more athletic, physically attractive, intelligent, witty, or honest. It seems that we have an ideal self whom we would very much like to be. It is against this self-ideal which we carry around with us inside our heads that we measure up our self-image—and usually find it wanting. Just how far we find it wanting, will vary for different individuals. Indeed, we can look upon self-esteem as one indication of the discrepancy that exists between a person's self-image and self-ideal. In general, the greater the discrepancy, the lower the self-esteem.

This view of the self as being composed of three major parts has considerable intuitive appeal. It makes good sense to both non-psychologist and psychologist alike. It is a self that is easily detectable in how and what people do and say. Indeed, an individual's self can be looked upon as forming a large part of what others view as his or her personality. It is largely a matter of perspective, in which self is me viewed by myself and personality is me viewed by others. These two perspectives very largely, but not entirely, overlap. There are certainly likely to be some aspects of myself which are not visible to particular indivduals I know. But it is also possible to imagine aspects of my character which are revealed in my actions and which are perfectly obvious to others, but to which I myself seem completely blind.

However, notwithstanding these complications, psychologists have generally found it relatively easy to elicit from individuals separate descriptions or measures of their self-image, self-ideal, and self-esteem. They have been able to make and test specific predictions about how these aspects of the self relate to one another and, perhaps more interestingly, how they may influence and be influenced by other factors whether inside or outside the individual.

Perhaps an even more important question they have asked is : how is it that we acquire this sense of self? What is it that leads some individuals to regard themselves as God's gift to the human race—or even to the police force—whilst others are paralysed by the thought of having to organize a raffle at a Brownie jumble sale? Where do our images, ideals, and evaluations come from? One view which commands considerable support among social psychologists has been called the 'looking-glass theory of self'. This view holds that the new born infant initially has no sense of self. It is unable to distinguish even between itself and the outside world. At first all is simply a 'booming, buzzing confusion'. Internal stimulation, such as pangs of hunger, is not distinguishable from external sources of stimulation, such as chafing nappies or a drop in temperature. Only gradually through constant contact with the physical world, does a sense of its separateness develop and objects come to have an existence distinct from itself. At the same time, as a direct result of the multitude of interactions with others during the continuous round of being fed, bathed, held, hugged, and talked to, the infant becomes aware of others' reactions to itself. And with this awareness of others' reactions comes a simultaneous awareness of itself as a distinct and separate being. Thus, in the process of realizing that it is an object of others' attention, the infant becomes an object of its own attention. It becomes aware of itself.

It is this becoming an object of one's own attention that we call self-awareness or self-consciousness. And it is in this process that we have the origins of self. The infant begins to see itself as others see it. Just as we look in a mirror to see how we appear to others, so we look to others' reactions to us to see who we are. The young child comes to see itself through others' reactions to it. It comes to value itself through others' evaluations. These reactions and evaluations become internalized. They become the child's reactions to and evaluations of itself. Thus, the images and evaluations reflected by others become the self-image and self-esteem of an individual. Just as others show that they regard a child as good or naughty; plain or pretty; clever of stupid; lovable or unlovable; quick or clumsy; so does the young child come to see itself in this light. Because it is the parents who initially have most contact with the young child and perhaps also because they appear to the child as both omniscient and omnipotent, it is they who usually have the major impact. The evaluations that they impose are often the most enduring, if only because the child will respond by acting in accordance with their evaluations even when with others outside the family, and thus will fulfil *their* prophecy. Of course, the possibility of change does exist, for as children grow up they are exposed to an ever widening circle of others—all of whom in varying degrees will reflect back to the child their images and evaluations. A perceptive teacher may have a dramatic effect in raising a child's self-esteem. But sadly, the reverse is also true.

Reference groups

This process of self-definition and self-evaluation in the light of others' reactions to us doesn't stop at the end of childhood. It continues throughout life. The self is 'on loan from society', as one writer has put it, and if society's evaluation of us changes, then our evaluation of ourself will also surely change. However, not all people we encounter have an equal impact on us. By middle childhood, for example, we have usually become increasingly susceptible to the influence of a peer group, especially our close friends. Normally, the values, attitudes, and beliefs of our friends map onto those of our family. When they don't, there is likely to be conflict. It is here that the social psychologist's distinction between a *membership group* and a *reference group* becomes important.

At any one time, you will belong to a number of social groups. For example, as a youngster you probably had an immediate family group and one or two groups of friends; you were in a particular class at school; perhaps you were a member of one of the school's sports teams; and even for an hour every morning a member of a group of newspaper deliverers sorting the daily papers at your local newsagent. In the case of most groups to which you belong, membership does not impinge very greatly on your life. Certainly, whilst with group members you are likely to behave appropriately, but otherwise the group will have little impact on you. Its influence will not carry over into other areas of your life. Such groups are called *membership groups*. At the same time, however, there will be at least one group—usually one of your membership groups—which acts as your *reference group*. What this means is that the values and standards of conduct held by this group are the ones which inform your life and against which you evaluate yourself. Your particular reference group may be your family; your immediate work colleagues; a specific part of the force; the force as an insitution; the local Methodist church; or whatever; and you will judge yourself as you believe others in that group would judge you.

It is probably the case, that for many police officers membership of the service is initially no more than one of simple group membership. However, as you gradually become socialized into the values, attitudes, beliefs, and standards of the serivce, spending more and more of your time with work colleagues, the service may become your reference group. For others, it may remain their family. For yet others, it can be both, in so far as there exists no discrepancy between the two groups in terms of values and standards. The most obvious example of this would be a police officer who comes from a 'police family', that is, a family with a strong tradition of sons and daughters entering and marrying into the police service.

Social roles

Whenever you engage in a social activity, you occupy what is called a *social role* or *position* and interact with one or more *role partners*. During the course of each day, you will occupy a number of different roles and on each occasion will act towards your role partners in ways appropriate to the setting—as spouse or lover; as parent or close relation; as work colleage; as friend; perhaps as member of a local sports club; as son or daughter should your mother telephone in the evening; and so forth. To each of these social roles are attached sets of expectations. These refer to how you should behave towards others as well as how others should behave towards you. They reflect the norms for behaviour which are deemed appropriate for each social situation. Thus, each new setting for social interaction will evoke from you appropriate role behaviour. Without effort, almost without awareness, you will alter your behaviour to meet each new situation and to fulfil the particular role expectations which hold in that particular setting.

An odd feature of this process is that for the greater part of the time, we are unaware of the pressure to fulfil role expectations. It is only when someone doesn't act in an appropriate way—perhaps due to too much drink, absent-mindedness or mental illness—that we are abruptly made aware of our expectations and of the social norms underlying social actions. Probably one reason for this imperceptible, but none the less very real power of social norms is that the process of socialization is a gradual one. The long period of childhood enables us to learn either through direct instruction from others or simply by imitation how to behave appropriately in a range of different social situations. By the time we are adults appropriate role behaviour has become as automatic and probably just as subconscious as changing gear becomes to the experienced car driver. As adults, it is usually only when we enter into a new social role—as perhaps for example when joining the police service—or when we encounter a novel situation and are not sure of the rules for behaviour, that we become aware of the considerable power of social norms and expectations. You will probably have experienced such occasions from time to time in your own life; perhaps for example, when first attending a funeral, or your first formal police dinner, or your first flight in an aeroplane—occasions when you were not altogether sure as to how to behave. What do I do at the graveside? When do I start eating and which knife and fork do I use first? Do I read the safety instructions on the card which the air hostess is pointing to? What you almost certainly did on each such tense occasion was to covertly watch what other people did, in order to be able to act appropriately yourself. You engaged in social comparison. You acted in just the same way that you would, if you were to suddenly find yourself among a tribe of Amazonian Indians and had to learn rapidly and without the aid of language how to survive in their social world.

What is of particular interest here is not just how quickly most of us are able to learn the roles and rules for novel situations, but rather how equally quickly we seem to forget the anxiety we experienced on the first occasion. What is more, we generally prefer to ignore the fact that the same situation—no longer unfamiliar to us—nevertheless still exerts just as great an influence over us as it did the first time. As we pointed out at the beginning of this chapter, people prefer to see themselves as acting on a situation, when what was experienced on the first occasion was the situation acting on them.

Role conflict

Once we have learned the roles and rules of social behaviour, most social encounters go smoothly. However, there are occasions when *role conflict* occurs. This refers to the psychological strain experienced by an individual when there is a clash between two sets of incompatible role expectations. For example, let us suppose that (in my role as father) I have promised to spend the evening helping my daughter with her revision for an important exam next day. Let us also suppose that (in my role as lecturer) I have to prepare a lecture for next morning. Both activities require more time than I have available. In my own mind, I cannot satisfactorily meet the expectations of both role partners, that is, my daughter and my students. I am likely to feel under pressure, whether actual or not, from these two quarters. I am likely to react to this by being irritable and bossy, especially if it is due to my own fault that I've put off writing my lecture until the last moment.

Since we enter and exit from a variety of social roles during the course of each day, the likelihood of our experiencing role strain is quite high. Fortunately, however, certain mechanisms seem to operate in society aimed at reducing its occurrence. Thus, for example, work and home are generally kept separate both temporarily and spatially, since these two sectors each make very powerful role demands. In particular, *multiple role occupancy* is usually avoided. This refers to those occasions when the same person simultaneously occupies two competing or conflicting role positions, for example, as mother and teacher. Schools usually ensure that teachers do not teach their own children and employers are likely to keep husbands and wives working in quite separate parts of an organization. There is also usually an agreed order of priorities for those occasions which cannot be avoided and which enable an individual to resolve the conflict without too much mental anguish. For example, when there is a death of a very close relative, the ties of family are seen as and agreed as having priority over the demands of work. However, on those occasions when there are no agreed priorities or mechanisms for reducing role strain, it is likely that individuals will act in accordance with what they perceive to be the demands of their reference group. The reference group or its members don't even have to be physically present. It is sufficient simply for individuals to believe that their actions would meet with the approval of the group and to use the standards and values of the group as a guide to action.

Most occupations have a period of training and probation during which new recruits acquire the knowledge and skills relevant to the job they are going to do. Also more informally they learn the particular ways of behaving considered proper in the organization or institution. Certain occupations, however, such as the police service and the armed forces necessarily have to make far greater demands on their members than do others. It is not surprising, therefore, that the socialization of new recruits into the police service is rather different from, for example, the apprenticeship of a car mechanic or the training of a hairdresser. There is nothing intrinsically more complex or difficult about any of these occupations. What is different, however, is the degree of commitment required of a police officer. It is this role demand which makes the period and type of training so very much more intense. In order to ensure the right degree of commitment, in order to ensure that the recruit identifies with the standards and ideals of the service, various strategies are used. These include during the period of 'basic' training a physical and temporal separation from previous social networks; reduction of signs of individual difference and of previous identity through the use of uniforms; the setting of group goals which require cooperation and foster a sense of dependency on the group; an initial stress on the inadequacy of the recruit and subsequent acquisition of status through the achievement of 'passing out'; constant emphasis on the traditions and high standards of the service such that final acceptance into the police service seems highly desirable and is achieved with a sense of pride and personal enhancement. Where such strategies are successful and the service becomes the police officer's reference group, the likelihood in the future of serious role strain will be much reduced.

Self-presentation

We have already pointed out that for each social role, there exists a set of expectations as to how the role occupants should behave towards each of their different categories of role partners. Similarly, there are expectations as to how the role partners should behave towards the role occupant. Thus, for all social roles and for all social situations, there are appropriate and inappropriate behaviours. However, this does not mean that all role behaviour is rigidly fixed. Only in the most highly formal or ritualized roles, such as that of a master of ceremonies at a banquet or of a sergeant-major on the parade ground, is the role behaviour restricted to a fixed pattern of actions. In most social settings, there will be a range of acceptable behaviour, from which the participants choose according to their personality, individual style, mood of the moment, or whatever. Thus, normally each role occupant will have considerable *role discretion* within which to operate. For example, as a lecturer addressing my students, I am expected to be informative, knowledgeable, coherent, well organized and clearly audible. Conversely, I am not expected to suddenly burst into song, suck my thumb or launch into confessions about my domestic life. However, whether I lecture standing formally at the lectern, walk slowly to and fro in front of the students, or sit casually on the desk at the front is neither here nor there. Each of these options is within the range of discretion attached to the social role of lecturer in the specific social setting of a lecture theatre. Thus, I am free to choose within the boundaries set by the situation and within these boundaries I will strive to fulfil the role. In doing so, I will attempt to manage the impression I create. I will try to present a self that is acceptable to the students. I will try to create an impression of being erudite, open-minded, witty, but above all of being an expert in my field. And I will avoid any actions which might discredit my performance or give the lie to my claim. I will slip into this role as I enter the interaction as easily as I slip into my clothes each morning—and I will slip out again just as easily. For police officers, of course, slipping into the uniform is the same as entering the role.

The implication of this is that each of us is all of the time attempting to present a self that is congruent with the situations we find ourselves in. We are engaged in an endless round of *impression management*, whereby we try to evoke from others the confirmation or validation of the self we are presenting. The self you present to the public when on the front desk at the station will be different from the self you probably present to your colleagues when backstage in the canteen. Each social encounter is a performance or set of performances in which each of the participants strives to present a self that is acceptable. It is essentially a dramaturgical or theatrical model of human social behaviour, in so far as it views social interaction as a social performance. However, this is not to suggest that we are all the time engaged in deliberate deception. There are two major reasons to support this view. First, we find it meaningful to distinguish between normal social behaviour and the behaviour of a con-man or trickster, who deliberately pretends to be what he is not in order to exploit others. Secondly, we find that most social encounters are a collaborative enterprise, in which each of the participants is not only striving to create or maintain an impression but is also willing to support the self-presentation of the other participants. We see this most clearly revealed in cases of *embarrassment*.

You cannot be embarrassed when totally by yourself, for example, when locked inside the bathroom. Embarrassment is essentially a social phenomenon. It arises when you do something which disconfirms the impression you are managing. It invalidates the particular self you are presenting. It reveals you as an incompetent performer. However, what is particularly interesting about embarrassment is that it affects everybody present. Your misfortune not only embarrasses you, it embarrasses everyone else. And what then usually comes into operation is *tact*, whose function is to restore the social interaction to its previous state. Tactfulness often consists of others pretending that the misfortune has not occurred and continuing as though nothing untoward has happened. Thus, others present at the spoiling of someone's performance will strive rapidly to repair the situation, so that the social encounter can continue to run smoothly. For social interaction to run smoothly, the participants must collaborate in accepting and supporting each other's self-presentations. It is not accidental, therefore, that reprimands or 'dressing downs' take place behind closed doors. For an inspector to reprimand his sergeant in front of junior police officers, for example, would not simply jeopardize the authority and status of the sergeant in their eyes but would be experienced by him as an acute embarrassment, even humiliation, in so far as the self which he normally presents to them is invalidated.

Summary

So far in this chapter, we have tried to show how important social influence may be in determining individual action. In doing so, we have necessarily introduced you to a number of concepts and theoretical ideas used by social psychologists in their attempts to understand human social behaviour. In particular, we have portrayed childhood as a period of primary socialization during which the values and norms of the child's immediate social group are learned and when the foundations of personality are laid down. Adopting a social psychological perspective, we have emphasized the key role that social comparison processes play both in the initial development of self as well as in its subsequent maintenance and modification through social validation. We have described how different aspects of your self and different rules of behaviour are activated as you move out of one social role and into another. Various societal mechanisms act to prevent role strain arising from incompatible sets of role expectations, but when such mechanisms are not available, you are likely to have recourse to the values and standards of your reference group. Finally, we have argued that every social encounter may be viewed as a set of role performances, in which each participant is engaged in impression management aimed at obtaining social validation of self. Any event which disconfirms the self that is being presented will create embarrassment for all participants and tact will be swiftly applied to repair the spoiled identity and restore the social situation to its former state.

Equipped with this social psychological perspective, we are now in a better position to examine some of the social psychological research which has been carried out over the past few decades into the nature and variety of social influence.

Part two

Social facilitation

One of the earliest findings to emerge from social psychological research was that the *mere presence* of other people seems to have a distinct effect on an individual's behaviour. This phenomenon is known as *social facilitation*. Historically, the study of social facilitation arose out of a desire by psychologists and sociologists to understand crowd behaviour. In the nineteenth century, official and unofficial reports of mobs, riots, and other violent gatherings often pointed to a distinct intensification or escalation of individual action as a crowd gathered in size and continued unchecked. However, riots cannot be produced on demand for psychological study, nor can they be easily simulated in the psychological laboratory. Consequently, the research focus gradually moved to more emotionally neutral situations and psychologists began to examine the effect of the presence of others on an individual's performance of a 'perceptual-motor' task such as riding a bicycle, typing, and quality

checking a production line, or of a verbal task such as learning and compre-
hending written material or solving anagrams.

The standard method employed was to compare the performance of
individuals working on their own with their performance when working in the
presence of others. This presence could be of two kinds:

(1) *audience*, where a group of others passively observes the individual
working at a task; or
(2) *coaction*, where others are simultaneously engaged alongside the
individual in working at a similar task.

Initially, the evidence suggested that the presence of others was beneficial, since
task performance was improved. Indeed, it was for this reason that the research
area came to be known as *social facilitation*. However, later evidence produced
a somewhat confusing picture, with some studies showing a facilitative effect
and others revealing the reverse.

This confused state of affairs lasted for a good many years during which
social psychologists could be of little help to anyone confronted with the issue
as a practical problem, such as, for example, an employer faced with a decision
as to whether or not to switch over to open-plan offices. However, in 1965
Robert Zajonc, an American social psychologist, reviewed the findings from a
large number of studies and came up with an explanation which seemed to
make sense of the data and account for the confusion. He argued that the
presence of others has an arousing effect on an individual. This increase in
arousal might affect a person's performance in one of two ways, depending on
the nature of the task to be performed. If the task were a well learned one, then
the effect would be to improve the performance. If the task was an unfamiliar
or difficult one, then arousal could lead to more mistakes being made and hence
to a poorer outcome. Certainly, his analysis of the many studies that had been
carried out in the past in terms of the complexity of the task being performed
provided strong confirmation for his view. Independent evidence also
supported his view that the presence of others leads to an increase in arousal,
since physiological measures of arousal were shown to be affected by the
presence of others as an audience.

Although there seems to be general agreement among psychologists that
Zajonc was right and that social facilitation or inhibition effects are due to the
interaction between an increase in arousal and the demands of the task to be
undertaken, there is by no means agreement as to why the presence of others
causes an increase in arousal. It would seem that we can rule out *competition* as
a likely explanation. Although competition certainly acts as a motivational spur
in many situations, it cannot easily explain the finding that a passive audience is
just as likely to have an effect on an individual's performance as a group of
coactors. Zajonc himself tended to view arousal in the presence of others as
being due to some kind of innate or biologically determined programming. In
support of this he cited evidence for social facilitation effects across a wide
range of animal and insect species. He has argued that the *mere presence* of

members of the same species will invariably trigger off an alertness response. This alertness or increased arousal primes the organism to respond more rapidly if necessary. Such a 'wired-in' mechanism allowing an animal to respond rapidly to the presence of another member of the species has obvious survival value, in so far as it will help defence of territory, protection of mates and offspring, and so forth. However, when it comes to trying to explain social facilitation effects in humans, the idea of an innately programmed alertness is less convincing.

An alternative view based on the outcome of empirical research by another American Psychologist—Nicholas Cottrell and his colleagues commands considerable support among social psychologists. He has argued that for both humans and animals the presence of others comes to be associated with both positive and negative consequences. Both humans and animals learn to anticipate rewards and punishments from others. It is this anticipation which is manifested as an increase in physiological arousal and which has a motivating impact on subsequent behaviour. We have argued earlier in this chapter that we are continually subjected to the personal evaluations of others in the form of approval and disapproval. Cottrell believes that anticipation of personal evaluation, or as he calls it, *evaluation apprehension*, is what causes changes in performance. He has carried out experiments which show that mere presence alone is insufficient to cause change, since the presence of a blindfold audience—and thus of an audience which could not evaluate the individual's performance—had little or no effect. Conversely, he has shown that an audience doesn't even have to be physically present to have an effect, since mere anticipation of evaluation of one's performance by others later is sufficient to alter the performance. According to Cottrell then, the facilitation and impairment effects observed by social psychologists are a reflection of the concern that we all have in varying degrees with what others may think of us. We want others to approve of us and we will feel apprehensive if we believe that this approval may not be forthcoming.

An explanation of social facilitation phenomena in terms of evaluation apprehension intuitively makes good sense. We can illustrate this very nicely by considering the extreme case of actors performing in the theatre. For experienced actors, a full house is welcome not only for its financial impact but also for its effect on their own performance; the bigger the audience, the better. Experienced and well rehearsed actors know their parts perfectly; they have a history of success in obtaining approval (applause) from audiences. Their task is a well learned one and one that has been performed many times. For them, a large audience constitutes a 'high'. Their evaluation apprehension acts as a spur to greater heights of acting. For beginners or for amateur actors, on the other hand, the presence of an audience may well have exactly the opposite effect: the larger the audience, the more daunting the performance. Thus, their performance may well be impaired on the first night, especially if they are not very well rehearsed. Stage fright is the result of overwhelming apprehensions of audience evaluation. In trying to cope with these apprehensions and the physiological disturbances that accompany them, such as butterflies in the stomach and trembling hands, the actors are in danger of forgetting their lines. Although a theatrical performance highlights social facilitation effects very clearly, they will be operating, albeit less acutely, in any social setting. From the extensive programme of experimental studies into social facilitation carried out by social psychologists, we can be fairly sure that the presence or even implied presence of others will have some influence on what an individual does. And there is no reason to suppose that police work will be any exception. Whilst you will probably be able to think of instances from your own experience, one of the most frequent occasions for social facilitation effects to operate is when you intervene in some action, such as, for example, when stopping a motorist or questioning a passer-by. The mere presence of colleagues or of other bystanders may lead you to react more sharply, even aggressively, to non-cooperation, than you would if alone. The need to 'create an impression'—especially in the case of an inexperienced police officer—is greatly increased in the presence of others and can easily lead to an escalation of feelings and eventual over-reaction. An awareness and appreciation of the social processes which can contribute to such outcomes may help you to maintain that firm but gentle approach, which is the hallmark of the experienced professional.

Conformity and deviance

We suggested earlier in this chapter that most of your actions are constrained within the limits of what others might regard as acceptable behaviour. Most of your social behaviour is normative in so far as it conforms to agreed rules and codes of conduct. Thus, your actions reflect and reinforce the customs and conventions of your social groups or of society. Not surprisingly, social psychologists have shown considerable interest in *conformity* as an aspect of social behaviour. However, before describing some of their findings, we need to spell out exactly what we mean by the term 'conformity' and show how it covers rather different kinds of social phenomena.

There is a sense in which the term 'conformity' is used to refer simply to conventionality and custom—without any implication of or emphasis on social pressure. Thus, the vast majority of our actions are straightforward reflections of convention, as, for example, when most people put on boots or wellingtons to go out in the snow. Such behaviour serves a useful function, but it goes no further than that. If an alternative and superior form of winter footwear became available, most of us would probably end up wearing it as our old footwear wore out. However, there is also another sense in which the term 'conformity' implies compliance with others' expectations despite *initial* reluctance and even on occasions despite *continuing* reluctance. This compliance may be a reaction to *explicit* social pressure, as, for example, when a police officer's colleagues might openly advocate putting in a slightly exaggerated claim for expenses. Or, it might be a result of *implicit* or felt social pressure, as, for example, when in a Police Federation meeting you might raise your hand to vote with the overwhelming majority of your colleagues on some issue, while privately disagreeing with them.

Just as there are at least two distinct forms of conformity, so are there two kinds of non-conformity or deviance. In the first instance, there is what we might call 'anti-conformity'. This applies when behaviour is a reaction against a particular set of norms and, at the same time, conformity to a different set. Thus, to take a very obvious example, the extravagant forms of dress and behaviour adopted by many adolescents is not only a symbol of non-conformity to adult standards but is also a symbol of conformity to the values and norms of adolescent culture. As one writer has put it : they are simply marching to a different tune. Thus, in general, deviance refers to types of behaviour which are non-normative from the perspective of the people applying the label and defining what is and is not acceptable. Indeed, the boundary between deviance and normative behaviour is a very fuzzy one, since there are always forms of behaviour which are in the process of becoming 'normal'. For example, just as premarital intercourse and cohabitation become increasingly the norm and so no longer deviant, we might equally expect cigarette smoking or even doing overtime to eventually be regarded as deviant behaviour.

The second form of non-conformity we might call genuine 'independence' or 'autonomy'. For the reasons which we have outlined earlier, we might expect genuine independence from social norms to be relatively rare, since it implies acting solely in terms of one's beliefs and values and risking social censure from others. The stand taken by Sir Thomas More against Henry VIII in refusing to accept the legitimacy of his divorce, as portrayed in *A Man For All Seasons*, is a good example. Fortunately for our peace of mind, we find most of the time that we *can* act in accordance with our beliefs and values without incurring social censure. This is because we are usually surrounded by others who share the same beliefs and values and who therefore provide social support. (Indeed, were it otherwise, society would fall apart, since the possibility of social life is premised on the notion of consensus!) We usually act, therefore, with what is really a *spurious* feeling of autonomy and independence, simply because our actions are underpinned implicitly by a large measure of social support. Nor does it have to be physically present; it is often sufficient for us to believe that our actions would meet with the approval of our reference group. Thus it is that religious and political dissenters have throughout history often been able to withstand imprisonment, torture, and other abuses for long periods while totally cut off from actual social support.

One of the most important effects of deviant actions is that very often they seem to arouse strong feelings in those who define the behaviour as deviant. Because we see others acting in ways which we consider to be neither right nor proper, we are tempted to classify them as unnatural or abnormal. Many forms of deviance challenge our view of the social, political, and moral order and, not surprisingly, they arouse in us feelings of uncertainty and doubt. For some individuals, these doubts may be difficult to cope with and they may be tempted to restore a sense of psychological certainty in the *absolute* rightness of their views by denying even the *possibility* that others' views may have some validity. One means of effecting this somewhat authoritarian stance is to stigmatize others we do not approve of by labelling them as 'wicked' or 'immoral' or 'sick'. Indeed, history contains many examples of the use of moral venom in trying to shore up sets of beliefs and values whose tenets and practices were being challenged. In defending the *absolute* rightness of our views and values, we run the risk of responding to those who do not share our perspective with intolerance and aggression.

For police officers there is a particular danger of over-reaction, not because there is any reason to suppose that they have a greater need than others for absolute moral certainty, but simply because their work inevitably brings them into frequent contact with a greater variety of social groups and forms of behaviour than is the case for most citizens. For many police officers, the kinds of occasion when response to law-breaking—or even sensitivity to the possibility of law-breaking—can become infused with strong negative feelings and a readiness to over-react will be when dealing with individuals whose deviance may have high visibility. Encounters with rastafarians, homosexuals or gypsies can all too easily escalate into confrontation, if police officers are motivated by a sense of moral righteousness. When law enforcement becomes a vehicle for the acting out of feelings of moral indignation, the essential impartiality and professional credibility of the police service as a whole is put very seriously at risk.

Conformity and social pressure

We have suggested that conformity can be divided into two classes of behaviour:

(1) conventional actions; and
(2) compliant actions, that is, actions which are the outcome of implicit or explicit social pressure.

For the most part social psychologists have tended to focus their attention on the second category and have tried to delineate those personal and situational factors which either facilitate or impede compliant behaviour. For example, in a number of laboratory studies, first initiated by Solomon Asch in the 1950s, it has been shown that under certain circumstances some individuals will go so far as to deny the evidence of their own senses rather than stand out against a group judgement.

The technique, developed by Asch, involved placing a naive subject among a group of strangers, who were—unknown to the naive subject—confederates of the experimenter. The task was presented as an experiment in visual perception and required them to make judgements of vertical line length by determining which of several lines presented on a screen was the same length as a standard line presented adjacently for comparison. Unknown to the subject, the seating had been carefully arranged beforehand in the form of a semi-circle around the screen so that the subject would give his judgement after all of the confederates had given theirs. On certain predetermined trials each of the confederates gave the same 'obviously' erroneous judgement. This left the subject with the choice of either giving into the implicit social pressure of the group and agreeing with the unanimous judgement or of acting independently by judging solely on the evidence of his senses. In the event, Asch found that approximately a third of his naive subjects tested over a long series of experiments conformed to the group judgement.

Subsequent research has largely been concerned with identifying factors which might influence the amount of conformity obtained in this context; for example, whether or not the size of the group is important and whether the presence in the group of a confederate who deviates from the rest of the confederates' judgements will have an effect on the naive subject. Although these and other situational factors have been shown to have an effect both on the number of subjects conforming as well as on the proportion of conforming judgements made by each subject, what is of major significance is the report by *all* subjects—both conformers and non-conformers—of the very considerable psychological tension and discomfort they experienced in the face of unanimous group error. When we realize that at no point was there any *overt* attempt by the confederates to influence the naive subject, we can begin to appreciate the power of *implicit* social pressure. The experiments do nicely demonstrate that whether or not others *actually* try to influence us to do something we don't want to, we nevertheless will find it extremely unpleasant and difficult to resist what is *experienced* as very definite pressure in our own minds.

We can also begin to appreciate in the light of this research why it is that corruption is often hard to detect and even harder to eradicate. Whether in the police service or in any other public institution, it is probably conformity in the face of implied or sometimes explicit social pressure from colleagues which—masquerading as loyalty—enables corruption and malpractice to go undetected.

Conformity and information dependence

Not all conformity occurs in the face of actual or implicit social pressure. Nor is the distinction between convention and compliance as clear cut as it might at first seem. Social psychologists have pointed to an intermediate area of social behaviour which, though certainly conforming, does not fit readily into either category. This type of conformity arises when we are trying to make sense out of our social world. To appreciate this point, we need to return to the distinction made at the beginning of the chapter between the *physical* world and the *social* world.

Whenever we have to make judgements regarding *physical reality*, we can usually apply objective criteria in the form of some sort of test or measurement, which will confirm or disconfirm our judgements. Thus, I can easily establish whether my car tyres have sufficient tread or enough air in them by using measuring instuments. Others will agree with the outcome, unless for some reason the instrument is thought to be inaccurate. Where no such instruments are available, as perhaps in making weather forecasts, then we make probability estimates based on available information, whose accuracy will be made apparent at a later time. However, there are large areas of what we might call *social reality*, where no such objective tests are possible and where the notion of accuracy does not apply. For example, my behaviour in court or in a Korean restaurant may be appropriate or improper; it cannot be described as accurate. Nor can my preference for certain kinds of entertainment; my tastes in food and drink; my beliefs in the area of religion and politics; nor my choice of clothing, hobby, or sexual partner. There is simply no objective reality to which I and others who think and feel differently to me can have recourse.

Although there is no objective arbiter for our opinions, preferences, and tastes, we nevertheless seem to have a need for social support. Thus, we feel more comfortable with people who share our religious and political beliefs and we are invariably pleased to learn that our friends like what we like—whether these be other people, late-night movies on TV, or brands of cat food. Thus it is that we seek and obtain from others social validation or support of the kind of person we are. Friendship acts as a mutual fan club in which each member obtains and provides consensual validation. Since we tend generally to surround ourselves with friends who are like us, this continuous process of validation goes for the most part unnoticed. However, on those occasions when we are uncertain (Will this curtain material go well with the chair covers?) or when the situation is ambiguous or novel (How do I cope with a close relative who seems to be on the verge of a nervous breakdown?), we tend to turn to others for opinions and support. The more uncertain we are, the more likely we are to be influenced by what others say and do. Thus, uncertainty often provides a fertile ground for one type of conformity.

This *information dependence* on others when we are uncertain about social reality has been nicely illustrated in a study by Muzafer Sherif, which made use of a visual illusion known as the autokinetic effect. This is an illusion of the apparent movement of a stationary spot of light. If an individual is placed at one end of a totally darkened room which has a small spot of light shining at the other end, then the light appears to move about in a rather erratic fashion, though it is in reality quite stationary. Sherif tested subjects individually over a number of trials by having them estimate the amount that the light had moved. Although an individual's initial judgements varied considerably, they gradually settled on a fairly stable estimate. These stable estimates differed *between* subjects. Sherif then put subjects together in a group and repeated the task. Surprisingly, although there was no instruction for subjects to agree and although the differences initially between them were quite large, he found that their judgements began to converge to the point where there was a stable group judgement or norm. When he then retested them individually later, he found that they stuck to this group norm rather than return to their original estimates.

Thus, since at no point had there been objectively any *actual* movement of light, what the subjects had done was to use each other as a reference point or source of information from which to base a judgement, such that they gradually converged on an agreed norm. They then used this consensual estimate or norm as the basis for any subsequent judgements. And, just as they were totally unaware that the movement was an illusion, so were they equally unaware that they were being influenced by each other.

At the beginning of this chapter, we argued that one of the most cherished beliefs that people hold is that they are the sole authors of their own actions. We are now in a position to appreciate how far that belief is a myth. What the social psychological analysis of conformity and deviance suggests and what much of the experimental evidence amply demonstrates is the ubiquity of social influence and the very considerable role played by social situational factors in determining individual action. To be aware of the power of these factors and to have some understanding of the social psychological processes which underlie them is an important step in liberating the individual from them. Police officers are expected to act in a considered, unbiased, and reasonable manner. To have any hope of doing so, it is important that you should know and acknowledge the various sources of bias and social pressure to which you are susceptible. Knowledge in this sense is power, for it confers at least the possibility of independent and autonomous action.

Obedience

The ability to act autonomously becomes of critical importance once we consider the issue of obedience to authority. The police service is an institution with an hierarchical organization. The chain of command starts at the top and works down through the various levels until it reaches the most junior police officer. The order of a senior officer is expected in general to be carried out without question by a subordinate. 'Disciplinary proceedings' are likely to be initiated against any individual who ignores or refuses to carry out an order. Obedience to lawful authority is therefore an integral element in police work. However, obedience to authority carries with it certain dangers, and requires an individual to consider whether that obedience is lawful.

Social psychologists for a number of years have been concerned with trying to understand how seemingly 'normal' human beings can perpetrate acts of frightful aggression and cruelty against fellow human beings. For example, how could large numbers of Germans have collaborated in the attempt at wholesale extermination of Jews, gypsies, communists, homosexuals, mental defectives, Jehovah Witnesses, and other 'deviants' from the Nazi ideal? Or how could ordinary American males recently drafted into the army slaughter innocent women and children on such occasions as Mai Lai? Whilst it might be reassuring for us to simply dismiss those involved as being different from us in some important way—whether by stigmatizing them as 'bad' or 'mad'—social psychological research suggests that such labels are inappropriate when applied to the vast majority of those involved.

In a continuing programme of experimental research first initiated by an American social psychologist, Stanley Milgram, three major factors have emerged as especially important in facilitating acts of inhumanity. They are:

(1) actual or perceived pressure from authority to obey;
(2) dehumanization of the victim; and
(3) deindividuation of the aggressor.

In a series of experiments Milgram succeeded in persuading subjects to carry out a violent act against another person in the form of giving them very intense, painful, and potentially lethal electric shocks. Subjects were people who had responded to a newspaper advertisement asking for volunteers to take part in a psychological experiment, for which they would be paid. The experiment was disguised as part of a programme of research into the effects of punishment on learning. By a toss of a coin subjects were assigned to one of two tasks: either they became the learner, whose job was to learn lists of word-pairs on the understanding that they would receive an electric shock every time they made a mistake; or they were to act as the experimenter's assistant and their job was to operate the electric shock generator whenever a mistake occurred.

Unknown to the volunteer subjects, the coin-tossing was rigged and they always became the assistant. The learner was in fact a confederate of the experimenter who had been carefully rehearsed in simulating pain and distress and who had also been programmed by Milgram to make a large number of mistakes. The shock generator was very clearly calibrated to deliver shocks ranging from very mild (15 volts) to extremely dangerous (450 volts) by stages of 15 volts. The subjects all thought that the equipment was genuine and that they really were administering electric shocks to the learner. However, in reality the machine did not *actually* deliver electric shocks and the learner simply pretended to experience pain and be distressed.

Throughout the experiment Milgram was dressed in a white coat and behaved in a very authoritative manner. The trials started at 15 volts and with each successive mistake Milgram ordered the subject to increase the voltage by 15 volts until he reached 450 volts or the subject refused categorically to cooperate any further. Despite the most distressing cries of pain and requests to stop by the learner, the subject was ordered by Milgram to continue increasing the intensity of the shocks. Although most subjects protested increasingly as the trials continued and the protests of the learner increased, nevertheless, some sixty-five per cent of the subjects continued to obey Milgram's commands to the point where they administered the maximum and potentially lethal 450 volts. In the light of these unexpected and rather extraordinary results together with the information gathered in interviews afterwards with the subjects, it would seem that they managed to abrogate responsibility for what they had done by attributing it to the experimenter. Thus by relinquishing their own moral responsibility and attributing it to authority, they were able to engage in actions which in other circumstances would have horrified them.

As part of an attempt to identify factors which might have been important in determining this observed obedience to authority, Milgram repeated the experiment a number of times with new groups of subjects and systematically varied a number of situational features that he suspected might be having an effect. These included:

(1) the location of the experiment and perceived respectability of the experimenter;
(2) the proximity of the victim (learner) to the aggressor (subject); and
(3) whether or not the authority figure (experimenter) was physically present or not.

All three factors were shown to have an effect. Thus, when the experiment was repeated in a shabby office hired for the occasion in a seedy part of the town and Milgram presented himself not as a university professor but simply as a researcher, there was a marked reduction, but by no means total elimination, of obedience. Also when the victim was placed only one and a half feet away from the subject rather than in an adjacent cubicle within earshot but out of sight, less than one-third of the subjects went as far as 450 volts without refusing to obey. And finally, when the experimenter gave some excuse for not being physically present and either relayed his commands over the telephone or left them on a tape-recorder, there was also a significant reduction in obedience.

Deindividuation

Extending the work of Milgram, social psychologists such as Philip Zimbardo have subsequently shown how situational factors, which have little or nothing to do with the personality of the individuals involved, can increase the likelihood of cruel and violent acts being committed against others. Thus the use of uniforms or any apparel which reduces the individuality, or rather masks the identity, of the wearer has the effect of making such acts more likely. Zimbardo has called this process one of 'disindividuation'—by which he means that in the process of conferring anonymity on an individual, normal moral constraints are weakened. If we cannot be recognized, then we cannot be evaluated. It is not surprising, therefore, that the increasing use of envelopping protective riot clothing without any clear means of identification should be looked upon by many social commentators as a worrying development—not because there is not a very clear need for police officers to be better protected, but because there is an increasing risk of breakdown of normal legal and moral restraints in the heat of riot control.

The same process seems to work in reverse, for it has been shown that the more we are able to dehumanize our victims, the more easily we can aggress against them. There are many ways in which we can do this. At the most obvious level, we can refer to *them* in a depersonalizing and derogatory way. Thus, in Vietnam, the term 'gooks' was used to refer to Vietnamese just as in the United Kingdom the more jingoistic elements of the popular press quickly adopted the term 'Argies' during the Falklands hostilities. It is somehow easier to justify killing 'Argies' than Argentinians. However, we can see the dehumanizing process in its most extreme form in the Nazi treatment of concentration camp inmates. By stripping them of all indications of their previous existence, forcing them to wear shapeless striped pyjamas, shaving their heads, and branding them with numbers, they effectively dehumanized them. Presumably, it was much easier psychologically for the guards to justify to themselves the brutality and torture, if the inmates looked less than human.

The psychological investigation of obedience to authority, deindividuation, and dehumanization has proved dramatic and highly controversial—not least because some psychologists argue that the experimental studies are often unethical. It is possible that some psychological harm is done to subjects in those studies where they are manipulated into acting with violence towards another person—despite the careful and thorough debriefing that takes place afterwards. This possibility of harm together with the deliberate deception of subjects by the experimenter is thought by some to more than outweigh the very considerable insights which such research provides into the relationship between authority, obedience, deindividuation, and violence against one's fellow human beings. Whatever your own personal view of the morality of such empirical research, there is little doubt that it does provide a very important corrective to the naive but popular view that it is only wicked or mad people who are capable of committing violent acts against others. Forearmed with a knowledge of some of the social processes involved, it is hoped that you will be in a stronger position—should the occasion arise—to resist any demand to carry out actions which you would regard as morally reprehensible.

Summary

In Part two of this chapter, we have looked at some of the ways in which the nature and structure of particular social situations and settings can influence individual behaviour. Pursuing the social psychological perspective developed in Part one, we have described experimental research into three important aspects of social life. Beginning with the phenomenon of *social facilitation*, we found that experimental evidence has shown that actual mere presence as well as implied presence of others are both capable of altering an individual's behaviour. We concluded that these effects may be largely due to the arousal of evaluation apprehension. We then considered the nature of *conformity* and *deviance* and described some of the classic studies which have thrown light on this important aspect of social behaviour. In particular, we described experimental studies of *conformity in the face of implied social pressure* and emphasized how very difficult it may be for an individual to act in opposition to others. We also considered work on *conformity through information dependence* and related it to our constant need for social validation. We concluded this chapter by examining the controversial experimental studies of *obedience to authority and violence to others* together with subsequent exploration of the nature of *deindividuation* and *dehumanization* as processes often involved in acts of cruely and violence.

Further reading

Aronson, E. (1980). *The Social Animal*, 3rd Edition, W.H. Freeman, San Francisco. This is a very popular and extremely readable American social psychology textbook. It deals with the areas covered in this chapter and many more besides. Aimed at the non-specialist, it is available in paperback.

Gahagan, Judy (1975). *Interpersonal and Group Behaviour*, Methuen, London. A small but condensed pocket-size paperback written for students on introductory psychology courses. It deals with topics covered in this and several other chapters of this book.

Wegner, D. and Vallacher, R. (eds) (1980). *The Self in Social Psychology*, Oxford University Press, Oxford. This contains chapters on various aspects of the self written by a number of specialists in the field. Aimed at the interested general reader as well as the student of psychology and is available in paperback.

CHAPTER 5

Dealing With The Psychologically Disturbed

Introduction

The police officer will surely learn about many aspects of the topic of psychological disturbance from many different sources, and will doubtless integrate those sources of information for him/herself. The aim of this chapter is decidedly *not* to offer some sort of lay guide to psychiatric diagnosis; still less is it a do-it-yourself psychotherapy manual. I merely offer a hopefully useful pot-pourri of fact, description, and even perhaps corrected misconceptions, which may be relevant to pragmatic decisions about how to cope in the immediate or short term situation with those psychologically disturbed persons most likely to be encountered in the line of police duty.

The reasons why a police officer may become involved with psychologically disturbed persons are not hard to glean. The judgement that a person is psychologically disturbed is made on the basis of disturbed behaviour, and such behaviour in turn is quite likely to 'disturb' a member of the public who will therefore turn to the police to do something about the situation. It is, however, not only disturbed behaviour in a public place which might first of all be referred naturally to the officer on patrol, but also disturbance in a domestic setting referred by a frightened neighbour, friend, or relative. To a frightened person, the police can often appear the natural effective helper, even if the police themselves would be the first in these cases to wish for a stage exit. Perhaps most importantly the police service is quite simply known to be a service which is available twenty-four hours a day, and this is not always the case with regard to what might seem the appropriate medical or social service. Last but not least, the ordinary man or woman is not usually in a position to know who other than the police may be the appropriate authority to turn to.

Background

Categories of mental illness

There are lots of difficulties with the term mental illness, which arise from the subjectivity and arbitrariness which are often present in judging who is and who is not mentally ill. The judgement is rarely based totally on observed behaviour, as the judgement of a physical illness may be based on a pattern of bodily symptoms. We can see this in an example. Imagine three people exhibiting this same pattern of behaviour: sleeping on a bench in Hyde Park, and seemingly having spent the night in the open. The first person is in his forties, and shabbily dressed; the second is a youth of eighteen or so with a rucksack beside him; the third you swear blind is the chief constable whom you caught a glance of only yesterday at the local station. The first you may judge 'down and out' but not necessarily mentally ill; the second is likely a perfectly normal foreign student 'doing' London on some small amount of currency per day; the third, if your identification is up to scratch (see Chapter 2) has likely 'gone off his head', which is about as meaningful a way of putting it as to say, by alternative, that he seems to have become acutely mentally ill. Context then is all important in judging mental illness. The person, the society, the culture all can be crucial in the interpretation of behaviour as in some way deranged. Thus to say someone is behaving abnormally should be as far as factual matters are concerned, merely a statistical statement and it does not of itself imply illness.

Having issued that caution, it is nevertheless usual to admit of two broad categories of mental illness: neurotic disorders and psychotic disorders. The behaviour of most neurotic persons is not likely to be a special concern of the police office, certainly not any more so than for an ordinary member of the public. We all tend to meet people at times with the varying symptoms of neurosis in varying degrees of severity. Thus we see people who appear unreasonably anxious about life in general, or phobic of something in particular, or obsessional, or who suffer despairing depression. These are all symptoms which lead to a diagnosis of some sort of neurosis if the symptoms are more severe and persistent, than circumstances dictate. Depression can be either a neurotic but understandable reaction to some precipitating circumstance or is sometimes seen as a cyclical 'out of the blue' mood swing, in which case it can be so deep and irrational as to be classified by some authorities as psychotic illness. Severe depression of any kind makes a suicide attempt a serious possibility and we shall discuss later in the chapter how a knowledge of some of the psychological research findings in this area can be of possible value in police work.

Psychotic behaviour is much more likely to be of a kind which will bring the behaving individual into contact with the police authorities. Psychotic behaviour is often bizarre, apparently totally irrational or at least incomprehensible to most onlookers; more to the point it is for those same reasons often frightening to those who witness it. For that reason, the police officer might find himself the *first* person being asked to interact with the individual; this will especially be the case if the psychotic episode is occurring in a public place.

Psychotic behaviour can occur in some cases as a psychological byproduct of a plainly physical assault on the brain, by the ingestion or inhalation of toxic substances, over a short period of time or a long period of time, wittingly or unwittingly. Deliberate ingestion of LSD might lead to 'bad trip' hallucinations; so also can incidental poisoning by lead. Most psychotic behaviour, however, is accounted for by a diagnostic category called schizophrenia. It will be the schizophrenic person whom we will consider when we discuss how a police officer might deal with any attendant disturbance. However, the advice which follows can sensibly be adopted in most cases of psychotic-type behaviour.

Schizophrenia

No one yet knows for sure the cause, or likely causes, of schizophrenia and this in itself leads to some difficulty in defining the term. Schizophrenia is really a group of disorders all sharing overlapping symptoms, and all characterized to some degree by irrational behaviour and a lack of contact with reality. There are, however, cross-cultural variations in who may or may not be medically diagnosed schizophrenic, depending, one sometimes thinks, on the degree to which eccentricities may be thought of as tolerable deviations from the norm. The British in this respect seem to require more deviation than Americans, who may sometimes diagnose schizophrenia solely on the basis of withdrawn behaviour, which the British psychiatrist might prefer to see as a sign of depression (or even perhaps an exaggeration of normal national temperament!). The criteria for diagnosis, however, are tightening in the interests of international research, and at least no one would dispute the florid symptoms which quite often are portrayed. It is these clearly noticeable florid symptoms which can alarm the public and lead to police involvement. We shall therefore give them pride of place.

An acute episode

Schizophrenics do not necessarily behave oddly all the time, with the exception perhaps of chronic institutionalized patients on some hospital wards. They enjoy periods of so-called remission, where they are free from symptoms, can hold down a job, and in fact have every right to be treated as full members of society, although the label 'schizophrenia' unfortunately often stigmatizes the patient and increases the stresses which may well play a role in determining the frequency of illness episodes. For one reason or another, and the reason may well be the failure to stay on 'controlling' medication when the patient thinks he is fully recovered, the patient may suffer a full bout of symptoms anew. This is what we mean by an *acute schizophrenic episode*, which probably heralds a period of illness, where the symptoms of irrational behaviour are never far from the surface, even if they are not being acutely expressed. We now consider these florid symptoms.

Florid symptoms of schizophrenia

These can be stated quite simply as

(1) delusions
(2) hallucinations

Delusion literally means false belief. Delusions are very common in schizophrenia, and the enthusiastic voicing of them is sure to attract attention and arouse a natural fear of the irrational. The hallucinations most characteristic of schizophrenia are most likely to be auditory. Seeing pink elephants or their equivalent is left to the craving delirious alcoholic; the schizophrenic hallucinator prefers to hear voices.

The content of delusions and hallucinations obviously varies, but these florid symptoms are particularly a feature of that subcategory of schizophrenia known as *paranoid schizophrenia*, where delusions and hallucinations are marked by ideas of incredible self-importance and persecution. Self-importance and persecution are natural bedfellows; after all wouldn't you feel persecuted if you believed you were the President of the United States? In fact delusions are rarely so simple. The patient may rather believe he is a friend of X, who is important, or even the real X as opposed to the imposter who people take to be X, and so on. In fact there is rarely a single delusion, rather a complex network of interlocking delusions emotionally tinged with the air of conspiracy. Sometimes, indeed, the delusional system, as it is sometimes called, is so internally consistent in its logic that one can be taken in for quite a time before one pulls oneself up with the thought: 'this really cannot be true.'

The voices can often be threatening to the patient, or abusive of him. When a patient starts abusively shouting back at them, or just talking to them, the craziness of it all can frighten an onlooker. Often the voices are overheard rather than heard. That is to say, they address the patient indirectly as a third party. The delusions which accompany schizophrenia often have to do with voices through the television, or radio, or science fiction notions of technological communication as yet undreamt of. They are more easily understood if we consider that the schizophrenic does indeed really hear voices and hears them so clearly and to his mind externally that he needs some explanation to account for their 'reality' to him. It is worthwhile to imagine what it would be like if you yourself heard someone speak, and knew that you had heard someone speak absolutely and without question, and then found that everyone around you denied hearing the voice. You may feel that you cannot deny the existence of the voice as something coming from outside, but you may feel that you do not wish to deny the fact that others did not hear it. Thus some delusion of private albeit zany communication is a way of resolving these contrary or dissonant cognitions.

As we have said, delusions and hallucinations are amongst the most florid symptoms of schizophrenia, and most likely to be the concomitant of a public disturbance involving the mentally ill. However, quite often the schizophrenic's behaviour may be merely socially embarrassing through its silliness: inappropriate laughter; the expression of odd ideas too vague or incoherent to constitute a fully fledged delusion; sometimes the need for police intervention may become apparent through the pestering of passers-by. No-one here is frightened or alarmed necessarily, but the nuisance factor can be considerable. No-one, including the most sympathetic petitioner on behalf of schizophrenic patients, would deny this capacity for tiresome behaviour. The question, now, is what do you do if you are the officer who is called to deal with an incident involving someone who is likely schizophrenic? How do you cope with the situation so as to bring about the best result, or at least not exacerbate the situation?

Dealing with psychotic persons

What the police officer can do

Essentially you are involved in what amounts to a 'holding operation' until either medical assistance comes, or together with colleagues you have the job of getting the individual to that medical assistance. If the latter is the case and the police effectively become an ambulance service then a lot will depend on your initial approach if the journey to the hospital or clinic is to be least fraught for both police and prospective patient. This is especially so if one is dealing with an aggressive or potentially aggressive individual.

One sure way of getting off to a good start and cultivating the right frame of mind is to be unfrightened by the bizarre behaviour yourself. Even if the patient is being verbally aggressive, the likelihood of unprovoked violence by a schizophrenic person is very small. There are undeniably cases of paranoid schizophrenia involving acts of great violence, but such cases are a very small minority. There is no reason to expect to be attacked *because* the person seems insane. In fact it is worth remembering that the statistics show you have a much *greater* chance of encountering violence if someone is sane rather than insane. Armed with those statistics, you yourself are therefore calm and collected, and that is the first important contribution you have made. If the incident has involved frightened members of the public or family or whatever, your calmness can be valuable to them.

In fact the question of dealing with others present is likely to be the first matter to cope with. Are those who are present making the situation worse by their presence? If they are carrying on talking to the person whilst he or she is 'raving', the chances are that the situation is not being helped by them and the individual's psychotic symptoms are being sharpened by this source of over stimulation. Might it not be better to remove them? Whether and how this is done will obviously depend on the situation.

Talking to the individual

Now the question is: can you do any better if you get talking? You might certainly wish to bear the following points in mind if you do get involved in what might well be a bizarre conversation. First there is absolutely no point at all in arguing against a delusion. That would only increase any hostility which was already present and arouse it if there were not. It would also serve to ensure that the hostility is directed towards you. As I indicated earlier, hostility is not likely in the case of schizophrenics to involve real physical violence, but you can do without even the verbal variety. In the rare case of encountering a violent or potentially violent schizophrenic individual, arguing against that individual's delusions is a sure way of increasing the odds of violence being shown to you.

In following the advice of the last paragraph, however, you should not go to the other extreme. There are dangers in acquiescing and going along with a patient's delusions. You may find yourself being drawn into a tangled web out of which it will be difficult to extricate yourself. If you agree that the head of the secret service is about to arrive and pick him up in half an hour, you will later find it difficult and inconsistent to explain why he must come with you to the hospital and miss this important engagement which you both agree has been arranged. Of course you may decide to out-delude the patient by playing his game: the head of the secret service has had to change the arrangement and will now meet him at the hospital. This is not likely to cut much ice, and may in fact be doing the patient a disservice. It is not necessarily the case that a schizophrenic during the acute experience is totally out of touch with reality. There is often a part of the person which is trying to cling on to that consensual reality and which is very frightened and confused by the strange experiences which he is undergoing. It does nothing to ease that fright if everyone agrees with every crazy statement he makes.

The middle path, then, is the positive path to take. The essence of this approach is to admit in general terms the kinds of experience which the person is going through, but to make it quite clear that this is what you understand the person to be *feeling*. The second thing that you can try to do is to establish yourself as a figure who is on his side in whatever battle the patient may believe he is waging. That is to say, try and be a protective influence and not an antagonistic one.

If the approach recommended seems vague, compare these two responses to a delusional statement.

(1) 'Don't be silly. The CIA is not trying to control you through the television set.'
(2) 'You're certainly feeling pretty terrified, but you're not going to come to any harm while I'm here.'

The second response is certainly preferable to the first. It neither confirms nor denies the *content* of the patient's delusion. However, it strongly confirms the reality of the patient's experience, and it offers a view of yourself as a possible protective influence. At the very least, this approach of trying to empathize just as far as you can with the person's feelings will avoid making the situation worse; it has a good chance of making it better.

The possibility of violence

The incidence of physical assaults by schizophrenics is, as I have said, small. However, such aggressive behaviour does occasionally occur in schizophrenic persons as it does in any other kind of person and it would be wise to say something about dealing with violence if it does present itself. This is especially necessary since it may well be the minority of potentially aggressive individuals who most attract the attention of the police. A more detailed and general discussion of aggression and violence is to be found in Chapter 6 of this book, so I will confine my remarks here to the specifics of dealing with aggression as an additional feature of psychotic behaviour.

First some repetition is in order. Do not do anything to arouse or aggravate hostility such as arguing with delusional statements. Secondly try to reach some conclusion about the likelihood of physical violence, independent of mere verbally threatening behaviour, if this is possible. If someone who knows the individual is at hand he or she may be able to tell you whether the individual has any past history of violent outbursts. Certainly past history often turns out to be the best predictor of behaviour of this kind. What is being said effectively is that predisposition to violence is to be seen as a separate component of a person's make-up from their psychosis. A violent person who becomes psychotic will likely turn out to be a violent psychotic. The psychosis and violence are not, however, intrinsically connected. Nevertheless, the distortions of perception and judgement which are part of the schizophrenic syndrome do mean that special attention must be paid to what can be termed the situational determinants of violent behaviour. If we consider a perfectly sane (or at least non-psychotic) violent person, even he or she is not violent every moment of the day. What we mean perhaps by the personality description of 'violent' is that such a person has a lower threshold for performing *acts* of violence in situations which might make any individual *feel* violent. He or she might also be adept at interpreting situations as threatening or requiring a physically violent response. Now these momentary and situational factors which can be seen as elicitors of aggression are no less important with respect to the potentially violent individual who is also psychotic. The difficulty (the additional difficulty) is that here we have the possibility that what you consider is neutral or even positive behaviour may be grossly misinterpreted as a threat and thus elicit violent behaviour. An example might be a sudden movement which you make, which in turn is taken by a confused, frightened, and deluded person to be the beginnings of a physical attack. Try therefore to announce your intentions, when moving about. Don't do anything suddenly.

The unpredictability of the schizophrenic's behaviour is what people generally find alarming: the unexpected gesture, the inappropriate or zany remark. If violence has realistically to be seen as a possibility, then it is only wise to treat the unpredictability in this respect with obvious caution. Thus it would be unwise to turn your back on the individual and so on (i.e. normal procedure but with added vigilance because of the added unpredictability factor).

Finally, it might be that the individual has to be moved somewhere and has no intention of being cajoled into moving of his or her own accord. It is probably redundant to point out that this is best not tackled on one's own. The myth of madmen having the strength of twenty men is only myth. However, it is true that a very frightened person can summon a great deal of hidden reserve and lash out in all directions. That person and you are better protected by more persons of the appropriate kind being in attendance. It has to be recognized that such undignified scuffles do take place, and should therefore involve the minimum of force, the greatest of tact, and only occur after the talking, which is cheap, has also been ineffective.

If the individual's behaviour has been alarming enough, the end result is almost certainly going to be hospitalization. Since your role has been a holding one rather than a deliberately therapeutic one, it is essential to congratulate yourself ('reinforce' yourself, to use psychologists' jargon) if this has been achieved even reasonably smoothly. Given that the end result is never a particularly nice result, it is important to guard against a feeling that your actions had no effect. All one can and must say in those circumstances is that the wrong approach might have made matters much worse.

Suicide attempts

Dealing with suicide attempts is a traditional crisis intervention role, associated in the minds of the public with a picture of a police officer (usually American) talking someone out of throwing themselves from a high building (New York skyscraper). The picture is good enough for our purposes, since it highlights the kind of suicide attempt most likely to involve police intervention, i.e. one involving the possibility of a quick and violent end in a public place. A police officer is not likely to be the witness of a private quiet grief followed by an over-dose in a hotel bedroom. In short the police are most likely to become involved if the attempt is threatened explicitly and is capable of being executed in a sudden all-or-none manner: the method may be by jumping from a dangerous height, it might also be by gunshot or knife wound or by some means of self-injury.

The first requirement of any police officer in this sort of situation is to be well informed about the likelihood of a person carrying out their intention. Perhaps I ought to put it more negatively. At least the officer should not be ill-informed. There are many people who seem to think that most suicide attempts are pathetic bluffs. More cruelly in modern times, in the USA at least, it has been known for onlookers to lose all sensitivity and invite the unfortunate actor in the drama to jump or pull the trigger, much as if the whole thing were a 'dare-you' sort of game. It cannot be said more emphatically that all suicide attempts are in some sense serious and this is reflected in the first of our statistics about suicide. One in four of all suicides have previously made one unsuccessful attempt. Moreover, compared with the tiniest chance that anyone taken at random will be killed finally by their own hand, the chance of an unsuccessful

86

suicide attempter finally ending up succeeding rises to a very significant five per cent. In other words one in twenty of failed suicide bidders do actually kill themselves good and proper within a five-year period. To increase your general knowledge, here are a few more facts and figures. Some of them will enable you to do what the Samaritans do, namely make a quick assessment of suicide risk and urgency even in the absence of detailed personal information.

Some statistical facts about suicide

Who commits suicide? The sex of the person attempting suicide is an important variable. A man will be three times more likely to succeed in a suicide bid than a woman. A woman, however, is more likely to attempt suicide. The likely success of male attempts has also to do with a sex difference in the method of suicide adopted. Success depends on the lethalness of the method chosen. Men are more likely than women to choose violent ends for themselves, and this means that death is very probable once the act is initiated. There is also a male-related stereotype which would identify failure with weakness and cowardice.

Age is another important variable. The older the person is, the more likely it is that they will guarantee themselves success. This may be due to seriousness of intent; it may also have something to do with a greater macabre wisdom: a young person may think that a handful of aspirin will serve their purpose whereas an older person is likely to know otherwise. Availability is another factor here. Aspirin might be the only drug available to a young person, whereas more lethal sleeping tablets or such are more likely to have been prescribed for an older person. Against the usual age trend, however, there has recently been a disturbing upturn in the number of adolescents committing suicide.

In terms of actual suicides, there is no difference in the rates amongst the various social classes. There is, in other words, no relationship between suicide rate and socioeconomic status. More suicide attempts, however, are made by persons in the poorer and more deprived strata of society.

All studies agree that being married confers some degree of immunity from suicide risk, whilst being divorced entails a higher than average risk. Being single, or widowed, is associated with a somewhat higher risk in some research studies but not in most. The statistics with regard to marital status and suicide can be broadly interpreted in terms of how isolated a person is likely to be on a dimension of intimate social acquaintance. In this respect, it is the divorcee who is most likely to feel cut adrift not only from an erstwhile spouse but from a network of mutual social friends. It is the maintenance of that close friendship network which is likely to make single persons and widows less prone to isolation than one might think.

It is often thought that someone who does commit suicide must have been mentally ill in some way. The very phrase 'took his life while the balance of his mind was disturbed' suggests such a view. However, this is not true except in the circular and useless sense that the person *must* have been ill *because* they committed suicide. A statement such as this is about as useful as saying one cannot sleep because of insomnia, or one has bad breath because of halitosis. The empirical truth is that about half of actual suicides have a record of depressive illness. This leaves a huge portion of cases who may have given little prior sign of being seriously depressed. The tragedy of much suicide is that it can be a relatively impulsive act in response to relatively acute pressures which nevertheless feel as if they are everlasting. The double tragedy is that if the pressures do precipitate an unsuccessful attempt, that attempt makes the person more vulnerable in the future, as we mentioned earlier. This may well be because the very act of attempting suicide alienates a person even further from remaining friends and acquaintances, who see the person as something of a perpetual risk. The closer they get to that person the more responsible they will arguably feel if the person does eventually succeed in killing themselves. It is thus an unfortunate but natural response for people to distance themselves from a 'failed suicide' and increase the unfortunate person's sense of isolation.

The incidence of suicide and something of the question why. The rate of suicide in the United Kingdom is about the world average. We are neither good nor bad in this respect. About thirteen people in every one hundred thousand kill themselves each year in this country, which means crudely and on average that someone kills themselves somewhere in Britain every hour of the day.

One of the ironies of suicide is that we can never ask a successful suicide why he or she did it. Can the objective statistics about who commits suicide, when they do it, and where they do it, shed any indirect light on answering the question why? We have already seen that the figures relating to marital status can be used to infer that feelings of isolation are important. What else? Some people have suggested that the different rates of suicide in different countries might give a clue as to why people commit suicide. Thus it is noted that industrialized countries have higher rates than relatively undeveloped countries, that Roman Catholic countries have lower rates than Protestant ones. It is sometimes therefore inferred that living a simple rural life, close to the land, with a simple faith and a strongly supportive and paternalistic church, innoculate against the types of concern which might otherwise predispose towards thoughts of suicide. However, it is unwise to read too much into cross-cultural differences in incidence figures, and that is because the figures cannot always be trusted. Sweden has a higher suicide rate than the Republic of Ireland. So here we do indeed have a Protestant, highly industrialized country on the one hand with a suicide rate apparently greater than, on the other hand, a Roman Catholic traditionally rural country. However, we must remember that record-keeping in Sweden is highly efficient and also that there is no strong taboo concerning suicide. The efficiency of record keeping in Ireland certainly would not compare with Sweden, and in addition a religious factor would militate against suicide verdicts and in favour of misadventure verdicts (except in the most cut and dried cases) so as to spare the feelings of the family.

However, certain kinds of statistics do give some understanding of why people commit suicide. Financial problems are traditionally the spur for social problems, and the tensions which follow in their wake. This it is no surprise to find that the suicide rate reliably goes up at times of economic depression. It also goes down during times of war. Cohesiveness and sense of purpose thrive during periods of the latter and dissolve during points of the former. No wonder that historians rightly see war as resulting from failure to solve economic and social problems. War offers a terrible but effective short term cure for national and individual malaise and alienation, an insight not entirely ungrasped by many generations of war mongering politicians the world over.

In Britain, people tend to have a preference for the months of November and April in which to kill themselves. Exactly why is uncertain. Perhaps the peak in November reflects the gloom of approaching winter—an added reason one might guess to kill one-self on top of other more personal reasons. The peak in April has been interpreted as being due to feelings of isolation being enhanced by having to witness the joy of others in the 'courting couple' season of spring.

In terms of days of the week, Sunday is peak incidence day. It has been suggested that more people succeed on that day because of less likelihood of help being available. Equally plausible is that Sunday is a traditional leisure day, a day for doing nothing, which is the worst thing a depressed person can do.

At this point we must conclude this section on research statistics. Some of it has been background material, but it can be of practical use. If you are called upon to minister to a potential suicide who is middle-aged, male, recently divorced, who has just lost his job at a time of economic recession, and if it is a grey Sunday in November, you would be advised to treat the threat extremely seriously. You might offer his only chance of survival. This is the juncture where we might profitably move on to some pragmatic considerations in dealing with suicide attempts.

Dealing with the suicide threat

Preparation

One of the first considerations, which is important if you are called in to deal with a person threatening suicide, is to avoid the temptation to rush into the situation without first doing some research. Because the situation appears to be a life and death one, the temptation to rush in can be strong. Normally, however, the sort of situation to which one is called out will be one in which the potential suicide has in some way publicized his or her threat. This in turn means that the person is possibly in no hurry to execute the deed, unless unwittingly prompted to do so by ill-considered intervention of some sort. Public or semi-public suicide bids are often of the type considered earlier, where the person concerned is likely to be male and the method is likely to be high on the scale of lethalness. This means, if you remember, that once the act of suicide is initiated it has a high probability of being successful. Hence ill-considered intervention is particularly hazardous.

The fact that the person has in some way publicized the forthcoming (or hopefully not forthcoming) event, at least has its positive side, and the positive aspects have the common denominator of allowing for a hiatus, a pause albeit a dramatic one, between the intention and the act.

The first positive aspect of a public threat is that measured by the at least objective criterion of giving notice of their suicide, the public threatener is implicitly giving the world (family, friend, or society's representative, i.e. you) a chance to convince them that their intention is misguided. The person may be admitting some residual doubt, which is not present in the case of someone quietly checking into a hotel and self-administering a lethal cocktail of pills. The second positive aspect also stems from the breathing space which the would-be suicide provides: that breathing space allows you the time to find out more about the person whom you will all too soon be trying to talk out of his or her intention.

Obviously this advice to move more slowly than feeling might automatically lead you is not always going to be appropriate. Sometimes you might be a late arrival on the scene after others have already filled the alloted gap between idea and reality. Sometimes the would-be suicide might only have publicized his or her intentions by default and without meaning to do so; they might have been discovered, if not *in flagrante delicto* as it were, at least in preparation. However, it still needs to be asked how much help you are likely to be if you are not prepared in some way. Thus rushing in is likely to be a course of action for fools rather than angels. Let us see therefore what can be done in the way of preparation.

Preparation is basically about assessing the person and the situation to the best of your ability in the circumstances. Given that attention tends in such cases to be clearly focused on the would-be suicide and the consequences for them of their own action, it is sometimes too easy to forget the broader situation and what might be the consequences for others. If the person is threatening suicide with a firearm, for example, it is a small physical event in space for that firearm to be redirected at you or a spectator, if disturbed psychological processes should whimsically take a change of direction. This general public security aspect might be the last thing to occur to a layman; hopefully, it might be the first to occur to a trained police officer.

The security of those other than the suicide threatener himself becomes most important when a firearm or dangerous weapon is in the hands of someone who is in some additional sense deranged. This additional derangement might be due to psychosis or confusion brought on by the use of drugs, including alcohol. One can in such cases only reiterate what was said in relation to a psychotic person who one has reason to believe may be violent. Extra caution is needed to take account of unpredictability and poor communication.

Once one has assessed the situation in terms of risks to all parties, certain preliminary actions might need to be taken, e.g. arranging for the removal by some means or other of people either for their own good or because they seem to be making things worse or both. This preliminary period is also the time to find out if possible all that you can about the person who is making the suicide attempt. When you come to talking with that person a little later, much will depend on a commodity called *empathy* (see below). Your degree of empathy may be more readily identifiable later if you can get some understanding of the person and his/her difficulties beforehand. What are the pressures that have led up to the event? Distinguish between long term and short term pressures, even ask about very immediate ones which might have been straws to a camel's back. Try to build up a picture of what it would probably be like to be that person from some convenient point in the past through to the present situation. At the same time let the picture be a deliberately tentative one, very much open to modification. Don't convince yourself you know what the person feels, just hazard an educated guess. Much more at the commonsense level, but equally important, establish what the here-and-now situation is. What is the person's mood? Are they agitated? Have they just reacted angrily to some prior intervention? Or are they sullen, resigned, uncommunicative? What has been said to them? How did they react? All this preliminary work can hopefully give you a feel about this person and this incident. Even straightforwardly factual questions may need to be answered. Is there any evidence that a gun is loaded? The answer will probably be 'don't know', but may be a certain 'yes'. In any event it is worth asking anything to reduce uncertainty. If the situation is particularly unclear, such as someone threatening suicide on the far side of a locked door, it is obviously beneficial to devote time beforehand to finding out the layout of a flat, house, etc. To assimilate information under these preliminary, calm conditions (looking before leaping) is better than letting a sudden escalation of events take one by surprise (which may force one to respond to them with a desperate search for information which has always been there for the asking).

Talking, listening, and empathy

It is now time to consider some guidelines for behaviour when you decide to enter into conversation with the suicide bidder. Any conversation is for any individual a mixture of time intervals given over to listening and to talking. We all know that the way different individuals partition their time between those two activities says a lot about their personality. One thing, however, that psychologists know for certain because research tells us so, is that the ability to listen rather than talk is the premium quality of a good, that is to say effective, psychotherapist. We can generalize from the field of psychotherapy to most verbal interactions. The worst kind of general practitioner, nurse, dentist, social worker, policeman, teacher, or 'man manager' of any sort is one who cannot listen. This weakness gives rise to two unfortunate effects. First the bad listener allows himself to remain ignorant of important facts which he might otherwise glean. Secondly he betrays a lack of empathy. We define empathy as the capacity for convincing another person that he or she is really understood. It might sound a bit vague, but psychologists have shown that people can independently show high agreement about how much empathy is shown by persons in conversation; empathy thus can be measured and has been shown to relate to successful outcome in counselling situations. A poor listener can show little empathy, because he inevitably shows that he has not taken in enough of the other person's point of view.

Counselling a potential suicide victim requires a good deal of listening. Indeed the problem might be to get the person talking so as to begin the positive process of listening. Do not be afraid to let the person open up, even if their talk seems self-destructive. Convince yourself that it is better for the person to talk about anything rather than clam up. Do not be tempted to say things like 'Don't be silly' or 'Stop talking that way'. Remember the obvious, which is that as long as the person is speaking, even distressingly about committing suicide, he is by definition not doing it.

Showing empathy has a lot to do with not being judgemental, and not being judgemental is perhaps the most important thing of all when faced by this situation. Positive remarks are likely to be non-judgemental if they are of the kind 'I see', 'I understand', if necessary with elaboration to test out that you have understood (and by implication that you have been an attentive listener), e.g. 'I see. You mean that....'. If the person says 'no' to your elaboration, accept that answer and ask for another go at understanding what he is trying to convey. Judgemental remarks are ones that appeal to 'oughts' and 'shoulds'. It rarely helps anyone to be told how they ought to be feeling, when they are in the grip of profound feelings of another sort. You cannot expect to 'cheer' the person up in any single way. The person can only be indirectly made less suicidal by a genuine feeling of being understood, and this will flow from honesty on your part, and recognition of feelings that *are* present for them in the here and now. You may offer the person a different perspective on matters, but make sure it is not a totally fake perspective, which is seen as an obvious artificial sweetener containing mere saccharine. Offering up depressing moments of your own life history as examples of a shared human misery can be a good thing to do, it can provide the person with a 'model' who has coped, and it is often a natural reaction. But just make sure such revelations genuinely match at least to some degree the supposedly parallel experience of the person. There's nothing more depressing than someone who begins: 'I know exactly how you feel. When I.....' and then goes on to show that they have no idea how you feel.

So far we have concentrated on the talking and listening related to the person's 'problems'. How does one address the question of the suicide threat itself? No advice can cover all eventualities, but the following has something to recommend it. Address the issue at the outset and clarify your attitude. It is wise to agree, as one American book puts it, that 'the person is to play the shots'. This makes sense because often in such cases you or others are not well placed to prevent the threatened injury, so why pretend otherwise? However, by giving permission, as it were, for the person to decide ultimately his own fate, you diminish the risk that the person will be accidentally pushed into the act by the misinterpretation of a movement or whatever; you also leave the person paradoxically feeling that they do indeed still have to make a decision, that they can choose life, and that if they do choose death it is totally up to them, which makes it that much more difficult. It is much easier to be pushed into something nasty rather than coolly to act alone. By giving permission in this way you also paradoxically assert a kind of authority and might well in come cases be cast emotionally in the role of a protective but permissive paternalistic figure. This could also be helpful if the end result is the safe return of the frightened prodigal child. Such almost Freudian aspects of the relationship between would-be suicide and would-be helper can exist, although we shall not pursue them at greater length. Suffice to say that the more you can make the present environment appear protective and non-threatening, and the more you can isolate the person's suicidal intention as something for him to resolve utterly on his own, but against the wishes of your caring but ultimately non-interfering self, the more likely it is that any but the most determined suicide bidder will hover sufficiently to wish himself rescued from the brink.

If what I have said reminds you of how a wise and loving parent steers their adolescent child away from some dangerous scheme, that is not strange. We are all of us most child-like when in the grip of emotional turmoil.

Of course the final result of all your efforts might be the carrying out of the attempt. What you do then will depend on factors outside the scope of a manual on psychology. You might or might not be able physically to do anything about the attempt, depending on the nature of the case. However it is worth noting that if the person is physically prevented from carrying out an initiated attempt, it is mildly cheering to know that once successfully stopped a peak moment seems to have gone and the person is likely to give up then without further struggle.

Some people are determined to go through with their threat, and it is important, if you are present on such an occasion, to guard against useless guilt. As long as you have done your best, you can do no more. However, the mention of guilt does bring us to a consideration of the aftermath of a suicide, which you may also be involved in. No act induces as much guilt and long term suffering as the suicide of a close friend or relation. There is little the police officer can do about the long term effects, but he can and should be especially aware of the need for sensitivity when dealing with the relatives of a person who has just committed suicide.

Finally, a brief word is in order about recognizing the potential quiet suicides, quite apart from the crisis intervention that surrounds a publicized attempt. Police officers are responsible for varying periods of time for a variety of persons in their custody. Recognizing signs of depression can therefore be important, since depression is obviously a major precursor of suicide. The obvious signs need not be dwelt on: weeping, despairing statements, even statements about suicide. Less obvious can be apathy, a slowing down of movements apparent in the person's gait, slow speech, indifferent appetite, sleepless nights and early waking, irritability.

If suicide is considered as a possibility, further sympathetic but direct questioning is in order as to whether the person has been thinking along such lines. No one can be made suicidal by talking about the matter. However, invaluable information can be got by directly raising the question and such information may be not only a simple 'yes' or a 'no', but an estimate of how serious such suicidal ideas have become. Is it still at the level of a general feeling, or has the person been thinking concretely about the ways in which the attempt might be made?

The advice then on the recognition of potential suicide cases is simple. Watch out for signs of depressed mood which might make suicide a possibility, and follow up any signs that you find.

Further reading

An American book, published by Pergamon in their General Psychology Series, is exclusively given over to crisis intervention, and deals with topics not covered here such as family disputes and victims of rape. It is suitably clear and forthright in tone and covers all topics well at an introductory level:

Goldstein, A.P., Monti, P.J., Sardino, T.J., and Green, D.J. (1979). *Police Crisis Intervention*, Pergamon, New York.

To develop an understanding of psychotic behaviour, I hesitate to recommend psychological texts as such; rather I would point the reader in the direction of a book written to help the families of schizophrenics cope with the disorder. It is far better than most texts in painting a concrete picture of schizophrenic behaviour. It also has a chapter on the law in relation to mental disorder, written by Dr. Henry Rollin, forensic psychiatrist to the Home Office; it is published by the National Schizophrenia Fellowship:

Rollin, H.R. (Ed.) (1980). *Coping with Schizophrenia*, Burnett Books in association with Andre Deutsch, London.

The small readable Pelican original on suicide by Stengel is something of a classic, and has now gone through new editions and revisions. It can be recommended:

Stengel, E. (1973). *Suicide and Attempted Suicide*, Penguin, Harmondsworth, England.

CHAPTER 6

Aggression and Violence

Introduction

This chapter aims to achieve two things. The first is to provide the thin coat of a reasonably scientific perspective on aggressive and violent behaviour as a whole. Without such a perspective, understanding is compromised and whatever practical implications there may be of psychological research findings, they would not be adequately drawn. The second purpose is, in fact, the explicit stating of some possible practical implications; others may be left to the reader to discover for him or herself.

A violent incident has causes. We can surely all agree on that. Some of those causes we shall take to lie within the individual who is exhibiting the violent behaviour. Such causes, then, are likely to be *historical* in nature. By historical, we mean that the person has become predisposed to act with violence in various sorts of situation (what sorts of situation we leave until a little later) because of his or her past history. Relevant questions here are: what sorts of parental upbringing favour the development of violent-prone adults? What sort of peer group experiences in childhood or adolescence are associated with later aggression? Such questions are developmental in nature and we shall have something to say about the relevant findings of developmental psychologists, particularly those psychologists interested in an area known as *social learning theory*. However, you might already have ventured an opinion or possibly a prejudice that certain violent individuals must surely be born not made. In the language of psychology, you are stating the view that individual differences in violence proneness have some degree of innate basis. Given the proviso that in reality nothing is all innate or all environmental but involves a complex interaction of both types of factor, we shall nevertheless look at the evidence for the view that innate factors may be important in the eventual determination of such individual differences as we have mentioned.

So much for the individual, who has weaved his way through history, to arrive at a violent encounter, to which we are witness. We cannot pretend that the causes of this encounter lie entirely within this individual. He is not some ball of fire, which sets alight everything in its path indiscriminately. Rather it is the case that some situations are more inflammable and flames spread more quickly; others are left untouched.

But our metaphor is wilfully contrary. It is better to think of the individual as having the fuse, the touch paper. It is the situation which sets alight the individual, even if an individual is said to spark off a conflagration. The metaphor is better this way round because it makes it clear that we are not talking about some minority only of violent-prone persons, we are talking potentially about all of us. We are all capable of being violent and aggressive, but we have different fuse lengths, we have different thresholds for letting our feelings flow into behaviour. Those, then, whom we have called violent-prone individuals interact with what we shall call *situational factors* and the result is violent behaviour. In looking at situational factors, we shall be looking at the here-and-now of aggressive behaviour, the immediate context which is needed to spark off the violence. Psychological research in this area is not only interesting, it is possibly pragmatic in its implications. Whilst there is not a lot one can do in the short term to alter an individual's character traits, there is something one can often do to alter a situation: diminish *cues* for violence (cool the situation) or, by mistake, add to or make more salient existing cues (escalation). Cooling a situation, which is preumably what we should normally desire, might sometimes appear almost 'instinctive', but we can all equally well think of times when our efforts have gone horribly wrong. If a knowledge of psychological research can be helpful in this area, it will be because it increases the tally of correct types of intervention, and lowers the incidence of mistakes. Even if your 'instinct' appears to need no improvement in this regard, it will be beneficial to have the nature of that 'instinct' spelled out. The trouble with 'instincts', 'noses' for things, and 'common sense', is that they are usually communicated in too vague a fashion either for firm verification of falsification, and fact and fiction, sense and nonsense, are all mixed together so that useless and even harmful 'noses' ride to victory on the backs of what might be worthy cousins of scientific truth. Of course the domain covered by your instinct might be a good deal wider than that covered by the existing knowledge which has been given a seal of approval by psychological science. If so, good luck to you; you can probably provide a research psychologist with some promising hypothesis to test.

Lastly a note of caution should be sounded in this introduction. Aggression and violence can and must also be looked at in a wider context; in short a socio-political context. Such a view of aggression goes way beyond the expertise of an experimental psychologist, and is in fact the rightful domain of the sociologist. We should, however, not fool ourselves into believing that the problems of a society can be properly solved by any approach which ignores the scientific analysis of society's functioning. Proper sociological analysis, however, even when undertaken with rigorous scientific method, is not always welcomed. That does not, however, make it any the less a necessary exercise. Possibly society does not really want the answers it hears, and the bearer of bad tidings suffers the traditional curse and cuff of he who pays the piper.

We can, however, hope that our limited psychological approach may at least have some practical implications at the palliative level of coping with problems of aggressions and violence, even if it is more limited though not impotent on the question of prevention.

Personality and aggression

The introduction should have served as a caution that problems of violence cannot be put down solely or simply to a person having a 'violent personality'. However, it is possible with caution to say that certain types of personality are more predisposed to become violent-prone, and moreover the personality types involved are possibly fundamental ones which may have a strong innate basis.

According to the psychologist H.J. Eysenck (1964), there are two fundamental dimensions of personality which in turn help to determine a multitude of lower-order personality traits. The dimensions which he specifies are *extraversion* and *neuroticism*. There is some evidence which strongly suggests that the personality differences associated with different degrees of extraversion and neuroticism reflect physical differences in nervous system functioning.

The typical extravert (i.e. person high on extraversion) is sociable, outgoing, talkative. The extravert has many good points, stemming from his sociability, but one of his drawbacks is that he is more impulsive than his introverted counterpart. In addition, he is according to Eysenckian theory less responsive to the socializing forces that are brought to bear on all of us as we develop into adults. In particular it has been suggested more recently that the socialization problems associated with the extravert end of this personality continuum may be specifically connected with difficulty in registering the incidence of punishing consequences (Gray, 1971).

The second of Eysenck's fundamental personality dimensions we termed neuroticism. This is a kind of emotional stability measure. One possible interpretation of it is a person's emotional reactivity to what psychologists term 'reinforcing events'—pleasurable and painful events. A person high in neuroticism is easily bounced up and down by the sea of such emotionally keyed events. In particular the word neuroticism suggests a particular disposition towards anxiety, but this should not obscure the more overall defining feature of general emotional reactivity.

If we put the two dimensions together we should predict that these individuals who are most likely to have problems connected with aggression and violence will be high on both dimensions, i.e. certainly extravert rather than introvert, and probably high rather than low on neuroticism. Being somewhat emotionally reactive (high neuroticism) and impulsive (high extraversion) and possibly undersocialized should predispose a person to aggression and violence.

This prediction of the Eysenckian model is in fact borne out. If we look at figure 6.1, we find that high extraversion coupled with high neuroticism is associated in children referred to child guidance clinics with conduct problems which often have a high aggressive component, whereas those children who are

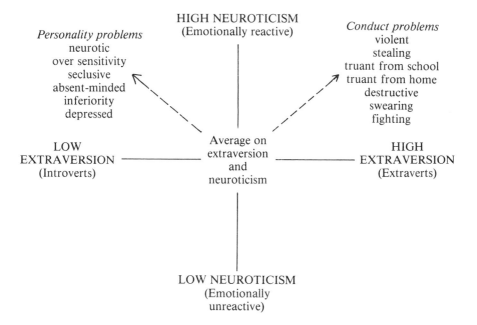

Figure 6.1 The patterning of personality problems in relation to extraversion and neuroticism (based on a sample of children referred to child guidance clinics). (After Eysenck and Rachman, 1965)

high on neuroticism but low on extraversion (i.e. introverts) are equally susceptible to problems but these are of a different type involving symptoms of guilt, anxiety, and depression. Thus neuroticism according to this theory predisposes towards having *some* problems, and extraversion determines the nature of those problems. With respect to aggression, extraversion is probably the most important dimension, with neuroticism playing possibly a more complex role depending on the type of aggression being considered.

Thus we can see that those psychologists interested in personality theory have had something to say about the type of person who is high risk as far as predisposition to violence is concerned, *but we should be extremely cautious about interpreting this information.* Remember that by definition half the population are above average in extraversion, and half are also above average in neuroticism. Thus a full quarter of the population fall in to the quadrant in figure 6.1, which we considered as a predisposing sort of personality. Most of the people are unproblematic citizens, because the same factors that predispose towards conduct problems can equally be channelled into a style of behaving which is not antisocial. Many people who are highly aggressive and violent are high on extraversion and neuroticism; *but more importantly* perhaps most people who are high on extraversion and neuroticism are not aggressive or violent by nature.

The same cautionary note needs to be sounded with regard to other arguments for innate components in the determination of violent-prone individuals. Males are more aggressive than females. This is a relatively undisputed sex difference, which is mirrored in most other animals. Alone, however, it tells us little of practical import, for dealing with problems of aggression and violence that arise. Even more of a red herring are speculations about genetic aberrations such as chromosomes like XYY which might be more common in criminal populations of men with histories of violence. The researchers who investigate such topics, would not pretend, and nor should we, that there is anything to be said in favour of the simple proposition that we could discover a genetic blueprint for the aggressive and violent individual. Such an oversimplified view of the criminal 'type', etc. has echoes only of nineteenth century pseudopsychology, when it was believed that a man's character might be read in the bumps on his head. No modern psychologist is ever going to claim for his personality tests what the 'phrenologist' claimed for his bump readings.

A further statement about 'types' may be in order here. It concerns that familiar label which refers to a dangerous violent criminal who in the collective unconscious of a worried nation is usually 'on the loose'. He is of course the 'psychopath'. In many ways the criminally insane psychopath is the extremest form of extravert. He has little control of his own impulses, and is severely undersocialized. Let us compare this with a personality profile given by Russell (1976), of violent prone criminals. The profile is the end result of a scientific study which sought criteria to predict 'dangerousness'. The researchers concluded:

> 'We see the dangerous person as one who has actually inflicted or attempted to inflict serious physical injury on another person; harbours anger, hostility, and resentment; enjoys witnessing or inflicting suffering; lacks altruistic and compassionate concern for others; sees himself as a victim rather than as an aggressor; resents or rejects authority; is primarily concerned with his own satisfaction; lacks control of his own impulses; has immature attitudes toward social responsibilities; lacks insight into his own psychological structure; and distorts his perceptions of reality in accordance with his own wishes and needs.'

Although this is virtually a description of the classic psychopath, it is important to realize that the authors saw it as the extreme end of a continuum for predicting 'dangerousness' across the board. This 'relative' approach to predisposing personality is in accordance with the Eysenckian one outlined previously. The descriptions are also virtually identical. Let us note, however, that the picture given above suggests a person who has learnt to have a 'chip on his shoulder'—he sees himself as victim, harbours resentment, etc. He has also learnt somewhere along the line that violent *behaviour* is an effective and/or acceptable way of expressing his 'personality'. It is time therefore to examine the question of upbringing.

A question of upbringing

As well as looking at aspects of personality in relation to aggression, psychologists have also examined the type of childhood to be gleaned in the records of those who later become offenders because of aggressive and violent behaviour.

A common argument which one hears espoused with regard to particularly the young offender is that he or she must have lacked discipline as a child. Parents of the next generation are constantly being admonished by the parents of the previous generation for a failure to discipline their charges. Is there any truth in this well worn cliché of an argument? As usual we shall prevaricate with the answer: yes and no.

All the research evidence points to *inconsistency* of discipline being the key parental pattern associated with all 'under-restraint' type problems later on, including those many problems with a component of violence. Thus the child, who is destined for future problems, will probably have had more than his fair share of disciplining occasions, and moreover the nature of the disciplining may even have been unduly harsh. However, the parent is likely to be inconsistent and confusing in the application of discipline. Thus a child might be told off for not being in bed by a certain time one night (perhaps because it suits the parents to be rid of an inconvenience), whilst the next night the about-to-retire child may at the same hour be ordered down to the corner shop to get Dad a packet of cigarettes (once again to suit a parent's convenience). Such an absence of consistent standards can be both confusing and 'morally' corrupting for the child who is at the stage of trying to internalize a moral sense, and a degree of self-discipline, which is the only form of discipline which is of lasting value.

Another aspect of bad parental upbringing is the failure to provide consistent praise for prosocial behaviour. A total emphasis on the occasional and inconsistent punishment of bad behaviours provides a child with no guidance at all about what is correct behaviour. Indeed in the type of example given above what might be wrong one day is right the next day—a very confusing state of affairs.

All of us, not just children, are great demanders of attention. Attention from others, it could be argued, reconfirms our existence to ourselves from moment to moment. There are those few among us who seem to need very little attention from others (the older one gets the more self-assured one gets?) but by and large we are all of us to some extent born and continued attention seekers. What, then, of the child who rarely gets any attention, except the reluctant recognition of *bad* behaviour to be followed up with a curse or a blow? Such children are effectively told to define themselves through their bad behaviour. Notoriety is better than being a 'nothing'. This 'reinforcing' of antisocial behaviour of an aggressive or violent form, has as much to do with couldn't-care-less 'parenting' by society or community at the later teenage stage as it has to do with earlier patterns of literal parenting.

A final observation with regard to upbringing factors associated with the development of aggressive individuals concerns the nature of discipline which is used. One of the most robust findings in psychological research is that parents who used naked power assertion (in particular physical beatings) as a method of checking a child's behaviour are *much* more likely to produce aggressive and violent adults for the next generation. It is glaringly obvious why this should be. When a child is successfully restrained from some behaviour by the threat of physical violence, unless that child is very stupid, he will learn that the use of violence gets results. With respect to his own behaviour he may learn not to bully the kid next door at least when father is around, but the general principle of bullying will seem to the child to be admirably vindicated. Despite the fact that this kind of imitative learning can hardly be exaggerated in its importance, parents, TV, films, comics, etc., etc., go on confirming that aggression pays off. We can therefore remain absolutely certain (as hard not soft psychologists!) that problems of aggression and violence will not even be remotely dented unless or until teachers, parents, and society at large change the climate in which *all* violence is seen. At the moment physical violence is sanctioned as punishment in school and home, although every bit of research either shows it to be ineffective or worse shows it to be ineffective *and* ultimately counterproductive. It is also glamorized in the media, despite the mounting evidence of its harmful effects. While sex is taboo, violence is to be applauded, it seems. The extent to which we reinforce aggression (especially in males, as part of a sex-role stereotype) is likely to be far more important in the long run than any biological factors in determining levels of destructiveness in our different societies.

We have dwelled on this last issue and if it makes us pessimistic about really 'getting to grips' with problems of aggression and violence, then that is rightly so. We can, however, add a postscript on the question *why* so many parents, teachers, and members of the public advocate violent punishment for violent behaviour, despite its being counterproductive. The answer is given by the famous behavioural psychologist B.F. Skinner, and is a very simple one. Such punishment makes the agent of punishment feel better in the short term, and it is hard to get people or rats in psychological laboratories to refrain from doing what makes them feel good.

The other universal finding with regard to physical punishment is that it engenders incredibly strong feelings of resentment and anger, which are hardly the emotions to cultivate in an offender who has already shown himself or herself to be prone to violent behaviour. There is all the difference in the world between slapping a child in the heat of the moment to terminate a behaviour (e.g. putting fingers near a fire) and using physical beating as a form of correction. There is an analogy here with adult offenders. No one would dispute that in (once again) the heat of the situation a police officer may need to use force to terminate a behaviour. That, however, is light years away from advocating some form of insitutionalized corporal punishment. And yet ritual beatings and other sickening types of child abuse too often form a part of the upbringing pattern of the later violent offender—a robust fact which should be studied by the more hard-hearted but soft-headed advocates of short sharp shocks. A hard-headed approach to social learning states that for violent behaviour to decrease in frequency in a society it must be seen not to pay—in psychologists' terminology it must not be reinforced at a behavioural level. This advice, however, must apply across the board and without exception. Where deviations are allowed by society in a good cause (violent acts deemed by authorities to be prosocial, perhaps the ending of a siege by the SAS) it should be in the full knowledge that any glamour and approval attached will *by definition* have unwanted side effects in the social learning of some children, and indeed, adults. It would be one hundred per cent better in such circumstances if society were to be more aware of the principle that it, like parents, should be as consistent as possible in its demands on its charges. Societal violence should be treated as a necessary unglamorous evil to be exercised with caution in narrowly defined areas of legitimacy.

Some views of aggression and violence

It may be noted that a moralistic usage of 'shoulds' and 'musts' has crept in at this point. Perhaps this is because the evidence which has accumulated on this matter is so relatively clear cut and yet apparently studiously ignored by the media. One of the most sober and diligent of psychological researchers in this area, (Zillman, 1979), squarely blames the media for having a vested interest in outmoded and discredited theories of human aggression. There is, for example, the 'theory' of Freud that a 'death instinct' which is innate in man, and ultimately self-destructive and self-directed, needs to be turned outwards towards others in the form of aggression. Such aggressive urges can only be checked by their 'sublimation', i.e. the instinctive energy has to be channelled elsewhere. Such a theory is not, whatever else it is, a scientific theory and cannot be said therefore even to have been proven wrong—only scientific theories allow themselves to be falsified. A more scientific-sounding theory, which echoes Freud's in some ways, is associated with the animal behaviour researcher Konrad Lorenz. Lorenz also sees aggression as an inevitable part of man's biological heritage. Like Freud, Lorenz sees aggressive 'instinctual' energy as building up ready to be elicited or triggered in appropriate circumstances. However, the critical aspect of Lorenz's theory is that as the energy accumulates so the need to discharge it increases in intensity until a point is finally reached where even in the absence of appropriate instigating stimuli in the environment, aggression spills out into behaviour. Such non-instigated behaviour Lorenz terms vacuum activity. It is obvious that Lorenz's theory makes one starkly pessimistic prediction: aggression is inevitable. The most we can hope for according to Lorenz is that some sort of channelling will occur, whereby pent-up energy will be relased harmlessly, e.g. in the form of sport. In so far as the release of aggressive energy is concerned, theories such as Freud's and Lorenz's advocate directly or indirectly *catharsis* as a way of controlling aggression. This 'letting off steam' under certain conditions has turned out to be a particularly dangerous notion that has been taken up by those who wish to justify a whole range of dubious practices. Thus half-baked therapies of the 'let it all hang out' variety abound on the one hand, possibly to treat on the other hand the aggressive victims of a diet of supposedly cathartic TV and media violence.

The evidence that does exist, however, gives no support for the notion that aggressive urges build up inevitably, and indeed environmental precursors of aggressive behaviour can never really be ruled out, thus making this aspect of the theory like Freud's virtually untestable. What can be tested, however, is the so-called cathartic effect of 'harmlessly' watching acts of aggression and violence. Here the evidence not only fails to support the catharsis view it indicates that when persons view such material, the likelihood of subsequent acts of aggression is increased. This is particularly the case, where the acts of aggression are seen to be rewarded (by material gain, status, or approval), where the actor has qualities which enhance imitation—highly admired, or seen as similar in crucial respects, and where the opportunity to similarly aggress is salient. The more harmful effects of TV violence on kids are possibly most in evidence when those kids are less gifted intellectually, particularly when they fail to make the clear distinction between total fantasy and what is or could be reality. Although no-one should say that the research evidence in this complex area is unambiguous, enough evidence has been forthcoming to put the burden of proof squarely on the shoulders of those who believe that their violence-packed schedules are harmless. If evidence were needed that TV schedules are so packed, then we can do no better than to quote the statistics from a random sample of one hundred hours during one week's TV in the United States, taken between 4 p.m. and 9 p.m., that is to say peak viewing time for children. Over half the time was given over to programmes in which violence played a major part. Disregarding cartoons and slapstick there were in the one hundred hours, twelve murders, sixteen major gunfights, forty-two non-fatal gunfights, thirty hand-to-hand fights, two stranglings, one pitch-forking, one stabbing, four pushings-over-a-cliff, two attempts to run over with a car, two mob lynchings, a horse grinding a man under foot, and a guillotining. Let us add to that statistical summary another separate statistic. It has been estimated that the average American prekindergarten child spends sixty-four per cent of his waking life watching TV, whilst even an eleven year old will probably watch about twenty hours per week. At the very least we should be wary of what this teaches a child in terms of how violent he or she perceives the world to be and how routine a matter it may be perceived to be. In this way psychologists have argued that we may desensitize ourselves to violence.

If Freudian and Lorenzian ideas of catharsis are unwarranted, there is another outmoded theory which effectively stresses the inevitability of aggression and was put forward by experimental psychologists of an earlier generation. It is called the frustration – aggression hypothesis (hypothesis rather than theory, since experimental psychologists are more cautious nowadays about grand theories). It suggested that aggression is an automatic sequel to frustration and that if we wish to look for the cause of aggression we should seek to find a source of frustration. Since frustration is an inevitable part of living, it follows that aggression too according to this hypothesis is in practice an inevitable consequence. Although it can certainly be illuminating to think how often aggression does stem from frustration, it cannot be maintained that frustration is either a necessary or a sufficient condition of aggressive behaviour. First of all, it is clear that many persons behave violently simply with a view to achieving certain ends. No emotion of frustration or anger need be involved. Much mafia and gangland violence can easily be seen in this light. The rewards, however, do not have to be material: approval by one's peer group or perhaps more importantly avoiding disapproval and being branded a coward are perhaps the most potent reinforcers of much violent behaviour among the young (and it has been said that with society's present male stereotype, growing old is the only cure for violence amongst young males!). Thus frustration is not a necessary condition of violence. Secondly, however, even amongst those who suffer the same frustration, it is evident that different people react in different ways to that frustration. Some, it is true, may respond with aggression; others, however, may cope with the frustration in very different ways. This indeed is the crucial point which needs to be made. It is social learning and experience, particularly the example set by parental and other 'models', which determines how a person translates his feelings into behaviour. Anger and frustration as feelings may naturally seem to go with aggressive behaviour, but it is clearly the case that in practice they can be decoupled. Thus frustration is not a sufficient condition of aggression. However, the frustration – aggression hypothesis does point to an important division of aggression into two types, which will be of importance later when we consider intervention in violent disputes. That division is into what contemporary psychologists term 'angry' aggression and 'instrumental' aggression. The frustration – aggression hypothesis concerned itself with the former and had little to say about the aggression and violence which is merely 'instrumental' in achieving some reward or avoiding some punishment, such as was mentioned earlier.

A current mainstream psychological theory of aggression would thus probably end up by saying aggression is likely to remain a problem for mankind not because of its being a part of man's biological luggage, but because it is unlikely to lose its rewarding value, or, as Zillman (1979) puts it: 'Man is hostile and aggressive, then, not because he follows inborn impulses, but because these behaviours have *utility*. It may be conjectured that if they had no utility, they would long ago have vanished in the evolution of man.'

This playing down of biological instincts does not mean that biologically laid down programmes for aggressive behaviour may not be wired into man's brain. What is being denied is that a need to play such programmes is also programmed. The environment alone can easily and parsimoniously explain why they go on being switched in.

Finally before we conclude this section on theory, it is instructive to think of the scope of rewards and punishments which might strenghten or weaken habits of responding violently to events. Whilst relief of anger or frustration provides strong 'reinforcement' for what we have termed 'angry' aggression, and whilst material reward or approval provides 'reinforcement' for much instrumental aggression, the reader may well ask what about those instances of aggression and violence which seem to be quite gratuitous, most aptly captured by the phrase 'for kicks'. Here perhaps psychologists have been inadequate in their theorizing, since they have tended to concentrate on motivational theories which have their organisms (including humans!) busy reducing arousal levels heightened by hunger, thirst, threat, frustration, etc. That humans may under certain circumstances seek out very high levels of arousal (and not just optimally middling ones either) has received less theoretical thought (see Apter, 1982, for an exception) even though the existence of big dippers and risky sports alone seem to testify to a need for stimulation. We may suppose that the circumstances which maximally evoke such a need are those in which a chronically and unpleasantly low level of arousal has been endured: in short, boredom. Such boredom may be unemployment-produced, in the sense that a lot of spare time is generated with little money to spend on pursuing sanctioned thrills. It is not surprising therefore that under such circumstances violence can be rewarded by its thrill value alone, or in conjunction with a feeling of getting back at the society which the aggressor may blame for his state of boredom, penury or whatever. Lorenz's suggestion that society may save itself from some of the unwanted effects of aggression through such channels as sport, etc., probably has some validity in this respect. However, the rationale has little to do with specific aggressive urges, and more to do with general urges to keep oneself active and stimulated. As it happens some contexts, such as a decaying inner-city environment, may leave little but fighting or burglary as a source of activity and stimulation. If you are thinking at this point that not all are affected equally then it may be pertinent to look back to the description of the extravert given in an earlier section. We might expect that someone very high in extraversion, and thus a chronically under-aroused stimulus-seeker, will be particularly at risk in this regard.

Immediate factors governing violence

Disinhibitory effects

First, we shall consider those factors which lead to a lessening of inhibitions against violence in a situation. Despite a lot of publicly expressed worry about violence on the street or on public transport, etc., the incidence of such behaviour is probably less than many would think. There are normally powerful constraints which most individuals feel against exhibiting direct aggression. These constraints come down to fear: fear of the consequences either in the form of immediate retaliation by the victim, or fear of being caught and punished by society's lawful agents. There might or might not be additional moral considerations. Most people in modern day societies are likely to feel extreme anxiety at the prospect of witnessing, let alone being involved in, real violence. That 'most people' will include a good proportion of those who sometimes *do* aggress. What then are the factors which lead people to lose this normal fear, which lower the inhibitions against violent behaviour, and escalate potentially troublesome situations? Any serving police officer will be aware of the single most important factor, and that is alcohol. In an analysis of police intervention in domestic disputes, Walter (1981) sampled fifty-six requests for help. All of the cases involved potential if not actual violence. Of those fifty-six requests, forty were alcohol related. That is to say, fully over seventy per cent of such calls involved intoxicated parties. Similarly it is well known that alcohol plays an important part in potentiating violent behaviour by football hooligans on the streets and on the trains. We may well ask what the nature of the effect is.

First of all alcohol is not a direct 'motivator' of aggression. In fact this is far from the truth since alcohol is a depressant drug which is likely to lower rather than heighten arousal. We also all know how often alcohol can promote the very opposite of hostility in the form of greater intimacy and feelings of camaraderie. It is now generally agreed that the effects of promoting hostility in certain situations is related to alcohol's disinhibitory qualities. There are at least two ways in which alcohol serves to disinhibit aggressive actions.

First alcohol has a direct effect on the emotion of fear. This 'dutch courage' which alcohol brings is well known in other contexts too: daring to ask for a date, for example. It is a straightforward effect which can equally be demonstrated on lower animals as well. Thus cats which have learnt to perform some laboratory response to avoid a mild grid shock from the experimenter's apparatus will respond less well after ingesting alcohol, simply because the anxiety which motivates the responding has been reduced. Thus if an intoxicated person finds himself in a situation in which aggressive action seems appropriate—someone has annoyed him or some gain is to be had by behaving violently—then the person will not be held back as he normally would by fear.

The second way in which alcohol promotes aggression comes from its disruptive effect on the higher cognitive capacities. Alcohol quite simply clouds both perception and reasoning. Thus quite apart from being less frightened, say, of the consequences of his actions, the drunken aggressor is also less capable of working out what the consequences are! He may also misread his opponent's ability to strike back, and of course his own strength. Thus a whole host of reasoning and perceptual mistakes may lead to a decision to aggress against another.

A further factor which may be included as a disinhibitory one in promoting violent behaviour is quite simply the presence of other people. Being part of a crowd or a gang has the effect of diluting responsibility for actions thus reducing the fear that would be felt normally. Secondly the crowd or gang will make the individual feel, according to the context, safer from counter attack and/or stronger in attack, once again diminishing normal fear. Finally even the threat of society's retribution is diminished since the statistical risk of being picked out for arrest seems less. All these effects are of course in addition to those we have mentioned in a previous section under the topic of rewards and punishments through group approval and disapproval. Lastly, and rather like alcohol, being in a crowd can involve the same sort of intoxicated effects of being carried away by group emotions and losing control of one's critical reasoning capacity.

Finally under this heading of disinhibitory factors, we might mention another factor which is related to the one given above. When an individual merges into a crowd and diffuses his responsbility he is said by social psychologists to be 'deindividuated'. Under these conditions persons seem capable of acts of great cruelty against particularly helpless victims. In some frightening experiments a psychologist called Zimbardo has examined the phenomenon of deindividuation. In one experiment his subjects either donned or did not don Ku-Klux-Klan-type hoods which made them either anonymous or visible to a helpless victim, who was in fact a confederate of the experimenter. The subjects were instructed for a credible reason to deliver painful electric shocks to the victim—in fact the victim's response was faked. Anonymous subjects were shown to be far more severe in their delivery of shocks. However, it was also shown that the 'cruelty' of the subjects was enhanced by playing them a recorded interview with the victim beforehand in which she was portrayed as rather obnoxious, conceited, and self-centred. Basically the deindividuated members of a group are capable of terrifically cruel acts of violence if they can first in some way derogate or dehumanize their victim through the operation of crude stereotyping. Such victims can often be assigned by the aggressor to a hated out-group, in which the victim's own individuality and humanity is swamped as much as the aggressors: he may be black, Jewish, homosexual, or even just an elderly person, since helplessness is no defence against prejudice.

The effects of weapon availability

Some of the worst consequences of violent behaviour stem from the simple fact that weapons were available at the time of an assault. This stark truth is the most damning indictment of politicians in the United States who, in fear of a powerful gun lobby, continue to refuse to legislate for some form of firearms control. The most tragic of needlessly fatal incidents are those involving what we have termed 'angry' aggression in a previous section. By its nature, 'angry' aggression involves very high levels of arousal with consequent detrimental effects on sober judgement. Thus a husband may shoot a wife (or vice versa) in the heat of a comparatively trivial domestic dispute simply because a gun was to hand. If the weapon had not been available, the incident may have ended with no more than a black eye and a few bruises. One of the most famous cases, along these lines, was an argument between a husband and wife over the contract arrived at through the bidding in an ordinary game of bridge. When argument failed to prevent her husband's criticism of the final bid, the wife went to the kitchen, produced the gun, and shot him dead. Bridge magazines were kept busy for years afterwards analysing the precise nature of the dealt hand which could wreak such havoc.

In addition to the factor of availability, some psychologists, notably a researcher called Berkowitz, have claimed to have provided evidence that the mere presence of weapon 'cues'—say, a picture of a gun on the wall or a ceremonial spear hanging up—can help trigger violence in a potentially hostile situation. Berkowitz has posed his position succinctly in the question: does the trigger pull the finger? Unfortunately the early experiments were not only methodologically unsound, but later experiments have failed to provide replications of this effect, and indeed some experimenters have found that the presence of a weapon has inhibitory effects. Even 'field experiments' in real life have produced ambiguous results. For example, one researcher drove a vehicle around with or without a rifle on the back and deliberately failed to move off when a traffic light changed to green. The measured variable of interest was how much angry horn sounding was elicited. The results depended on so many other variables—whether the driver was visible or not, etc.—that no firm conclusions could be drawn. Nor, anyway, is horn sounding a violent act, although it may be an illegal aggressive nuisance! Certainly the effects of aggression-linked incidental cues is not an easy area to reach conclusions about.

De-escalating tactics

In talking about methods of controlling violent behaviour, in the short term, we can make a twofold division in our discussion. First of all, we shall need to reiterate the distinction made previously between 'angry' and 'instrumental' aggression, since research would indicate that different considerations may be necessary in dealing with these different forms. Secondly, we need to differentiate between the situation where the police may be forewarned of trouble and have the job of advance de-escalation, so to speak, and incidents in which trouble has already flared and a police presence is called for.

With regard to the latter distinction, psychological research would tend to corroborate normal police practice, which, in essence, is to remove or minimize the presence of those disinhibitory factors mentioned in the previous section. Thus, other things being equal, the discouragement of crowd formation, over-consumption of alcohol, and the removal of potential weapons would be an ideal achievement. However, the phrase 'other things being equal' masks the practical difficulties. The achieving of the above ends would no doubt in certain circumstances arouse a degree of anger and resentment which may be counter-productive. Certainly there must be room for a multitude of methods of trying to achieve the above aims, depending on the exact nature of the situation. Rowdy football supporters on their way to a match, and a planned carnival in Notting Hill, are both potential flare-up situations but presumably call for very different modes of preparation. The results of general psychological research

108

can only point to general principles, which may, however, be helpful in giving some direction to the operational experimenting with methods, which must ultimately be done by the police in a real context.

We now move on to a consideration of how best to handle a violent incident which has already begun or is in its initial stages. In this instance, we are going to assume that the incident involves but a few persons and we are not going to get involved in discussing aspects of crowd control. We shall also initially consider encounters where anger is minimal and instrumentality is high, perhaps where a 'victim' is being threatened either for gain or for fun, and where the aggressor or aggressors are not themselves acting out of heated resentment or anger.

Perhaps the greatest inhibitor of violence or continued violence in such cases is the injection of authority by the presence of the police, in so far as this represents in concrete form the threat of punishment which is, *especially in the case of non-angry violence*, the only established deterrent. We should particularly distinguish between the meanings of the words 'deterrent' and 'corrective'. A deterrent refers to the threat of future punishment for transgression, whereas the supposedly corrective role of punishment is to prevent further transgression after punishment for a past transgression. Now whereas there is a lot of evidence which suggests the weakness of punishment as an effective corrective, this evidence has nothing to to with the role of punishment threat as a deterrent. Indeed psychologists are now agreed that punishment threat is an extremely effective deterrent, especially if the likelihood of punishment following the behaviour is (1) highly likely, (2) sufficiently severe. Once a police presence is obtained, it stands to reason that the first and major requirement of effective deterrence is already established. If the person continues to misbehave then the likelihood of punishment is high. Given therefore that nothing is more important than threat of punishment, what can go wrong? At least two things.

First of all, the beginning of the last paragraph begged a question by assuming that the police presence consituted an injection of authority. The extent to which this will be true will depend on both the quality and quantity of police presence. Lack of firmness, for whatever reason, is likely to reduce the punishment threat, which may in turn lead to a failure to terminate the aggression or the turning of the aggression against the police themselves. Although we speak here of concrete matters, they do follow inexorably from the premise that threat of punishment is an extremely effective deterrent but only when it is thoroughly believable.

The second thing that may go wrong is more easily avoided by police awareness. The only reason why a person might go on aggressing even when they know they face certain punishment is if they accept such punishment (*at that moment*) as a lesser evil than the lost face of giving in to authority, perhaps especially in the presence of other peers. Thus it would be extremely counterproductive to say or do anything which increased the aggressors' ego involvement in their activity. Slurs on manhood are probably best avoided! What this amounts to is that threat of punishment is not so effective a deterrent for angry aggression and so it behoves any peacemaker to avoid that transition in the aggressor.

In summary then, for instrumental aggression, a cool, firm, professional response which heightens awareness of punishing consequences of further action is recommended. Revealing one's own anger is likely to increase the likelihood of a transition on the part of the offender(s) into angry aggression. It also quite possibly 'reinforces' the offenders by giving them more attention than they need.

We now move on to a consideration of angry aggression. We have suggested that the threat of punishment is not such an effective deterrent in such cases. This is indeed confirmed in laboratory experimentation. A social psychologist called Baron looked at three levels of threatened punishment—low, medium, or high probability—on subjects' aggression in a contrived laboratory situation. Subjects were either angered or not before taking part. The results which are shown in figure 6.2 indicate quite clearly that threat of punishment was not

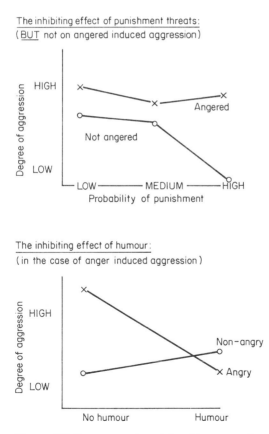

Figure 6.2 Some experimental evidence on the inhibition of aggression. (After Baron *et al.*, 1974)

effective for the angry subjects. Although the laboratory experiment sacrifices true-to-lifeness for precise measurement, the results do reflect what we might expect from real life. Baron *et al.* (1974) give as an example, a soldier who has just seen his friend killed by the enemy. He may virtually run amok amongst them with no thought for his own safety. Equally a child who has been constantly bullied may eventually turn on his tormentor, despite having been threatened with severe punishment if he is caught fighting.

This is not to deny that threat of punishment may not be of some importance, since the division between angry and instrumental aggression may not after all be as neat in reality as we have perhaps been suggesting. However, the incidence of angry aggression does indicate that the first priority should be to reduce the arousal which is characteristic of such cases. It is the high arousal which clouds the cognition of the aggressor and makes him relatively impervious to threat of punishment. Reduce that arousal and threat of punishment again becomes a more powerful tool. Thus we may profitably look at guiding principles for the reduction of arousal.

First of all it is most likely that the victim himself will be the source of the aggressor's anger. He will have in some way legitimized the attack by some prior action. Thus the removal of the victim from the scene will immediately deprive the aggressor of powerful arousal cues. If both parties are angry aggressors, physically touching either might be dangerous, especially where weapons are involved. The correct action may well depend on a sensitive reading of which party is the more aggrieved and therefore more likely to be dangerous.

An aggressor will, however, continue to generate his own feelings of anger and resentment even in the absence of the victim. It is thus useful to remember that psychological *distraction* can be a powerful changer of mood. An attempt to focus the person's mind on something totally different may have the desired effect of reducing their arousal sufficiently for them to get a better grip on reality.

It is worth quoting some evidence that the injection of humour into a situation can be especially valuable in de-escalating incidents of angry aggression. Once again the results are from a laboratory experiment but are nevertheless illuminating. Subjects were either angered or not angered by a confederate of the experimenter; they then had the chance to aggress against this confederate in a laboratory exercise involving delivering electric shocks. Half the subjects in each condition were in addition shown funny cartoons immediately before the exercise began. Results (see the lower part of figure 6.2) showed that the injection of humour occasioned by the showing of the cartoons reduced subsequent aggression *but only* in the group of subjects who were angry, and who otherwise showed high levels of aggression.

Finally it is worth remembering that the person feels angry because he believes he has been badly done by in some respect. One method of reducing that anger is to present mitigating circumstances for the victim's behaviour if that seems appropriate. The general form of such a presentation might be: 'he didn't mean it'. In reality a better and more plausible excuse for the victim might be offered according to the exact context.

Postscript

As a postscript to this chapter, let us reiterate some of what has been said earlier. Physical violence is not as far as psychological research has shown an inevitable expression of human nature. There is every reason, however, to be pessimistic about its continuation in every society at present foreseeable for the simple reason that it achieves a variety of 'rewarding' ends. Even in the case of angry aggression it appears to be the case that people can be taught habits of responding to angry emotional *experience* with *behaviours* other than aggressive ones. It is further the case that progress would be made in the control of aggression and violence if the idea was less prevalent that we need to purge ourselves of aggression by its inevitable expression in some form or other. It is a view with no clear scientific support and, apart from being potentially harmful in its effects, is rather insulting to the many people who do inhibit the expression of aggression, by suggesting that this inhibition may be itself a form of pathology.

It is appropriate to end with a quote from Zillman (1979):

'A person's right to punch obviously must end where another persons's nose starts.'

Suggested further reading

Baron, R., Byrne, D., and Griffit, W. (1974). *Social Psychology: Understanding Human Interaction*, Allyn and Bacon, Boston.
Zillman, D. (1979). *Hostility and Aggression*, Erlbaum, Hillsdale, New Jersey.

CHAPTER 7

Stress

Few people are likely to disagree with you if you say that police work can be stressful (but see Lester and Mink, 1979; Lester and Gallagher, 1980). Memories and imaginations will readily provide examples of exposure to danger or horrific circumstances, of working long hours, or of intense striving for outcomes demanded by an anxious public. Of course there are other potential sources of stress for people in all occupations. Police officers are exposed to pretty well all of them and vulnerable to most. Indeed, Hans Selye, doyen of theorizers about and researchers into stress, writing in the first issue of *Police Stress*, placed the police at the very top of the occupational stress league. Noting this, Marilyn Davidson and Arthur Veno (1980) point to its very serious implications, including the impaired functioning of individuals and a deterioration of performance which can result in a corresponding deterioration in response to the needs of the community that the police are expected to serve.

And there lies our cue. To officers accountable for management in the service, surely those implications strike at the very heart of their personal and processional commitment. That they are concerned for the safety, health, and well-being of their subordinates and colleagues is a truism. We may reasonably assume that their advancement in the service is at least in part attributable to their having been perceived as giving a proper priority to the needs of the community. As supervisors, coaching, monitoring, and evaluating the performance of subordinates may well be among the most effective acts they perform contributing to meeting those needs. They, and the subordinates themselves, by understanding stress can not only be on their guard against it and the strain which may result, but also, as I hope to show, can help protect their colleagues.

The aims of this chapter, then, are three: to try to show what stress is and some of the ways in which it might arise (and most of the chapter will be about that); to consider some of its effects and how managing officers might be alerted to them; and to offer some prescriptions for action which police officers might take or initiate to lessen the stress or alleviate its effects upon themselves or their subordinates and colleagues. The chapter will not be a recital of stressful experiences with which police officers have had to try to cope—although some general observations of that kind are as desirable as they are probably unavoidable.

There are many sound reasons for reading the collection of papers *Social and Psychological Factors in Stress*, edited by Joseph McGrath. (If you are really interested by this subject, then do read them.) One reason might be to seek a definition of stress. If you did that, you would quickly gain a vivid impression of how difficult it is to define and of how much attention psychologists have had to give to that problem alone. The most superficial analysis will show you that, of the seventeen chapters, at least nine make direct reference to it, and three appear to be dedicated to it. Tom Cox too, devotes much of the early passages in his book *Stress*, to the issue, and to developing a satisfactory descriptive model.

Is stress something which *happens* to a person? That is certainly the opinion of some. Sells, writing in the McGrath collection reminds us that it is a view that had generally prevailed in medicine and psychiatry. In psychological terms, those holding such an opinion regard stress as a *stimulus* to which an individual responds in some way. An officer who agreed with that might be led to the conclusion that stress could be quantified and understood by, for example, counting the number of supposed stresses to which a policeman is subjected. Doing that might conceivably have some constructive outcomes, but achieving a fuller understanding of stress, or accurately assessing individual states, would not be two of them. The stimulus model is too simplistic, and therefore not satisfactory.

Could it be, then, that stress is a response? Hans Selye says so, and that the response is essentially the same regardless of how specific the demand which induces it. That has something more than intuitive appeal, since something very like it does seem to take place: some event or sequence of events produces responses which, it might be said, *are* stress. There are questions which test that idea rather severely though. Why, for example, do different individuals respond so differently to the same stimuli? Or, indeed, why do an individual's responses to a stimulus differ on separate occasions.

Tom Cox offers a simple example which seems to show very well the difficulty which accepting either of these models—stimulus or response—poses. He asks about fatigue. Is fatigue a stressful stimulus or a stress response? A moment's thought will convince you that the answer is 'Yes'—to both. The experience of fatigue could very well be stressful. It could certainly contribute to a stressful experience. Imagine the police officer who, for whatever reason, is so fatigued that he is not sure that he can adequately support a colleague at risk. On the other hand, is it not a fact that exposure to some demanding but not especially exerting situation induces in some people sensations of extreme fatigue?

If both the stimulus and response models are potentially useful but neither is entirely satisfactory, it is clear that stress is a more complicated phenomenon than appears to be the case. Psychologists generally agree now that it is the outcome of an interaction or transaction between an individual and his (or

114

her—but I shall not keep on saying it) environment. By environment I do not simply mean a person's surroundings. Environment includes everthing which can influence a person in a given situation. Two conditions are necessary if stress is to be an outcome:

(1) the individual must perceive that his capabilities are insufficient for him successfully to respond to some demand he perceives being made of him by (something in) his environment; and

(2) it is important to him that he responds successfully.

Put into the simplest language, stress is what affects a person who believes he must cope but is not sure that he can.

Actually, that simple language helps us understand an important source of stress which surprises some people. Implicit in the first condition is the notion that somehow the person stressed is not up to meeting the demand placed on him. In a more useful conceptualization, Van Harrison (1978), invokes the idea of person–environment fit (P–E fit), which allows for the extent to which the job environment provides what he calls *supplies*, to meet individual needs. That allows for the possibility that an undemanding job can be stressful. As a matter of great interest to us here, Van Harrison cites evidence to show that work *underload* does *not* lead to job dissatisfaction among policemen. (Job dissatisfaction is a form of strain; a job-related strain.) Van Harrison offers a reasonable explanation for this unusual finding. It is that policemen have to be available to deal with heavy or sudden work loads; and while they hold themselves available they perform some humdrum routine tasks. Van Harrison suggests that they perceive that as being all part of their jobs. The result is that, although they perceive the P–E misfit, they do not experience it as a stressor. No stress, no strain.

The objective and the perceived

Let us go back now, though, and take a look at the two conditions which are necessary if a situation is to be potentially stressful. It can hardly have escaped your notice that the word *perceived* is a feature. This is very important indeed; as important in this context as it was in the sections on memory and witness behaviour, for instance.

So often psychologists in laboratories and other research settings are, quite properly, dedicated to the discovery or manipulation of objective facts. Outside the laboratory, these same psychologists are likely to find that, for the individuals with whom they are concerned, the operative facts—what we might call *their* truth—are entirely subjective. Effective truth, like beauty, lies in the eye of its beholder. Nobody knows this better than clinical psychologists. Many of them expend a great deal of effort trying to help people for whom the truth is so different to objective facts that they behave in ways which are often bizarre. But for those people it is the truth. It is only the extent of the difference between their and everybody else's truth which determines that they are in a category we call disturbed. In fact I would not be alone in asserting that it is *only* perceived facts which determine our behaviour. It is only our perceptions with which we can work. For each of us, then, there are two environments: one objective and actual, the other that environment as we perceive it. These need by no means be identical. It follows that a demand upon us from the environment will have two versions: the actual, objective demand, and the perceived, subjective demand. The luckier ones among us perceive fairly accurately—Van Harrison would say we have a good grasp of reality. But if you want a demonstration of the impotence of objective facts against perceived facts, just try denying a rumour.

More seriously, what often happens is that an individual in a situation in which demands are made of him, perceives those demands as even greater than they actually are. Can you remember preparing for your last set of examinations? Or having to face an interview panel? Did you not expect the questions to be even more testing than in fact they were? I do not meet many students who do not feel something like that. They think they have to know and be able to handle even more information than can reasonably be expected. I leave it to you to remember or imagine the sort of effects this has on, for example, preparation for the examinations.

As if that were not enough, people in situations like that very often underestimate their own capabilities. Did you not seriously doubt your ability to pass that examination? Or to field the questions likely to be thrown at you by those interviewers? If you have been answering the questions in these last couple of paragraphs in the affirmative, then you have experienced stress. For some people examination stress is an interaction having temporary but very seriously incapacitating effects.

Cognitive appraisal

That homely example is given to illustrate the nature of the differences between the actual and perceived environment and the actual and perceived self. It also serves to point us towards the next feature implied by our two conditions, a feature which is absolutely crucial. Its presence is essential if stress is to be experienced. *The individual must weigh his perception of his capabilities against his perception of the demands made of them.* In other words, he must carry out what we call a *cognitive appraisal* of the situation. Only by going through this process can he decide that he can cope (no stress) or may not be able to cope (stress).

It is exactly in this feature that the difference is found between arousal and stress. Psychological arousal is an important phenomenon influencing human performance in significant ways. If a person is too little aroused his performance will be at a very low level (he might fall asleep). Too much arousal is incapacitating too (people freeze in terror). For each individual there is an optimal arousal level at which they perform at their best. (It varies also with the complexity of the task on which the individual is engaged.) But the response to arousal is automatic. Sleep-deprived people who perform better when subjected to noise (Corcoran, 1962) do not have to decide 'Ah! noise! good! now I can cope better'; they are simply aroused by the extra environmental stimulus, and their state more closely approximates to their optimum state of arousal. Stress is probably like arousal in that some is desirable and there are optimum levels. It differs in this concise cognitive way though. Imagine somebody trying to solve a difficult complex problem by a certain time. Suppose he is distracted by an unpredictable noise made by somebody aware of but seemingly indifferent to the intellectual striving taking place nearby. Probably his concentration will be seriously disturbed, and he is quite likely to find the problem becoming more complex and his abilities less adequate as the deadline draws nearer. He may soon come seriously to doubt his ability to produce a solution. He will not only appraise the balance between the factors but may frequently review his appraisal. The greater the apparent imbalance in favour of the problem remaining unresolved (and assuming that finding the solution is important to the individual) the greater the stress.

Roles

Social psychologists have developed a theory of roles (Biddle, 1979). Each position occupied by a person in society is seen as a role which he plays. Often the role is determined for him because it carries with it obligations or the expectation that he will do certain things and not do certain others. The person also has rights by virtue of his role position, and has expectations of others with whom his role interacts. A role under consideration during, say, an analysis of behaviour, is called the *focal role*; and the total role network interacting with and including a focal role is known as a *role set*. Each actual role set is, of course, an individual thing which needs to be carefully plotted if it and its influence is to be understood. It is possible, however, to imagine typical role sets. Consider the role set of an hypothetical police officer (figure 7.1). Even with the relatively coarse analysis shown, the different sorts of expectations of and by members of this role set are easily imagined. Figure 7.2 shows another, smaller scale role set of a more local nature, but one similarly full of potential demands. Look at the same role player in yet another role (figure 7.3) and we realize the possible complexity of role sets which may at any time affect an individual and make demands of him. A role set is a very useful way of representing an individual's environment. Before we stop looking at role sets, consider for a moment the demands implicit in one more (figure 7.4). There may be some rather incompatible expectations and obligations existing there.

Role stress

That brings us to the first of some important potential sources of stress: *role conflict* (Kahn, 1973). Role conflict arises whenever the expectations of (or obligation to) different members of a role set are clear but incompatible. The greater the incompatibility the greater the demand placed on the focal role; and

Some examples of role sets

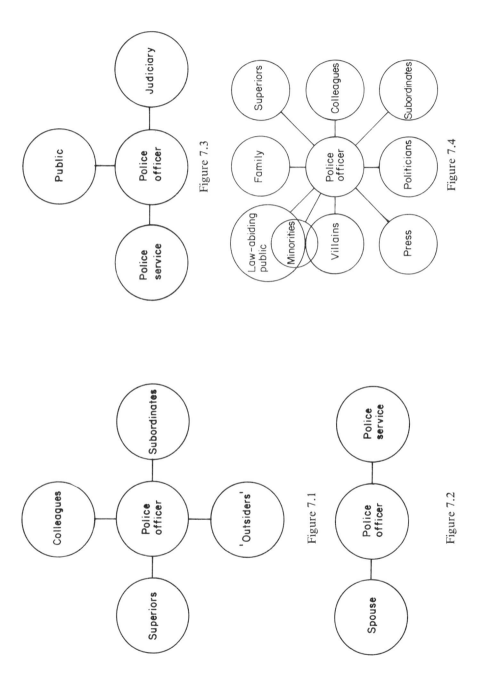

Figure 7.3

Figure 7.4

Figure 7.1

Figure 7.2

if the role player does not possess, or cannot call upon, the power or the skills to resolve the incompatibility, stress may be the result.

Another potent source of stress, also described by Kahn, arises when the focal role does not receive enough information about his obligations and the expectations of others. The resulting uncertainty is known as *role ambiguity*.

We might not expect to find high levels of role conflict or ambiguity arising from work within the police organization. Formal communications among members or units are necessarily as unambiguous as possible. Nevertheless, some goals are unavoidably general rather than specific (keep the peace; prevent crime; protect citizens). Socialization and other training may be expected to make the paths to their attainment clearer than their generality might suggest. Nevertheless, Kroes (1976) has pointed out that the policeman's need to respond to a variety of situations makes it impossible to prescribe actions very closely. Awareness of direct responsibility for people coupled with the need (often swiftly) to make a choice among decisions in fraught situations, can lead to ambiguity, or sometimes to conflict, which could well prove stressful.

Interaction with the public

Such situations, however, are not entirely 'within-force'. They typify the aspects of the police officer role which require interaction with the public. These have long been recognized as potentially stressful for the police officer. Reference has already been made to the needs of the community. Our police are confidently expected to serve these. Yet it sometimes seems that they have (or are prepared) actually to decide what these needs are. In England in 1981 we have heard strident claims from some sections of communities that these decisions have not always been wisely made. There have been examples of what Eisenberg identified in 1975 as the potentially conflictful obligations of the police role in preventing crime: maximizing efficient law enforcement while ensuring constitutional rights and civil liberties. The effects of a gross (perceived) imbalance between these are potentially disastrous—and the potential may already have been realized in some situations. One effect may be that, prompted not only by their perceptions of their own role but also by the expediency of some political bosses, senior police officers fall back on law and order as their prime concern and justification to such an extent that they risk appearing to act unnecessarily repressively, and so of exacerbating the situation. Kroes (1976) sees role conflicts stemming from negative attitudes among the community as a potential stressor unique to police work. It might be foolhardy of managing officers to assume that attitudes *towards* the community among their force members are to any great extent uniform. It is quite reasonable to expect that among more recent entrants will be some, with social attitudes born of today's experiences, who are receptive and flexible in ways not automatically responsive to appeals to 'law and order at all costs', just as the public can no longer be relied upon to respect the law simply because it is the law.

Of course it is not the role of this book to debate the rights or wrongs of such issues (for which I am grateful) but managing officers need to be aware that, to the extent to which they exist, they are potential sources of concern, dismay, frustration, *and stress* for those with whom they serve. And that is so even before any are called upon to risk their lives and protect their colleagues in confrontation with an aggressive hell-bent mob, who may themselves be stressed beyond further endurance.

Davidson and Veno (1980) argue that, if the negative image the public have of the police and poor community—police relationships are the stressors with which the police can least easily cope, then surely here is something requiring much more research. It may be that Robert Miles offers a framework within which this can be conducted, as well as one which helps to appreciate the importance of this difficulty which police officers invariably meet. He writes about what he calls 'organization boundary roles'.

Boundary roles

Organizations, he says, have boundaries which are apparent to us chiefly by the activities performed across them. *'An organisation boundary is a region in which elements of organisations and their environments come together and in which activities are performed of such a nature as to relate the organisation more effectively to the outside world'* (Miles, 1980). People carrying out activities which, as it were, span the boundary, occupy *organization boundary roles*.

Boundary role occupants link systems. The goals and expectations of the linked systems are quite likely to be at least to some extent conflicting. In most situations, boundary role occupants can find themselves acting without formal authority. The authority given to them is little acknowledged in the other system in which they are acting. While that cannot be entirely true of our properly constituted police forces, when conflict obviously arises across boundaries it may be that the essence of the authority which is delegated is in need of review ... or at least research.

A glance (below) at the categories of boundary-spanning activities revealed by Miles's work may serve to remind readers of police officers' activities which fit into them.

1. *Managing the 'face' of the organisation*
   1.1 *Representing the organisation.* This consists of presenting information about the organisation to its external environment of other organisations, groups, or individuals in service of the focal organisation.
   1.2 *Protecting the organisation.* This means warding off external environmental pressures and influence attempts that otherwise might disrupt the ongoing operations and structures of the focal organisation.

120

2. *Processing environmental information*
   2.1 *Scanning the external environment.* This is searching for and identifying changing or emerging environmental events and trends that might provide threats or opportunities to the focal organisation.
   2.2 *Monitoring the external environment.* This means tracking environmental trends or events that have been established as strategic contingencies (that is, definite or highly probable threats or opportunities) for the focal organisation.
   2.3 *Gatekeeping environmental information.* This consists of translating and selectively communicating information about the external environment to key decision-makers in the focal organisation.
3. *Managing relations with environmental elements*
   3.1 *Transacting with external elements.* This means acquiring the resources needed by, or disposing of the outputs of, the focal organisation.
   3.2 *Linking and coordinating.* This is established and maintaining relationships between the focal organisation and important organisation, groups or individuals in its external environment.
   (Miles, 1980. Reproduced with permission.)

There are other characteristics of boundary roles, activities, e.g. whether they are routine or non-routine, and Miles lists and explains these. The objective here suggests the conflict latent in such activities and hence their potential for producing stress. More than that, though, it is to ask whether it is not the case that to a greater or lesser extent, *every* police officer is active in a boundary role. It is in the very nature of the job.

Some other job stressors

As well as role conflict and ambiguity, other aspects of jobs are known to give rise to stress experiences. One of these is *work overload.* French and Caplan (1972) have made the useful distinction *quantitative* and *qualitative* overloads. Quantitative overload arises when there is too much work to be done. Davidson and Veno (1980) cite evidence that this seems *not* to be a serious problem in American and Australian forces, and now that there is less of a shortage of manpower in Britain's forces the same may be true there. This finding is important in a more general way too. It shows how objective investigation can establish empirical facts at variance with conclusions reached simply by sitting and thinking about issues: the difference between what Henry Clay Smith (1973) refers to as scientific and mythic thinking. The same sort of difference is illustrated by the work overload problem. Some theorizers speculate that boring spells of routine patrolling (for example) have deleterious effects. Those who take the trouble to investigate individual responses to such periods of low demand, however, find no adverse effects. Roy Payne, investigating stress and strain among managers, and employing a model about which I shall say more later, lends further weight to the argument that finding out is superior to speculating. He could find no manager who reported that the demands made of him were at all excessive. Contrast that with the popular image of executives—and while doing so, bear in mind the fact that it is the *perceived* environment and self which determine whether psychological stress is experienced.

One more aspect of work load is worth discussing, since it does seem to be a feature of the perceptions of many police officers. Like other professionals, police officers find it objectionable and frustrating to have to do work they do not accept as part of their jobs. Johnson and Stinson (1975) discuss (and measure) this general phenomenon in terms of person—role conflict. Davidson and Veno discuss it in the context of work underload because it is associated with boredom. However it is categorized, it is clearly a person—environment misfit and worthy of managing officers' consideration. How, among policemen, does this particular phenomenon show itself? Paperwork!

To round off this limited picture of some of the sources of stress which are aspects of the job or organization, we shall consider three more which could well affect police officers.

Responsibility

Responsibility for people is consistently identified by researchers as a potential stressor. Alan McLean (1979), in somewhat anecdotal vein, relates how executives dealing with money, markets, and material, take those decisions and actions in their stride. Those involving people, however, and especially the implementation of unpleasant evaluative, disciplinary or layoff decisions are often harrowing. Cooper and Marshall (1976; 1978) emphasize the importance of this factor and its strong association with stress-related illness. They remind us, too, that the association shifts in the opposite direction as the responsibility for people is reduced and that for 'things' is increased.

Police officers have a general responsibility for people, one which from time to time becomes acute. Reference to this has already been made in connection with possible ambiguity and conflict; but Kroes has pointed out that the responsibility itself is a possible factor in police stress; the ambiguity, etc. serve to heighten the effect. It might be valuable to study the influence of this factor on the experiences of managing officers who, it is reasonable to assume, may find themselves responsible for public *and* subordinate officers in situations making great demands upon them.

Career frustration

The second of the final group is that of career frustration. Cooper and Marshall again have highlighted the impact of lack of security and status incongruity. The latter is more likely to be a factor in stress among police officers, comprising as it does under- or over-promotion, frustration at reaching one's own career ceiling, thwarted ambition etc. Leaving aside the possibility of over-promotion which may or may not be a factor, repeatedly we find investigations that point to the stressful effects of limited promotion opportunities. Davidson and Veno have found repeated evidence for this; and in conversation, some managing officers from British forces related recently how their backlog of officers formally qualified for advancement is reaching distressing proportions. This might not only stress the frustrated officers but also adds to the burden upon the superiors responsible for them, in their tasks of maintaining morale and of motivating their teams. It also serves to emphasize the urgent need for meaningful, reliable, and valid formal evaluations and associated systems. If a host of people are equally qualified for posts, it is probable that the evaluation of them and their performances will be relied upon to differentiate among them. As Gowler and Legge (1980) argue, the practice of evaluation may itself be a potent source of stress for the evaluator. Attention ought to be given to its effects in the circumstances prevailing in police services.

Physical danger

Policeman I have spoken to do not discount physical danger. At a moment of hazard, though, say during a pursuit, they do become temporarily obsessed with not letting a miscreant elude them. The danger then is presumably not a factor in their cognitive appraisal of their ability to cope. Nevertheless, that may not always be the case. Patiently confronting a rioting mob, before attempting to quell their behaviour but while still within range of their foul missiles, affords plenty of opportunity for a cognitive appraisal involving self, colleagues, opponents etc. Isolated incidents, particularly those involving self or colleagues in injury, may well occasion reappraisal. Kroes records that the physically dangerous situations in which police officers find themselves can be beyond their abilities to cope with emotionally. Davidson and Veno note that situations involving violence are the most anxious and the least liked by American and Australian policemen. These are not confined to situations of personal hazard, though. Encountering child beating is one example; and delivering messages about death (one of the most difficult tasks carried out by police officers—Georgiades, 1976 personal communication) is another. Evidently some officers welcome some situations of physical danger and tension. Others may react differently to them as they gain experience. In that context it is, perhaps, worth bearing in mind that studies of parachutists show that both inexperienced and experienced jumpers show psychological and physiological signs of stress—but show them differently. Those without experience show greatest stress symptoms in the plane at altitude immediately before a jump; experienced practitioners show them hardly at all then, but do so earlier and more selectively (Fenz, 1975).

Despite comparatively few research findings, relationships with others at work is often cited as an important potential source of stress. Because this factor is not being treated in this section it should not be thought that it is being overlooked. There are some positive findings about relationships which I wish to consider in a different context: that of combating or alleviating stress and strain.

Individual and social factors in stress

Reaction to potentially stressful situations is very much an individual matter—indeed, it may vary within an individual. It seems likely, then, that there will be factors at work which are aspects of the individual; and factors which he brings into the situation and which help determine his perceptions, appraisal, and responses. To put it another way, should we not look to see whether there are things about individuals which, perhaps at some moment, make them more or less vulnerable to stress?

Following the 1976 review by Cooper and Marshall of research into occupational stress and personality differences, Marilyn Davidson and Arthur Veno (1980) go a stage further by seeking specifically police-related aspects. They look at work done to try to identify the so-called 'police personality', but conclude that features which have been isolated tend, in fact, to reflect particular cultures and even particular police forces within some cultures. In other words, they are not inherent personality traits. Usefully, though, they point out that some characteristics, such as rigidity and conformity, may well benefit their bearers when they are in situations of conflict stress.

There is some evidence that your sensitivity or responses to different stressors depend on your personality type. For example the situations in which nurses work differ in many ways. One is the nature of the stressors inherent in them (e.g. mental health wards, operating theatres etc.). Quinlan and Blatt (1972) showed that best performances in these differing situations depended on the nurses' cognitive styles. Another personality dimension which has been implicated is that which indicates the extent to which individuals characteristically believe that events in their lives, and their consequences, are determined by either powerful others, luck, fate etc., or are under their own control. If you believed you were not in control, then it would not be altogether surprising to find that you were more susceptible to stressors. This has been shown to be the case for teachers. Those who believe in *external* control (Rotter, 1966) also tend to report greater stress at work (Kyriacou and Sutcliffe, 1978).

There are, it is true to say, some interesting consistencies among the results of psychometric studies. It is also fair to add that much remains to be done if managing officers are to be expected to place any reliance on them in their professional roles.

For the population at large, social factors are now known to be important in determining the amount of distress that stressed people may suffer. Kessler (1979) has shown that that is largely attributable to the different impact that stressful events make upon members of different classes. That has not been demonstrated within a single occupation yet; the Kessler research is concerned with the effects of stressful events in life rather than with work stressors. Nevertheless, the results alert us to yet another source of difference among people in their susceptibility to stress or strain.

Life events

In fact some life events (as they are invariably termed now) are known to be stressors, and research for over fifteen years has shown how significantly associated they often are with the onset of a variety of stress-related disorders. Perhaps the major momentum in the work arose in the 1960s when Holmes and Rahe (1967) published their ranked and rated schedule of recent life events. In that original schedule there were forty-three of these ranging from 'minor violation of the law', worth eleven points to 'death of spouse', valued at one hundred points. By no means all of the events listed have negative connotations. The benchmark event against which all were originally compared, ranked seventh and rated fifty points, is 'marriage'; and only just below that at ninth and forty-five points is 'marital reconciliation'. Ranked twenty-fifth and worth twenty-eight points we find 'outstanding personal achievement'. But whatever the nature of the event, be it favourable or unfavourable, the points are all positive and *cumulative*. There was found to have been an increase in subjects' life-change-unit (LCU) values in the year or two preceding illness; and there was a clear relationship between the total LCU value in the year immediately before an illness and the severity of that illness. In one study, seventy per cent of the comparatively few subjects who clocked up more than three hundred points in a year also experienced serious illness in the next year.

There is a questionnaire which can be given to individuals in order to assess the impact of life events (Dohrenwend and Dohrenwend, 1973). Davidson and Veno—who note that the former has employed that questionnaire in studying police stress in Australia—clearly attach great importance to the whole issue of life events in studying police stress. Alan McLean (1979) speculates about the potential value of a study involving only life events which are *not* related to work and assessing the predictiveness of high LCU scores on them for reaction to stressors at work. That would be difficult to control; but the idea may serve to alert us to a possibility. Since these events are held to be cumulative in effect, may not exposure to them heighten an individual's vulnerability to the next stressor, whatever its source? Fenz's work with parachute jumpers shows that this is very likely. Finally, in relation to this subject and with sympathetic, if speculative reference to police work, some of the Holmes and Rahe events are very suggestive:

'Change to different line of work'
'Change in work responsibilities'
'Change in work hours, conditions'
'Change in sleeping habits'

Change

It is not without significance that those events are described first with the word 'change'. Years of experience of dealing with stress and, more especially, its victims, have led Alan McLean to the conclusion that change is a factor in all events that are perceived as particularly stressful, Another source of change and, McLean is persuaded, of varying vulnerability to stress, is the common process of ageing. He cites Levinson who has mapped out the series of adult developmental stages through which most of the men he has studied passed. Crucial to this discussion are the several transitions Levinson has noted: periods of change in themselves, but which frequently occasion desires for, or actual, changes in a man's environment; and those changes may contribute to the stress on the individual.

Type A behaviour

This leads us back to individually determined stress and strain, and to another important line of research of which much has been written, and of which we should take note. Friedman and Rosenman (1974) have spent more than twenty years investigating the relationship between behaviour patterns and the likelihood that people will suffer heart attacks. Their work has led them to the conclusion that there are two fundamentally important types, or clusters of behaviours. Type A behaviours are shown by people who appear driven to achieve, who chronically engage in an incessant determined struggle to accomplish more and more in less and less time; and to do so, if it proves necessary, despite all opposition. Extreme type A people cannot bear to have time on their hands, always programme and timetable events closely, are highly intolerant of delays, are fiercely competitive and play games to display their powers, interrupt others or finish their sentences for them, and quickly bring conversations around to topics of concern to themselves. They thrive on deadlines and if there is no deadline imposed, will create one for themselves. They tend to be over concerned with status and recognition. They set high standards for themselves. McLean speculates that the outward confidence of type A people may be deceptive and that they are often insecure individuals, unconvinced of their ability to perform to their self-imposed standards. A moment's reflection on the nature of our basic model of stress, with its perceived demands and capabilities, will strongly suggest how very vulnerable to stress effects such individuals risk being. Certainly Friedman and Rosenman found three times the incidence of heart disease among type As than among their counterparts, type Bs. Type Bs, are relaxed, contemplative, uncompetitive, and content that there is plenty of time. Even if they neglect themselves by smoking, not exercising, eating a fatty diet, are hypertensive, and come from families with a history of heart attacks, they were found to be still less likely than type As to develop heart disease.

Even after discounting the methodological shortcomings which may have influenced the type A behaviour results, Kasl (1978) concludes that type A behaviour is a serious risk factor for coronary heart disease. He also warns that we do not yet know how work is implicated in this behaviour, what demands in particular settings trigger it. Some people, however, clearly have a disposition which predisposes them to respond to some environmental stimuli with this sort of behaviour; and that seems to heighten their vulnerability to stress and its effects.

One last factor, or group of factors, which may be brought by an individual to the work situation or which may be stressful, is that which arises outside the organization. Jokes and anecdotes abound which tell of the irritability with an aspect of work of somebody who sets out from home at odds with his family. The review by Davidson and Veno indicates that there are indeed very serious versions of those situations. The resulting strains, both at work and domestically are usually sad, sometimes tragic.

Some effects of stress

'Tragic' may be no exaggeration. Stress has been closely associated with suicide—although as Kasl is careful to point out, the relationships may not always be as direct as they appear. Some researchers have disclosed exceptionally high suicide rates in some (but by no means all) police forces (Davidson and Veno, 1980). Cooper and Marshall (1976) record how long term effects of stress can include physical and mental ill health. The health hazard most commonly associated with stress and frequently employed as an index of stressfulness of occupation, is coronary heart disease. Once again there may sometimes be an element of self-selection, by those at risk for other reasons, into jobs which also appear stressful (Morris *et al.*, 1956), and other confounding variables may affect findings, but aspects of occupation which may be considered to induce stress are certainly implicated in the incidence of coronary heart disease (see the work of Hinkle and his colleagues in the 1960s) (Hinkle, 1973). As one more example of stress's potential for tragedy we need only remark the finding by Margolis *et al* (1974) of a positive relationship between job stressors and escapist drinking. Davidson and Veno make it clear that they regard this as a possible problem deserving careful research and, if shown to be a real threat, sympathetic countermeasures.

Always sad and sometimes tragic, too, are those cases in which stress leads to impairment of the performance of previously proficient personnal—one of the serious implications regretted by Davidson and Veno and mentioned at the outset of this chapter. Individuals, their colleagues, and their managing officers will be anxious to avoid these consequences; and may wish to be sensitive to the behavioural and other signs which may alert them to the existence of strain or stress in a person's experience. It is important immediately to say that the signs to be noted here need not invariably indicate that somebody is stressed. The short term physiological indicators listed by Randall Schuler (1980) could equally well be (and often are) responses to other classes of stimuli and situations, e.g. anxiety, or arousal. Similarly, the non-specific physiological indicators are certainly not specific to stress. Schuler is at pains to indicate all the difficulties associated with attributing his three classes of stress symptom.

A look at Schuler's table (7.1) gives an idea of the variety of effects for which concerned people will be on the alert. There seems little point in going through the list and commenting in detail. One or two observations are, however, in order.

The first point worth making is that, understandably, all of the symptoms involve change—that word again. Noticeable symptoms usually do, of course. But what I am trying simply to say is that we need to be alert to changes in our behaviour, in that of our colleagues or (especially?) in that of those for whom we have responsibility. Some of the changes listed under behaviour might not attract concerned attention: improvement in dress? change of hair style? They might casually (and accurately) be attributed to causes other than stress. At least, though, we need to acknowledge the possibility that the person changing might be stressed. No evidence is offered for the cumulative diagnostic value of the symptoms listed; but intuition is there to be checked out. If I thought I saw several of them displayed by one individual, I would suspect stress.

A word about voluntary turnover. This certainly is a symptom which has been associated with stress, but its absence should not be interpreted to indicate the absence of job stressors. Nina Gupta and Terry Beehr (1979) investigated the relationship between four job stresses (role ambiguity, role overload, underutilization of skills, and resource inadequacy) and two behavioural symptoms (absenteeism and turnover). They found that the correlations of stress with *intention to leave* were higher than with actual voluntary turnover. In other words, stressed individuals may want to quit but (for all sorts of reasons which are not too hard to imagine) do not.

Just to complicate matters, Carver *et al* (1976) have observed that type As actually suppress some symptoms which might be thought stressful. Even though type As objectively worked harder on a treadmill than type Bs, they reported less fatigue. What is more, their suppression is greater if they believe that their work is not completed than if they believe it is (Weidner and Matthews, 1978). Chesney and Rosenman (1980) believe that it is when the pressure of work is off that type As become distressed and fatigued—and so they hasten back to their stressful existence in which they are less distressed. Watch workaholics!

Self-esteem

Change in self-esteem is not specifically mentioned in Randall Schuler's table of symptoms, presumably because it is implied in some of the psychological symptoms he does list. He mentions it, however, as one of the variables most frequently used to represent psychological symptoms (along with satisfaction, job involvement, tension, anxiety, depression, boredom, and psychological fatigue). Perhaps it is a pity that it does not receive separate billing: a change in

Table 7.1 **Individual symptoms of stress.** Reproduced with permission from Schuler (1980), *Organizational Behaviour and Human Performance* Vol. 25.

Physiological
Short term: heart rate, GSR, respiration, headache
Long term: ulcer, blood pressure, heart attack
Non-specific: adrenaline, noradrenaline, thymus deduction, lymph deduction, gastric
acid production, ACTH production

Psychological responses (affective and cognitive)
Fight or withdrawal
Apathy, resignation, boredom
Regression
Fixation
Projection
Negativism
Fantasy
Expression of boredom with much of everything
Forgetfulness
Tendency to misjudge people
Uncertainty about whom to trust
Inability to organize self
Inner confusion about duties or roles
Dissatisfaction
High intolerance for ambiguity, do not deal well with new or strange situations
Tunnel vision
Tendency to begin vacillating in decision making
Tendency to become distraught with trifles
Inattentiveness: loss of power to concentrate
Irritability
Procrastination
Feelings of persecution
Gut-level feelings or unexplainable dissatisfaction

Behaviour
Individual consequences
Loss of appetite
Sudden, noticeable loss or gain of weight
Sudden change of appearance: decline/improvement in dress
Sudden change of complexion (sallow, reddened, acne)
Sudden change of hair style and length
Difficult breathing
Sudden change of smoking habits
Sudden change in use of alcohol
Organizational consequences
Low performance—quality/quantity
Low job involvement
Loss of responsibility
Lack of concern for organization
Lack of concern for colleagues
Loss of creativity
Absenteeism
Voluntary turnover
Accident proneness

so relatively global a characteristic may be intuitively perceived (and checked out). Even though we note the liability of self-esteem to fall into Kasl's aptly named triviality trap, we should be aware too that many investigators take it seriously. Davidson and Veno are concerned by the results which indicate relatively low self-esteem among police. They mention the work by Garrity, Somes and Marx which indicated that success in coping with stressors is greater among those high in self-esteem.

Concern for colleagues

Among the behavioural consequences for the organization, Schuler lists 'lack of concern for colleagues'. There are many occupations which seem to be characterized by a high level of concern by members for one another. In my own experience I have noted it among seafarers, read and heard of it among coalminers, been told of it among firemen, and am assured of its priority among police officers. I do not say it is not present among other categories of worker; a friendly interest exists in all the job situations I have been in; but having been in one of the occupations I have mentioned above, I think I have been aware of a large qualitative difference between the sincere interest in other categories and the genuine concern in that. I do not sentimentally ascribe all the concern to altruism. One feature which seems to me to characterize those occupations is the interdependence of their members. This is not just an organizational or functional necessity; it is an intuitive awareness, of what amounts to an unwritten role obligation, that if things get tough members can depend on one another. (The occupations in which I have become aware that this exists are also characterized by some operational remoteness and potential hazard—but that may not always be the case.) Socially, too, the police are effectively a minority group. They behave like one, with their own rituals, taboos, and special cohesion among members.

Not only, then, may we expect this change in concern to be very readily noticeable in the police force, where its opposite is the norm, but also we may be justified in suspecting some extremity of stress on the individual concerned.

Physical disorders

The range of physical disorders which have been associated with job stress is astonishing. They include asthma, thyroid problems, dermatitis, arthritis, obesity, ulcers, migraine, tuberculosis, gastrointestinal disorders, hypertension, and diabetes, as well as heart disease (Cooper and Marshal, 1976). Brown (1954) observed that well over ninety per cent of all industrial dermatitis is psychosomatic in origin. Of course it will usually first fall to a medical practitioner to help sufferers combat these ailments; but it is perfectly possible for the perceptive managing officer to collaborate or otherwise contribute to their alleviation or avoidance.

The alleviation and avoidance of stress and strain

There is a host of techniques available by which individuals may hope to minimize the effects of stress: to cope with it. Before mentioning one or two of those, however, I think it might be sensible to go back to where we started, to our definition of stress and our model of it. If we look at the contributory components we may get some ideas; some ideas which may not need special expertise or surprising insights to bring them to fruition.

Recall that we perceive stress when our cognitive appraisal of demands and capabilities shows imbalance. Both demands and capabilities are in two forms: objective or real, and subjective or perceived (see figure 7.5).

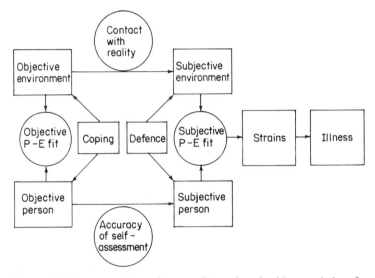

Figure 7.5 The perception of stress. Reproduced with permission from Van Harrison (1978)

Our *perception* of demands in our environment may be different to the actual stimuli which our senses detect. (Sorry to keep on labouring that point, but it is *always* important.) Nevertheless those objective demands do exist. They are the necessary starting point. There, too, lies the first point at which the managing officer can have an impact on the problem of stress. He can help avoid stressing a subordinate by manipulating the actual demand. By pitching demands at an attainable level, other things being equal, the managing officer can make more probable a balanced outcome from the subordinate's cognitive appraisal.

On the other side of the inequality we have capabilities. Any manager can aim to help reduce or avoid stress by training subordinates. Training in knowledge or skills which directly increase a person's capabilities for a particular task is the way to increase his objective capability to meet the environmental demand imposed on him by the task. A striking example of the recognition of the importance of this is contained in written evidence to the Scarman enquiry into the 1981 riots in Brixton, London (England). This particular evidence was presented by the Police Superintendents' Association. It seems entirely reasonable to assume that they may have had in mind the reduction of stress, even if only incidentally, when they complained that a new entrant to the police force should be better equipped *by training* to deal with the problems which will confront him. Ill-conceived solutions to those problems, the superintendents posit, could have contributed to the riots. Consider, if you will, in the light of earlier parts of this chapter, the following paragraph from the evidence:

> After only 10 or 12 weeks from being an electrician, schoolteacher, plumber, clerk, or whatever, he is expected to act, often alone, and make decisions of considerable importance to individuals. These are decisions which may result in loss of liberty. It is no wonder that, occasionally, mistakes are made through ignorance and lack of confidence.

For those two strategies (making demands realistic and enhancing capabilities) to have any hope of success, at least two processes are necessary: the demands must be objectively established and the capabilities of the individual objectively assessed. It is perhaps because of the close involvement of immediate superiors in situations and with subordinates, and the probable intrusion of their own values, that the necessary objectivity may be difficult to obtain. If that were so, it would be desirable that managing officers welcomed and trusted the intervention of third parties as training advisers.

We now turn to the next factor suggested by our definition of stress: to the subjective or perceived demand and capabilities (environment and self). Van Harrison offers two important linkages which are shown in figures 7.6 and 7.7.

Figure 7.6 Links between the objective and the subjective. Reproduced with permission from Van Harrison (1978)

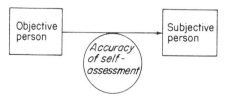

Figure 7.7 Links between the objective and the subjective. Reproduced with permission from Van Harrison (1978)

Counselling

An obvious line of attack on the problem is to try to increase a person's grasp of reality or (perhaps and) the accuracy of his self-assessment. Here, if straight talking and sympathetic discussion do not bring about convincing changes, there may well be a need for rather special abilities. In exceptional cases of course, failure to grasp reality, or persistently inaccurate self-assessment, will be components or symptoms of severe clinical disorder. More often they are not, and it is reasonable to hope for some resolution with the help of competent counselling. At this point I want to speculate a little. I hold what amounts to an ideological position, which I want briefly to present because, to the extent that it is a true position, it is important in this context of combating stress through correcting perceptions.

Meyer *et al.* (1965) have argued in another context the incompatibility of the conventional roles of judge and counsellor. A counsellor's task is often to help a person recognize and articulate a problem—a difficulty he is having in living effectively. That person is not likely honestly to explore the evidence with another who he thinks is evaluating him and what he says. There is nothing very mysterious about that, no amazing insights are called for to see it; that is just how people are—very sensible too. In some counselling processes, understanding may be sought through the counsellor confronting the client with some apparent contradiction, perhaps between what the latter says is important and his actions which might suggest other priorities. The discrepancy might be between a person's real and perceived abilities; or between the demands made of him and his perception of them. That sort of thing not only has to be tackled very sensitively indeed, but also cannot be productively done if the client, who after all is being invited to evaluate his own discrepancy, perceives that the counsellor is evaluating it and him. The confrontation needs to be achieved dispassionately and in an atmosphere of security. Even the suspicion of evaluative behaviour can produce defensive behaviour and a failure to engage in the desired problem-solving activities. That is why people trying to learn the techniques of effective counselling are taught not to respond judgmentally (Carkhuff, 1969; Egan, 1975) or at least not to show it.

I cannot imagine a situation in which a manager, however sympathetic, is not or will not subsequently be evaluating his subordinate's behaviour, abilities, responses, ... whatever. He cannot avoid it, it is his job most of the time. Even if a manager could achieve that improbable condition, is it conceivable that his subordinate will believe that he has? Could the subordinate construe a discussion of such issues as demands, capabilities, problems (to be) overcome, however apparently sympathetically they were handled, so as to perceive his boss's attitude as one free from evaluation of him? *Should he*? In other words I do not believe that any manager or managing officer, no matter how able at counselling, can succeed as counsellor to his subordinate—ever.

Of course, some convincingly reassuring experiences at work might cause an individual to reappraise his own abilities or to reassess environmental demands. Failing that, it is entirely possible that counselling will prove an efficient way for the individual to be helped to do so. I happen to think it can. I do not think that counsellors have to be psychologists. I know of no evidence that psychologists, including those clinically trained, make especially effective counsellors. Carkhuff strongly implies that they train badly for it; and Henry Clay Smith (1973) shows that in at least one important respect—sensitivity to people—they are not at all superior to people in general. (Nor are psychiatrists.) In any case, we all know that many effective counsellors are not psychologists at all.

The managing officer's task, then, would seem to be to make available to officers evidence that their capabilities are clearly adequate to deal with the demand they are about to meet. They may need to be aware of when that is not succeeding (very difficult); and a force owes to its members the supporting services which will minimize the risk of damage to them. The reduction of gaps between objective and perceived environments or selves may often be the key to a balanced outcome of the critical cognitive appraisal.

The only person who can bring out that reduction is the individual himself. All right, so he needs help sometimes, but his is the perception. The 'straight talk' bit by the boss is usually doomed. Ellis (1978), however, claims that some straight talking can sometimes be very productive in countering stress. He does not pretend that there are not some situations which are so genuinely stressful that most people would not suffer if exposed sufficiently to them. On the other hand he maintains that all too often the stress some people experience is largely self-imposed. They convince themselves that the strain is just awful. Then, says Ellis, a little direct (but not harsh) talking can help them rejig their ideas: cognitively reappraise the situation; or as it is sometimes called, cognitive restructuring. Ellis calls it rational-emotive therapy. Behind the racy, sometimes flip language Ellis affects is a serious and apparently successful therapeutic technique, which he claims can induce a self-helping approach of some power. By challenging any irrational beliefs about what he thinks *should* be the case, the counsellor forces the client to recognize the realities of the situation which is proving stressful. The client is shown how to dispute his own irrational beliefs and so recognize and abolish avoidable strains, while coping as sensibly as possible with unavoidable stressors.

Other techniques

There are other methods advocated for coping successfully with stress, or for avoiding some. Relaxation, meditation, dietary control, and exercise are all recommended. People likely to behave in the type A manner, for example, are recommended to find times when they can stop planning, timetabling, striving, and force themselves to relax. They should also try to avoid interacting with other type As and so keep out of a competitive spiral.

Alan McLean is an advocate of meditation for some people. While suggesting that it is always as well to seek professional advice, he outlines a simple procedure devised by Carrington and recommends her book (1978).

Benson (Benson *et al.,* 1974) has developed what he calls a *relaxation response*, easily learnt and, he and his colleagues claim, effective in combating stress effects.

Organizationally much can be done to reduce the risk of stress and strain by obviating role conflict and role ambiguity, and by managing job content and work loads. But there is another very important counter to stress, with a brief discussion of which this chapter must close. The influence of the organization is significant here too, although much can be achieved informally or conventionally—as the police experience probably shows. Let me continue the build-up by recounting the gist of an answer given by Roy Payne to a questioner at the British Psychological Society's Occupational Psychology Conference in 1981. The questioner asked how he should advise a client manager who wanted to relieve his subordinates of stress. Roy replied that, if he wanted to recommend one action likely to have a profound effect, he should tell the client to do his best to ensure that his subordinates enjoy plenty of *social support*.

Roy Payne's model of stress

Roy Payne (1979; 1980) offers a model of stress which, if adopted by managing officers, could guide them in their dealings with their own stresses as well as those of others. It analyses the whole process into useful, sometimes clearly identifiable stages at which the perceptive individual might intervene. The whole model is illustrated by figure 7.8. The model has the merit of being largely self-explanatory, particularly if you have borne with this chapter this far. A general word about the two appraisals, primary and secondary, might, however, be in order.

The outcome of the primary appraisal is the conclusion by the individual that he is indeed threatened by some demand. Concern, anxiety, fear ... any or all may be his reactions. Of course, this is a subjective conclusion, Payne (1980) goes on, though, to suggest the separate existence of his important secondary appraisal during which the individual tries to decide upon his best course of action for dealing with the threat that he perceives. It will be evident that help can be effective at either of these stages. What is more, probable substages constitute the secondary appraisal, at any of which, intervention may be made. He points out, for example, that the whole process outlined in figure 7.8 is a rapidly reverberating one and that at a first stage—which he calls the identification stage—the individual may well benefit from help in recognizing the actual problem with which he is trying to cope. Stages at which possible solutions are thought up, chosen, and their implementation prepared all follow; and wise counsel during these phases will be of especial value. The remaining stages (of what you probably recognise as a typical problem-solving process) are those in which the chosen solution is actually implemented and, finally, evaluated. It is at these points that the guidance and watchfulness of able and concerned people may be expected to help. The message to individuals and their managing officers is probably clear; Payne's model seems to me to help its clarification.

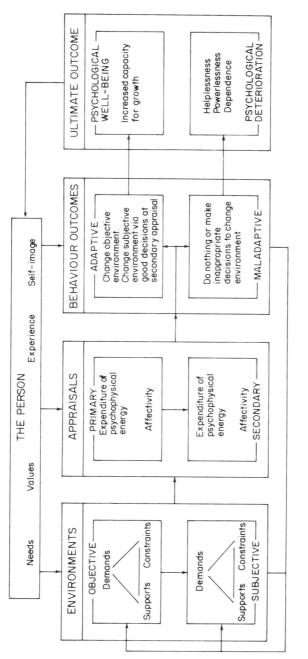

Figure 7.8 A model of stress. Payne (1980)

136

There is a further aspect of the model to which I want to attend briefly. It is the ingenious conceptualization of the environments (objective and subjective) in terms of demands, constraints, and supports. Events, processes, or influences in any environment can be clarified in those terms. Once the definitions of the categories are understood, most people can readily carry out the classification if asked. This affords investigators the opportunity to measure the categories. It would also seem to make assessment relatively straightforward for managers and others. The concept of support from the environment has proved particularly fruitful.

Social support

Support is envisaged as the extent to which resources are made available. One category of resource is *social*. (For a full and analysed table of organizational supports, see Payne, 1980.) Social support is provided by any who make a person feel valued for his own sake and not for what he does. It can moderate two relationships: that between a stressor and the experience of stress; and that between experienced stress and its ill effects, or strain. For example, social support has been shown to lessen the experience of psychological battle stress. It has been found superior to life events as a predictor of some psychiatric symptoms (Lin *et al.*, 1979). In combination with life events it is a powerful predictor of clinical depression (Brown, 1979). La Rocco *et al* (1980) showed that social support can also 'buffer' between occupational stress and strains such as mental and physical ill-health. Their data, gathered from over six hundred men, in no fewer than twenty-three occupations, include policemen.

An important fact elicited by La Rocco *et al.* concerns the relative effectiveness of sources of social support. They assessed three: co-workers, supervisors, and family and friends. And that is the order in which they were found to be effective. Co-workers appeared to be about twice as influential as either of the other two sources.

Managing officers, you will do well to encourage, if you need to, the development among your subordinates of mutual social support. You should give it too.

I hope you receive plenty.

Suggestions for further reading

'*Work Stress*' by Alan McLean. This is one of a series published by Addison Wesley. It is a distillation of the author's experience. It pays due regard to some major contributions to the field. It will be a good introduction.

'*Stress*', by Tom Cox, published by MacMillan. Although a book for psychologists and quite technical, this is a very accessible text and highly recommended.

Society's Victim, the Policeman—An Analysis of Job Stress in Policing, is by Kroe and published by C.C. Thomas in New York. The title commends the book.

Any or all of the Wiley series on *Studies in Occupational Stress*, edited by Cooper and
Kasl. You may wish to start with—'*White Collar and Professional Stress*', edited by
Cooper and Marshall, because of the Davidson and Veno chapter, *Stress and the
Policeman*—an excellent and a valuable source work.

'*The Mechanisms of Job Stress and Strain*', by French, Caplan and van Harrison, the
latest in the series at the time of writing this, is an account of a large scale study. It is
excellent.

Finally, also from Wiley, *A Behavioural Approach to the Management of Stress: a
practical guide to techniques*, by Beech, Burns and Sheffield is interesting and prac-
tically helpful. There are detailed instructions on learning to relax.

CHAPTER 8

Management 1—The Manager's Role; Communication

As has been said, writing this book is one consequence of running a short introductory course in psychology for British police officers. The content of that course was decided almost entirely as a result of responses by the prospective participants. They had been asked which issues most intrigued, perplexed, or concerned them. The target group for attendance was those who in industry would be called lower and middle management. In fact the police officers who attended thought of themselves in exactly that way: they saw their jobs largely and increasingly as those of managers of human resources. (We quickly coined the term managing officers, and used it throughout the programme.) It is hardly surprising, then, that one large subset of the topics they requested group very readily under the general heading *management*. What is more, as the course progressed the relative importance of some items changed. The outstanding example is that of performance evaluation, or appraisal. It had been the intention to use it as a helpful and interesting bridge between two other topics which seemed likely to be more important than it. In the event, discussion of appraisal and some shortcomings of some methods being used seemed to touch a collective nerve, and the topic assumed a prominence I had not suspected that it deserved. It must retain some of it here of course.

Indeed, in this chapter and the two which follow it the aim is to try to reflect those concerns expressed by the members of our first course. If the selection and allocation of topics seems at all arbitrary or wilful, though, I am to blame. The treatments vary. They range from the frankly prescriptive to the merely descriptive, from empirical to what will seem musingly speculative. Because the topics and issues are common to management and work, irrespective of context, no special effort has been made to gather material or experience exclusive to the police service. If there are some ideas or suggestions with which you find it hard to agree, or some techniques which you find it difficult to envisage applied in your own setting, do try to resist the temptation to dismiss them. The 'Ah-but-we-are-different/special/unique' syndrome is so often symptomatic of an unhealthy underlying elitism, sometimes complicated by the usually terminal condition popularly known as having a closed mind. The aim, as it was on that original course, is simple. It is to offer some of the work and ideas of psychologists and allied scientists which can provide insights and techniques which managing officers may wish to put to work.

What do managers do?

Perhaps, as I have, you have received management education as a student, or attended management training courses. Could it be that you too were solemnly taught about the functions of management immortalized by Henri Fayol (1916, 1950)? Were you told that a manager plans, organizes, coordinates, and controls? What an impressive ring those words have. Aspiring managers can be forgiven a slight nod of recognition and even a faint smile of satisfaction on hearing that their tasks are those. Indeed, some of the recognition may be justified. Those terms could conceivably describe, albeit vaguely, what managers set out to achieve. In one organization in which I had the genuine pleasure to work we actually strove to write managers' job descriptions in sections under those very headings: planning, coordinating, organizing, controlling ... and it can be done; but I am bound to say that we were sometimes perplexed to find the number of activities which stubbornly refused to fit neatly into one and one only of these categories. But, Fayol had spoken .... Are these the things, then, that managers actually *do?*

The answer seems to be *no*. For one thing, managers are just too hectically busy. Guest (1956) studied the work of foremen. He found that, with no real let-up in the pace at which they performed, they carried out, *on average*, five hundred and eighty-three activities a day. That is faster than one a minute! Stewart (1967) reports that the middle and top managers in her study worked without interuption for half an hour or more perhaps every other day. Mintzberg (1971, 1973, 1975) observed an unrelenting pace of work by top executives. He records that, *on average*, they processed three dozen items of mail, participated in eight meetings, (of which four were not scheduled), engaged in five telephone calls, and made a tour of some kind ... every day. And that was what passed for a normal day. Those managers' working weeks might not seem particularly long—just over forty hours—but Mintzberg points out that outside office hours they would spend a great deal of their time on work-related activities too. He concluded that managers do not seem able to escape from work and from their own predisposition, which becomes one to search continually for new information.

An interesting observation of Mintzberg's and one which, on the face of it seems at odds with the stateliness implied bv the Fayol pronouncements, is that he could observe no pattern to managerial activity. Successive activities were directed at issues which differed widely. He commented that a manager is somebody who has to be able to change mood quickly and often.

Variety we might expect. It is more surprising, though, that quite important issues were separated by some which were relatively trivial. In no particular order either. And they were brief. Almost half of all of the activities observed lasted for less than nine minutes (although the very few activities which lasted over an hour used more than half of the managers' time). Mintzberg's impression was that the managers he studied preferred short tasks and encouraged interruption. The sheer weight of demands on him (or her, but I shall not keep on saying so) forces a manager to treat issues abruptly and superficially.

His sample of managers also showed a marked preference for ad hoc rather than regular routine reports. Over ninety per cent of the verbal contacts made by them were ad hoc. All but one (out of over three hundred and fifty) were related to particular issues. Only that one could be described as being about general planning. (Top executives remember; although the other studies referred to here and in Mintzberg's writings support his contention that his findings are typical not special. Indeed, he comments (1975) that 'no study has found important patterns in the way managers schedule their time. They seem to jump from issue to issue, continually responding to the needs of the moment'.) Current, uncertain information is what managers seek out. The certain and historical is not highly regarded. Evidently what they want is something to which they can react.

What all this boils down to is that managers are not reflective planners in any classical sense. The environment within which they work, far from being conducive to reflective activity, does not allow it. It does produce adaptable information processors who prefer live, concrete situations, and who relish action.

A manager is essentially a user of information. My own casual observations lead me to believe that the manager who can use most most effectively is going to be the most successful. Mintzberg asserts that a manager's output ought to be measured in terms of information. He, like Sayles (1964), observes that a manager places himself, as it were, at the hub of a complex network of contacts from whom information is gathered and among whom it is distributed. Senior managers have large numbers of their contacts outside their immediate organizations. They also tend to receive far more information than they transmit.

Information may be gained in a number of ways: from mail, by telephone, at meetings, during tours. Study after study turns up managers' clear preference for the spoken word, and especially for face-to-face interaction (Jablin, 1979). Two-thirds of contacts recorded by Mintzberg were brief telephone calls or unscheduled meetings. The executives in that study disliked documented communications, initiated very little mail, and such things as operating reports tended only to be skimmed.

One of the other characteristics of managers' work which Mintzberg notes is too important to overlook. It is that managers *can* exert a lot of control over their own affairs. Other writers (e.g. Carlson, 1951) conclude otherwise: that managers can only react, cannot initiate; they are driven by events. Despite the apparent outcome of irresistible demands on their time, which he acknowledges, Mintzberg argues persuasively that managers determine a great many of their activities. They do this by establishing their own communications networks, by setting up projects which are going to need their attention later, and by joining committees etc. They also have the opportunity to exploit situations in which their participation has all the appearances of being obligatory. Could it be, as Mintzberg suggests, that this (is one of the things that) distinguishes the successful from the less successful managers. Do those who succeed impose themselves on their situations and take advantage of whatever it is they are obliged to do? And are the other managers those who cannot do this and, swept along by the torrent of events, submerge?

Managerial roles

Mintzberg said that all of the activities which he observed related to one or more of three categories of behaviour: interpersonal contact, information processing, and decision making. Within those categories there can also be grouped the ten roles which are able to account for all the observed activities. These are: the *interpersonal roles* of figurehead, leader, and liaison; the *informational roles* of nerve centre, disseminator, and spokesman; and the *decisional roles* of entrepreneur, disturbance handler, resource allocator, and negotiator.

Some of the role titles mean exactly what they seem to mean and therefore require no special comment here. One or two have meanings rather special to their context. The roles are important, not simply for the better understanding of what it is managers do but potentially also for directing training and development efforts. It ought to be fruitful if trainers were to help managers acquire or improve actual role behaviours. So, briefly, here are descriptions of the more unusual roles.

Liaison

This refers to the manager's activities in establishing and fostering a complex net of contacts through which he, and therefore the organization, gains information and favours. This applies to all managers irrespective of their level in the organization's hierarchy.

Nerve centre

This again relates to the manager's information-gathering activities. Nerve centre activities are those activities in which the contacts are gainfully used. Very senior managers have among their contacts these performing in nerve centre roles in other organizations. If your part of the service is one in which lateral communications are free, you will find each level's and line's nerve centres interacting.

Disseminator

When occupying this role a manager passes factual and what Mintzberg calls 'value' information to subordinates. The latter class of information is that by which philosophies, performances, styles, etc. are communicated. This is an internal role. It is in the *spokesman* role that information about the organization is passed to those outside it.

Entrepreneur

This is given special meanings which take the term beyond its rather dull dictionary definition or its more glamorous unofficial implications of enterprising commercial initiative. In Mintzberg's scheme it means the manager's role as initiator and designer of change, as seeker after whatever will lead him to start improvement projects.

The three categories of interpersonal, informational, and decisional behaviours have recently been re-examined in two studies by Shapira and Dunbar (1980). They concluded that only two categories are necessary and that they include all the activities identified by Mintzberg. One of these is the generation and processing of information; the other category consists of activities concerned with decisions. The interpersonal roles of figurehead and disseminator fit into the information group; the leader role is one of the decisional cluster. That seems to deny leadership due prominence. After all, Weick (1974) thought that the leadership role influenced all the others. He is probably right. The method chosen for this study (in-basket exercise) may not allow the role the scope it really enjoys in other situations—perhaps in most.

Those studies serve to emphasize, if emphasis were needed, the enormous importance of information processing in the managing officer's work, and to remind us that the work's main purpose is forming or making decisions. There is also in Weick's speculation a realization of the pervasive significance of the managing officer's leadership behaviour. The first and last of those elements of management will receive special attention in this chapter and the next.

But it is not simply the convenience of the structure of Mintzberg's findings which have influenced the decision to give them so much attention here. After all there are other studies of managerial work (e.g. Stewart, 1963; 1967; 1976) which produce valuable insights into its nature. Mintzberg's, though, is the work which first produced in me the 'Of-course' response so often accompanying what feels like insight. In it I felt that I recognized a description of what I thought I saw around me. It also asks very serious questions about what management training and education are—and ought to be—about. It successfully challenges several cherished notions about a manager's work without in any way diminishing it. Indeed it helps us understand the sources and nature of the sheer unrelenting intensity of the managerial way of life. It is also reassuring in that, despite an admittedly restricted and special group of subjects, the findings appear widely generalizable. There seems on the face of it to be no reason why we should not assume their applicability to managing officers in the police service.

Communication

An important part in information processing is that played by communication. I like to torture an analogy somewhat and liken organizational activity to that in the body. If you will allow that the actions of people and equipment can be compared to those of our nervous systems and muscles, then you will agree that to function properly they will need adequate supplies of the equivalents of blood, sugar, and oxygen. I am prepared to butter up to the controllers and say that finance is the lifeblood of the organization, and that cash is the sugar—the fuel that makes any effort possible. But I want to add that unless the blood is oxygenated with enough information, the activity will be ineffective—if indeed there is any. Communication is the system and process which delivers them all to where they are needed. It had better be healthy.

If all that seems too far-fetched, then perhaps you will accept Katz's and Kahn's (1966) concept of communication as the glue that binds an organization together. Or again, Bavelas and Barrett (1951), note that an organization may be regarded as 'an elaborate system for gathering, evaluating, recombining, and disseminating information'. They go on to declare their belief that communication is no mere secondary aspect of organization supporting other fundamental functions but 'the essence of organised activity and is the basic process out of which all other functions derive'. Quite a lot of the psychological writing on interpersonal communications is descriptive. It stems from the physical technology studied by communications engineers and information theorists. It is about as factual as most metaphor, but has often provided managers with ideas which help them improve their own practices. Other more empirical work helps towards a clearer understanding of the influences on communication. Despite years of effort though, researchers have not provided us with an altogether clear picture of what happens when two people, for example, try to pass information one to the other.

The metaphor mentioned depicts two equally important parties to any communication: a transmitter and a receiver. 'Obvious', the reader will say. But most of us will know some transmitters who behave as though the receiver were of little if any importance; and who, having uttered their information, take for granted that their edicts (or whatever) are complied with. So it is not always obvious to everybody.

The metaphor also says that the transmitter takes the meaning he intends to convey and encodes it—puts it into words, figures, diagrams, whatever—selects the medium he believes most appropriate—face-to-face voice, phone, paper, computer data, statement of accounts etc.—and transmits it. The receiver, on detecting the signal has to receive it accurately, decode it precisely, and infer from the result the meaning intended. At each stage along that process errors are possible—some would say probable. The managing officer who would communicate effectively with a subordinate or a superior be it a sender or receiver, needs to be sensitive to that.

As if all that were not enough to contend with, the model provides for the probability that all messages are communicated in an environment full of *noise*. This noise is not necessarily physical stimuli competing with the actual stimuli which represent the true message. Noise is anything misleading or distracting which can be mistaken for the message or cause the message itself to be misunderstood, distorted, or overlooked. Of course it is not necessary to envisage communication in this way. Some people though, do find it helpful to do so. All investigators of interpersonal communication are concerned about the factors which interfere with its effectiveness. It is true that not all of them originate within the transmitter or receiver. Many do.

It is generally accepted that no matter how carefully a transmitter plans his message (encodes it) and how judiciously he chooses his medium, *if he and the receiver work within different frames of reference the message will probably be misunderstood.* Roethlisberger (Rogers and Roethlisberger, 1952) finds it extraordinary that, given their probable differences in backgrounds, experiences, and motives, any two people can ever understand one another. If people do not see and assume the same things and do not share the same values (he wonders) how can communication be possible? You hardly need to run an experiment to recognize the validity of that remark. Politicians thrive on it: they generally ensure that any remarks they allow to be attributed to them can be construed in a way sympathetic to them however situations may change and despite any reasonable challenge. The world of industrial relations provides demonstrations almost daily of the futility of the unitarist approach (Fox, 1968) by which management (choose to) assume that their aims and those of their subordinates coincide. Neil Rackham (1971) and his associates have based a very successful training process on exactly this point: that the intention of elements in communications are often misunderstood, and the effects therefore unanticipated. Burns (1954) observed that the intentions of a surprising number of communications between members of a departmental group were not perceived by receivers. When a superior transmitted an instruction or a decision, these were being received as information or advice. Weinshall (1979) observed interactions among managers in European organizations, and found that in a majority of them the participants did not agree about their nature. Whatever may be causing this failure, its implications are potentially serious. Rogers and Roethlisberger stress how important it is that (all) parties to a communication must perceive identically its meaning and character. Given enough misunderstanding of the nature or intention of communication between boss and subordinate, efficiency must suffer. Tom Burns attributed the failure to a tendency an individual has to protect his own status. However speculative that may be, it does have an uncomfortably plausible ring to it.

The medium

What of the medium? There is now overwhelming evidence of managers' preference for the spoken word and face-to-face rather than on the telephone. We have seen what Mintzberg (1971) had to say about it. He was not the first by any means. Berkowitz and Bennis (1961) and Lawler *et al.* (1968) observed it, as has Penfield (1974).

The effects, though, of different media are readily envisaged. Suppose your own superior stuck his head around your office door and said: 'We must do something about these street crimes.' As well as agreeing, you would probably make a mental note to expect some follow-up to the remark. Unless the superior had shown unmistakeable signs of having suffered personal assault, you might suppose that the message did not imply imminent top priority action. What, though, if the same words had been telephoned by your boss to you? Would it feel the same? If he had scribbled it on a scrap of paper and dropped it on your desk? Said it in a typed memorandum? A memorandum copied to your peers? and to his own superior?

Clearly the choice of medium will be dictated by circumstances. And it will matter. Stuhr (1962) showed how employees preferred to be kept up to date with company affairs and progress; and the preferences differed according to how well informed the employees kept themselves. There was always a high degree of interest in meetings with immediate supervisors as a source of information.

Wall and Lischeron (1977), both in their review of the literature on worker participation and in their own researches in that area, were able to show that participation through face-to-face contact at the 'local' level of an immediate superior is by far the most desired form for participative communication and action.

Also, Housel and Davis (1977) show that the satisfaction of subordinates feel about communication with their superiors is highest when they are conducted face-to-face, less when by telephone and least when written.

Language

The choice of language is of considerable importance too. It will determine the effectiveness of the communication. Words are extraordinarily powerful, even single words. In 1946, Asch gave subjects short lists of adjectives which purported to describe a person. With one exception the lists were identical. The exception was that whereas in one list the word *warm* appeared, in a second list it was replaced by the word *cold*. That single simple difference induced subjects to infer widely different characters for the two hypothetical individuals. The individual whose description included the word warm was seen altogether more favourably. Not unreasonably some people criticized the method saying it was unrealistic. After all, they complained, you do not gain information about people in the form of lists of adjectives. Warr and Knapper (1968) dealt ingeniously with this objection. They embedded the Asch adjectives in simulated newspaper accounts of an incoming manager of a local soccer club. They were the only evaluative terms in an otherwise neutral story. They then sought readers' opinions of the manager. Asch was vindicated. This time though, the critical word was one in a great many, not merely one in ten.

Further to demonstrate to yourself the need for care in selecting words when communicating, just think of the newspapers. Think of the different ways different papers report single events. Actually this was done quite carefully, entertainingly, and illuminatingly as long ago as 1939 by Sargent. He recalled the words used by a right wing newspaper and a more temperate, neutral newspaper covering the same stories. He had the emotional rating of the words assessed. Never mind the ratings. Just look at the two sets of words, recognize which sort of paper used which, and ponder the implications for general communications:

Radical	Progressive
Government Witch-Hunting	Senate Investigation
Regimentation	Regulation
Communist CIO Leader	Maritime Leader
Labour Agitator	Labour Organizer
Inquisitor	Investigator

The difficulty with some of these words is that they are excessively (or insufficiently, depending on your political stance) emotionally loaded. Rogers (Rogers and Roethlisberger, 1952) is of the opinion that it is when emotions intervene that it is most difficult for one communicator to accept the frame of reference of another. And he goes on to observe that it is exactly then, when emotions run high, that that sort of acceptance is essential if clear communication is to be established.

Emotional loading is not the only property of words which can hinder communication. Sometimes clarity is lost by the inclusion in instructions (for example) of negatives. Far too often communicators tell people what not to do instead of what to do. Sometimes negative instructions are very effective, sometimes unavoidable too. In general though, if you want somebody to understand a communication of any complexity at all, it helps them if you avoid negatives. And negatives can be implied. 'No', 'not' etc. are obvious and direct negatives. 'But ...', 'except ...', 'notwithstanding', 'excepting only ...'—the language beloved of lawyers and others whose livings depend on their right to interpret—can be depended upon to confuse. While all the reasons why this should be so are not yet understood, many are. Wason and Johnson-Laird (1972) deal with the subject at some length. Sheila Jones (1969) deals with some very practical applications of the principles implicated, as well as giving a great deal more sound advice on improving the communication of instructions.

There is another aspect of comprehensibility which is very important in organizational settings. It has been given the unfortunate and incomprehensible name semantic-information distance (Jablin, 1979). What it boils down to is that there is far too often a significant gap in the information and understanding of superiors and subordinates. They use different terms in referring to the same things and events, describe themselves differently, use different criteria when making judgements, and a superior's perception of his subordinates' attitudes to him is often at odds with their real attitudes. What is more, the larger the 'distance' between superior and subordinate, the lower the subordinate's morale will be. All of these effects, results of this phenomenon of semantic distance, must threaten the effectiveness of communications. Indeed, Colin McCabe (in a recent broadcast) suggested that language is sometimes used by some members of a society to set themselves apart from or even render themselves incomprehensible to other members of the same society. The British police do not struggle to give the impression that they are above that sort of thing, especially the former. (Do I hear 'psychologists too'?)

Distortions

Bass and Ryterband (1979) offer some other reasons why communications become distorted. They list:

Adaptation
Association
Closure
Condensation
Expectation
Memory bias

and explain:

Adaptation is a special effect of the good news—bad news game. The receiver of generally bad news will overvalue the first piece of (even slightly) good news which is communicated. This is because his adaptation level (Helson, 1964) has shifted towards the bad news end so that, if you like, his average incoming message is 'lower' and the better news is further above average than it would have been before all the bad news came flooding in. Of course the reverse effect is possible: a preponderance of good news can lead to a piece of bad news being (exaggeratedly) perceived as worse than it actually is.

Association is a very powerful influence on a great deal of human behaviour. Memory is often more efficient in states or environments in which the material to be recalled was originally learned. This is because of the association we form between the information and the context in which we first process it. If, for whatever reason, we come to associate a type of event with a set of circumstances, then a report of such an event in approximately those circumstances may be interpreted as one of the events taking place actually in those circumstances. Or a report of an event something like those we associate with particular circumstances may, if those circumstances are present, be wrongly interpreted as a report of *exactly* such an event as we have learned to expect. It is not difficult to imagine the frame of mind of a police team sent to an area notorious for incidents of interpersonal violence following a report of an argument there.

Closure is a time-honoured concept in psychology. It refers to what the Gestalt psychologists claimed is a persisting human tendency to resolve ambiguity in a familiar and highly probable way. Bass and Ryterband's argument, then, is that the receiver of an ambiguous or incomplete message will tend to fill in (bring closure to) the gaps in it. Ambiguity and incompleteness are often characteristic of rumours: early rumours that something *may* happen become messages that it *will* happen.

Condensation refers to the tendency of people allowed discretion to shorten and simplify messages that they relay. If their memories are relied upon then there will be other processes at work. Bartlett (1932) showed how messages freely and successively relayed changed to reflect the experience of people passing them. This is akin to the next distorting influence, expectation.

Expectation is the name given to the process which leads people to hear what they expect to hear.

Memory bias refers to our tendency to remember not only those parts of messages we hope to hear, but also—and often more dangerously—those parts most likely to please those to whom we shall have to pass the message. This is one explanation of a well known phenomenon: an unwillingness to pass the whole message upward.

Evaluation

When considering the adverse effects that emotion and emotional involvement might have on communication, brief reference was made to the Rogers and Roethlisberger (1952) analysis of barriers to communication. In that, Rogers's main point is that his research and experience all indicate that a major, perhaps *the* major, barrier to communication is receivers' tendency to evaluate what is said to them or to evaluate the person saying it. Evaluation is the culprit. Unfortunately it is an almost instinctive response. Our education system, social system, judicial and legal system, impose evaluation on us all. Management is all about evaluation—of information, people, equipment, etc. Even our parents measure our (and their?) progress by the rapidity with which we acquire *approved* behaviours or the apparent relish with which we display those of which they disapprove. Osgood, Suci and Tannenbaum (1957) developed a psychological technique for measuring individuals' reaction to objects or events. It is known as the semantic differential method, and relies upon people's ability to discriminate between favourable and unfavourable adjectives' power to describe aspects of the object under consideration. When Osgood and Tannenbaum looked carefully at the sort of factors people used when responding, they found that there were essentially three: activity, potency, and, accounting for forty per cent of the total response, evaluation. So most of our response to anything probably is evaluative. Perhaps all of our initial response is. Small wonder then if we tend immediately to evaluate what is being said to us. The question is, will evaluation inhibit communication?

In the counselling and therapy literature the belief is that evaluation inhibits the establishment of the helpful relationship which is held to be essential to progress (Egan, 1975). More appropriate perhaps to the sort of situation we have in mind, in an organizational setting, is the work done on creativity and problem solving. There is some evidence relating to the process known as *brainstorming*.

Brainstorming is a technique by which groups of people or individuals try to generate ideas about a specified topic or object (Osborn, 1953). The first essential step in a brainstorming session is to free everybody from the inhibiting effect of self-criticism or criticism from others. It is held that only by first suspending judgement on your own ideas and those of others will you or they feel free to express suggestions which at first sight might seem silly or impractical, but from which novel solutions to problems could well develop. In other words, pariticpants are obliged to resist their natural inclination to evaluate. They also are freed from the anticipation of evaluation.

That the latter may not be fully realizable is suggested (Taylor *et al.,* 1958; Dunnette *et al.,* 1963) as a possible reason for the consistent finding that individual brainstorming performance is superior to that of groups. Collaros and Anderson (1969) found that performance by members of a group known to include experienced brainstormers was inferior to that of members in a group who knew nothing about the expertise of others in the group. They explained this in terms of the new members' anticipation of evaluation by experts, and the lack of this influence in the absence of information about individuals' experience. When Maginn and Harris (1980) tested this, however, they found that the anticipation of evaluation did not inhibit individual brainstorming productivity.

Admittedly the conditions imposed by Maginn and Harris were not exactly those a subordinate talking to his superior is likely to find himself in. For example, the evaluators were not in the room with the subjects. Nevertheless this experiment does show that cherished notions need challenging and can be challenged. In at least one kind of situation, knowing that what they would say would be evaluated did not inhibit some individuals. Of course trust was not an issue, neither were subjects likely to feel that the judges could affect their wider success or progress. Those two factors have been shown to be important in at least one form of communication—that from subordinate to superior.

Trust and other factors

Mellinger (1956) demonstrated the importance of trust—or rather of distrust. Distrust of a superior makes it unlikely that a subordinate will reveal feelings. Concealing feelings is often associated with evasion, compliance or aggressive communication behaviour by the subordinate. The superior will often overestimate or underestimate the amount of agreement that exists.

Another factor militating against frank communication with a superior is ambition. Cohen (1958) and Read (1962) showed that aspirations to advancement or increased status reduce the likelihood of accurate upward communication to a superior who has power over the sought advancement. So powerful was this effect according to Read, that aspiration could actually overcome trust. This is not a universal phenomenon though: O'Reilly and Roberts (1974) confirm the importance of trust, but could not find a strongly influential role for promotion hopes. Certainly Jablin (1979) reports one study (by Krivonos, 1976) in which intrinsically motivated subordinates may distort upward communication less than those who are extrinsically motivated.

An interesting observation, and one whose importance in the police service might merit examination, is that of Maier, Hoffman and Read (1963). They compared the freedom people felt to communicate to superiors who had or had not held their own jobs previously. Greater freedom was felt to communicate to the latter: to those who had *not* previously held the subordinate's positions.

The Organization

The nature of the organization in which people work is known to influence how they communicate. Young (1978) found that subordinates were likely to communicate more freely to superiors in a mechanistic than in an organic organization. Those two types of organization were described by Burns and Stalker (1961). The mechanistic is the traditional hierarchial organization, relying on specialists and the division of the overall task into carefully defined parts. In the extreme case only somebody at the top of the organization knows what the overall task is and sees to it that the parts are relevant. The command structure is based on the assumption that complete information about the organization, its condition, and real aims ought only to be available to those in ultimate authority within it. It is difficult to imagine a police service thriving when organized in so extreme a manner. On the other hand, to the observer there would appear to be much in that brief (and incomplete) description which reminds them of their image of the police service. To the extent that they are right, we may expect subordinates not to risk free and complete expression in their communications to their superiors.

Openness

What we are talking about is one (important) feature of a larger aspect of communication within the organization: openness. If members of an organization can frankly disclose feelings, bad news, and importants facts about the organization to others prepared to permit—or preferably to encourage—the frank expression of opinions they do not share, or who will listen to the bad news etc., then communications can be said to be open. Much is made of the concept by consultants working in organization development, who preach the virtues of trust as essential to a healthy organization climate. It is difficult, perhaps undesirable, to gainsay the desirability of trust in human relationships.

The effects of openness in communication, on effectiveness of management—as distinguished from the satisfaction felt by subordinates—is not consistently demonstrated. Willits (1967) finds a close association between openness and effectiveness; Rubin and Goldman (1968) find none. The important factor seems to be accuracy; and accuracy, at least of upward communication, seems to depend upon trust (Fisher, 1981).

It is difficult to see how enough trust can be established to increase the chances that communication will ever become satisfactory. In 1962 Nichols wrote that by the time information passed across five boundaries between organizational levels, from directors to workers on the shop floor, eighty per cent of it had been lost. His case was that much of it was lost by inefficient listening. Perhaps. But most people have heard of the 'need-to-know' principle, whereby those in authority pass to their subordinates only the information they judge it to be appropriate that they pass. Presumably they cannot trust them with more. Are they entitled to expect their subordinates' wholehearted trust? I well recall the chief executive of a major (but declining) British manufacturer beset by industrial relations problems declaring publicly (on television) that 'his workers' would be sensible because 'they' knew that 'we' could sell every product 'they' made. *The very next day* that company announced thousands laid off because the retail outlets were unable to shift that product. That man is still in his job three years or so later, probably much better paid; but trusted? (Is it possible that it does not really matter after all?)

Feedback

Returning to more formal issues, we should consider the subject of feedback. Feedback is another of those analogies psychologists gratefully grasp. In the world of engineering it has a quite precise meaning and intention; and, when applied, an equally precise and desirable outcome. It conveys to a system information about its progress and enables immediate corrections to be made to the controls.

In human interaction the intentions are very much the same. Happily humans are not so readily controlled as other machines are, so the corrections do not necessarily follow from information about performance. Indeed, as we shall see in our discussions of motivation and evaluation of performance, by itself such information is of little if any use. Also we shall note that some forms of feedback are more effective than others.

Used more loosely when considering human communication, feedback tends to mean information about the suitability, appropriateness, or acceptability of an individual's current communicating behaviour or of the content of the communication under consideration. Clearly there is already a difference between human and mechanical feedback, since the latter needs to be immediate, sometimes instantaneous. To a greater and less simple extent than its mechanical model, feedback to humans depends for its effectiveness not only on its accuracy but also its target's receptiveness to it. It is possible to improve one's receptiveness by the simple expedient of deliberately lowering one's resistance to the information. For example, if a person hears adverse criticism of the content of something they say, their first reaction—impulse almost—is often to defend their intention by attacking the other's interpretation: 'No no, I didn't mean to imply ...' Too late, and misguided. The fact is that to at least one individual the speaker had given a clear impression (that he wanted to imply...). The intention is for the time being irrelevant. The important question now is: 'What did he *do*?' If on reflection he can recognize that he worded something unfortunately and created an impression he would sooner not have created, then he can reword the message. Perhaps with further help he will be more careful in future too.

The critical words in that last-but-one sentence are 'on reflection'. Taking time to reflect can do more than enable a person to identify what is unfortunate (or excellent) about what they said—although that may be the most valuable outcome. Reflection's first duty is to prevent the almost instinctive reaction of resisting or defending against the criticism in the feedback. (Or praise: it is quite difficult for some people to accept compliments, and their instinctual response is to shy away or deflect the remark: a sort of verbal blushing). A quite simple and widely known technique by which you can impose a first pause on yourself, as soon as somebody feeds back to you, is to say thank you. I have not read of any research on the matter, but it does not seem impossible that by that simple expedient you also reward the other person, simultaneously creating an impression of receptivity. If that is so it seems reasonable also to suppose that you will receive more feedback.

Without wishing this to become too convoluted, I do want to speculate further that, by going on to feed back in turn to the person being critical of your performance, you can improve the quality of the information you receive. This is important.

To be useful, feedback needs to possess certain characteristics. Randall Schuler (1979) has listed them. He noted that effective feedback will be:

(1) *specific* not general. It may be that you can convince a communicator that people do not understand his message. You will be more likely to help him if you tell him he uses too many long words.

(2) *about behaviour*, not personal or in terms of personality. The last example works again. Telling the failing communicator that he is too complicated a person or too intellectual or pedantic is not constructive. Telling him that the words he habitually uses are too difficult for most people to understand is telling him about something he does (not is).

(3) *about behaviour the receiver can change*. This seems self-evident yet is all too often overlooked. There simply is no useful purpose served by giving information about behaviour that a person cannot control. The communicator in the example probably cannot become less complex: he can use other parts of his vocabulary.

(4) *consideration given* in *usable quantities* of *information* (not advice). He uses words which are too difficult not: 'You should use simpler words when you write.'
(5) *timely*. Although feedback does not operate in exactly the same way as reinforcement, and can be delayed, the evidence from training studies is that it is ineffective if it is delayed beyond the onset of the next similar event.
(6) *expressed in terms of what is done* (not why it is done).
(7) *checked for clarity* as most communications probably ought to be.

Schuler also insists that feedback should be sought and not imposed. I think that he is writing about receptiveness. Ideally people communicating will be actively receptive (seek feedback); at the very least the effectiveness of feedback requires passive receptivity, a willingness to learn directly about the clarity, impact, comprehension, or grasp of intention of your message. Schuler's catalogue of characteristics, however, reminds us also that the effectiveness of feedback depends on the ability of its originator every bit as much as on the receptivity of its target.

That feedback is a useful component of communication is easily demonstrated. At its most rudimentary it does not even have to be verbal. An encouraging nod or a smile can quite easily tell a speaker that he is not flagrantly breaching too many conventions. A change of expression can readily convey that the speaker has finally gone too far. Unable to see the receiver of his message, a human transmitter must practice and contrive if he is to communicate proficiently. Just think of the conventions of conversation on the telephone, and how special efforts have to be made to provide substitutes for the visually conveyed feedback of face-to-face interaction.

It is also a valuable part of more formal communications. Some of its effects were ingeniously investigated by Leavitt and Mueller (1951), when they examined the influence of feedback from a group to an instructor giving quite complex instructions. It is the sort of experiment which you could repeat for yourself or adapt to provide a demonstration of the value of feedback in the same or similar conditions, so some detail will be recounted.

For their first experiment Leavitt and Mueller created complex arrangements of six rectangles touching one another and in various orientations. The instructor was given one of these and his task was always to convey to his audience the layout before him, using only words. His objective was to enable his audience to reproduce the arrangement on paper. This had to be done in four conditions of feedback:

(1) a *zero feedback condition* in which the instructor sat behind a blackboard, unable to see the group who were to remain silent;
(2) a *visible audience condition*, in which the instructor and a silent audience could see one another;

(3) a *yes—no condition* in which the instructor could see an audience and ask them questions which they were only allowed to answer either yes or no; and

(4) a *free feedback condition* in which questions, comments, interruptions by the audience were unrestricted.

The accuracy with which subjects completed the task improved as the amount of feedback increased. So did their confidence in their own accuracy. The time it took instructors to give their instructions also increased with the amount of feedback. That last finding posed a new problem. Might it not be the case that the increase in accuracy only resulted from having to spend more time on the task?

Leavitt and Mueller investigated that. In another set of experiments they used different geometric patterns, and compared only the two extreme feedback conditions, zero feedback and free feedback. Each instructor carried out a series of trials under each condition. Once again, free feedback proved more accurate but also more time consuming. Every instructor obtained better results with feedback than without, and took longer.

However, there were some additional findings of great interest. While the average accuracy of subjects improved with experience in the zero feedback condition, it never did reach even the starting level of those feeding back freely to the instructor. That starting level was very high and very near to the maximum attained in the free feedback condition. What is more, while the average time required to complete the task was low in the condition without feedback, performance did not become even faster with experience. Even over the small number (four) of trials conducted in these experiments there was a progressive reduction in the time taken by subjects when they were allowed to feedback freely.

Leavitt and Mueller report some other results, one of which is qualitative but intriguing. The way in which the experiments were conducted meant that some instructors addressed groups allowed to feed back and who had not previously been prevented from doing so. Other instructors worked with groups allowed to feed back but who had already and recently experienced the zero feedback condition. The differences in the feedback received at first were very interesting. The new group using free feedback gave reasonable feedback, generally seeking repetition or clarification. The experienced group, however, who had had to function in the no feedback situation, asked plenty of questions, but they were hostile at first, often adversely critical of the instructor. They were not hostile to the method; they preferred the feedback method. Uncertainty about success is frustrating; feedback reduces uncertainty.

There is one finding which serves to emphasize the importance of feedback in reducing uncertainty. Instructors and subjects were asked to state how confident they were of the accuracy of the reproductions. *Instructors were always less confident than subjects*. Without feedback they were not sure of what the subjects were receiving. They could not know how adequate their communication was. Leavitt and Mueller believed that the really important differences produced by the two circumstances, communicating without feedback or with free feedback, were those of the feelings of certainty, adequacy, and hostility.

Of course what we are into now are the relative merits of one-way and two-way communications. Almost by definition one-way communication is communication without feedback. It is fast and orderly. It is also convenient. It spares the sender the embarrassment of criticism or contradiction. It also allows the sender the luxury of attributing failures in communication to the receivers—who were not attending or were incapable of understanding a simple message.

On the other hand it can be frustrating for the receivers. Around three times the number who were frustrated by two-way communications found the zero feedback condition frustrating in the Leavitt experiments (Leavitt, 1958).

Two-way communication is not only more accurate, it is also more enjoyable, if we may judge by Leavitt's findings. Over four times as many two-way communicators reported enjoying the task. It also seems to be the case that people want—perhaps need—to communicate upwards, but have to be encouraged before they will do so (Kelley, 1951). Genuine two-way communications can satisfy this urge, relieving whatever pressure might have built up had the desired opportunity not been there. Not all claims to have provided two-way communications, however, are genuine. Sometimes they are the results of supervisors' fond imaginings. Likert (1961) records a study in which nearly three-quarters of foremen asked said that they always sought subordinates ideas, yet only a sixth of their subordinates actually experienced this.

The mutual nature of two-way communications is indicated by Jablin (1979) who writes that one of the commonest complaints of superiors and subordinates is that the other does not provide enough feedback. Feedback *to* a superior certainly can have important effects. This is illustrated by Fodor (1974) who showed how being disparaged by a subordinate can affect a supervisor's behaviour, notably in the way he then uses power. Butler and Jaffe (1974) found that feedback to a supervisor can determine what sort of leader behaviour he will tend to exhibit. Positive (favourable) feedback tended to induce more emphasis on carrying out the task efficiently. Negative feedback led the supervisor to express more of what Bales (1958) calls socio-emotional behaviours—those associated with fostering and maintaining group and interpersonal relationships. They also note the Simpkins and West (1966) finding that feedback delivered publicly can lead to an increase in socially desirable behaviour—a not altogether surprising effect, but a procedure most of us might want to think about at least twice before trying it in an organizational setting, especially if it was negative feedback we had it in mind to deliver.

Listening

Among trainers, and psychologists acting as trainers, increasing attention is being given to listening. It is treated by them as a separate and special subset of behaviours, performance of which can be improved. Even in one-way communication this is important. If the communication is anything more than the most peremptory, the receiver needs to be working every bit as efficiently as the transmitter. Two-way communication has an advantage though, for it allows the receiver to check out that the transmitter's message has been accurately received and correctly interpreted (perceived).

The process of checking out reception and, especially, perception is sometimes called active listening. It can always be practised and can be deliberately rehearsed by trainees in simulations or role plays. Practising active listening implies good intentions. It bespeaks a wish to understand not only the surface content of a message but also its meaning, the intentions of the transmitter, perhaps sometimes the feelings beneath the surface. It is an act of goodwill.

We have seen how Rogers has come to the conclusion that evaluation of a speaker prevents accurate listening—listening with empathy, he might call it. Schuler offers some other activities which will interfere with a hearer's ability to listen accurately and sympathetically. He warns us against:

(1) *prejudging* what a person's message is about or his intentions are. Prejudging issues too, will predispose towards closing the mind and not hearing what we prefer not to hear.
(2) *assuming similarity of opinions or attitudes* which can obviously lead a listener to infer wrongly from whatever is being said. Schuler does not mention dissimilarity of attitudes. This is just as potent a source of inaccuracy as its opposite. Social psychologists have long known the powerful urge individuals have to seek consistency in their transactions between themselves, others, and attitude objects (see for instance Brown, 1970). It can be powerful enough to distort incoming messages.
(3) *allowing one's mind to wander*. Little need be said about this, except perhaps that it is common and all too easily done. The busy managing officer may (almost certainly will) have many pressing tasks, some of which intrude upon his attention while he listens to a subordinate stumblingly trying to convey some issue which is of paramount personal importance.
(4) *wishful hearing* which means hearing selectively. This is an aspect of communication already touched upon in this chapter. Variations are to stop listening to the answer to a question which contains matter in addition to that you hope for, or attribute to a respondent words or meanings never uttered or intended. This latter has been known to happen during selection interviews.
(5) *talking too much*. Enough said.

I would like to add one more based on bitter experience: *thinking about what you are going to say next*. This is especially disruptive if you do not have a clue about what it will be but you know you are going to have to say something. An example is when interviewing and you do not have a question ready.

It is well worth practising to listen. As has been written in at least two other chapters in this book, any difference between sensual fact and reality is caused by misperception. Perception is a process involving a mass of experience, memories, expectations, and such like. The effectiveness with which we communicate always depends upon the reality of our percepts (the products of perception), never more so than when we receive a message. Learning to listen dispassionately but interestedly is a way of improving the process and its product.

By the way, do listen to yourself.

Summary, look ahead, and comment

The nature of management behaviour is not easily grasped. These studies borrowed from in this chapter show that it is not as classical description of it would have us believe. It is characterized by brief, unscheduled, unpatterned activities, with a preferred predominance of face-to-face interactions. Written material is skimmed or used minimally. It is likely that managers seek opportunities for action; reflective planning is not prominent. Commitment extends well outside nominal working hours. The currency of management is information. Information gathering and dissemination is a manager's central activity. The pace is hectic and unrelenting.

Information gathering and dissemination is communication. Communication is not something easily accomplished without care; the ability to communicate effectively ought not to be assumed. Some major barriers to effective communication have been considered, and the properties of some of them examined. Barriers may be erected by the environment (organization) but many are produced by transmitters or receivers, often involuntarily, sometimes wilfully. Language itself can, in the wrong hands, be a barrier to communication. This could even be the result of a deliberate policy. Two-way communication, although slow and sometimes uncomfortable, can remove barriers and help communicators understand one another's intentions and meanings. An important feature of effective two-way communication is called feedback; and the quality of feedback can be improved, as can our receptivity of it. One of the most effective communicating abilities we can develop is the ability to listen.

Leading and obtaining from followers high levels and standards of performance depend upon communicating with them, notably, but not especially, when evaluating their performances. Making and taking sound decisions depends almost entirely on the evaluation of information sought and gathered from a variety of sources, and the clarity of perception of that information is crucial. It is impossible, for example, to select a new member of an organization without obtaining manageable amounts of pertinent information, principally by in some way communicating with candidates and they with you. I only mention these because they are obvious examples of tasks carried out by managing officers. Leading, motivating, and evaluating performance are also what the next two chapters are about.

I hope it may not be considered impertinent if I step outside my self-imposed brief and offer a comment. It is obviously crucial that police officers become expert at communicating with each other. They will manage their service more effectively if they do. Comments in the British Parliament recently, and some unfortunate events which provoked them, have included criticisms of one police force's ability to manage itself. There is no overwhelming reason why that must continue. We must hope it does not. But at least as important is communication between the service and those it purports to serve. All of the problems discussed in this section, as well as the ways in which they may be solved, apply with equal force to these channels. The big difference is that the rewards will be greater for more people.

I wonder how you perceived that.

Further reading

Suggestions for further reading for Chapters 8–10 appear at the end of Chapter 10.

CHAPTER 9

Management 2—Leadership; Motivation

Leadership

Few topics of interest to managing officers have received as much attention from psychologists as leadership. In a service and service-like context (such as a police force) it is probably fair to say that few topics exert the fascination that leadership seems to. Library shelves groan under the weight of books about it: books descriptive, books academic, books prescriptive, books exhortatory ... think of an approach, double it, and you will find a book about it. This phenomenon may be particularly noticeable in the libraries of institutions dedicated to the production of managing officers.

Writing about leaders and leadership has gone on through the ages. That is entirely understandable. The glamour of the prominent leaders, the historical figures, no matter how malign their aims or inhumane their methods, demands our attention. What is more, some of that glamour rubs off on to the many everyday acts of apparent leadership and to holders of leader positions, giving to them a source of excitement and potential satisfaction peculiarly their own.

Psychologists too have tried to make a contribution. They have tried to isolate the strain of personality which is leadership, to identify what it is about effective leaders which differentiates them from the rest of us. They have sought the constituents of leader behaviour; the characteristics of the situations in which leaders flourish, or of the leaders which flourish in them; and the nature of a leader's influence over us. It would be encouraging if after all this time and so much diligent effort we could claim to know very much that is useful. We do not. In introducing his massive *Handbook of Leadership*, Stogdill (1974) almost despairingly writes: 'It is difficult to know what, if anything, has been convincingly demonstrated by replicated research. The endless accumulation of empirical data has not produced an integrated understanding of leadership.'

Not the least of the difficulties facing the student of leadership is that of trying to define the phenomenon. Stogdill estimated that there were nearly as many definitions as there had been attempts to define it. In other words, little agreement exists about what it is. The nearest to any consensus seems to accept leadership as a process of social influence. But as Pfeffer (1977), and McCall (1976) more bluntly, say, so is most social interaction that we want to understand. House and Baetz (1979), for the purposes of their review try to define what they call the construct of leadership as '... the degree to which the behaviour of a group member is perceived as an acceptable attempt to influence the perceiver regarding his or her activity as a member of a particular group of the activity of other group members.' If you accept the idea (Calder, 1977) that leadership is something that one person attributes to another after the event, then that definition may suit your purposes too. Perhaps, however, you want leadership to be about what somebody does, or what they have the power to do, which persuades others to comply with his (or her, but it is too disfiguring to keep saying so) wishes. Then attribution will seem dissatisfying, however plausible.

Instead you may favour the Katz and Kahn (1966) notion of leadership as something they called incremental influence. That is to say, some influence a person has over and beyond that which the organization assigns to him (by rank, authority, whatever). That could be an implicit factor in the Davis and Luthans (1979) representation of leadership as whatever it is which links what leaders do to what their subordinates do and to the consequences of the subordinates' actions.

That hardly does justice to the Davis and Luthans proposals, but it does help to point up the ever increasing difficulty of grasping what it actually is we study when we study leadership. Indeed it sometimes seems that the harder and closer we look at leadership the less visible it becomes. At least one investigator (Miner, 1977) has been moved to recommend that the very concept of leadership should now be abandoned because it is no longer useful. I do not agree with that. Something happens sometimes when individuals comply with the wishes, instructions, orders of another and do something which they would not have done anyway. I am content sometimes to call that leadership, and I should like to know much more about it.

Quite recently attention has been drawn to factors implied by words in that description: ' ... which they would not have done anyway.' Kerr and Jermier (1978) point out that in many situations leadership behaviour is actually redundant. If, for example, what somebody has to achieve and how it is to be achieved are both entirely clear, then no leadership is required to get that particular task successfully completed by a competent subordinate who is adequately motivated. It would be a (common?) mistake to attribute the success to leadership. Similarly (to give only one or two simple examples from what is a quite complicated set of ideas) subordinates who regard themselves as professionals and those who are members of professions, may not require leadership to direct or support them when performing their duties. Nor may those who are indifferent to whatever rewards the organization provides. In situations where survival is not a reward and where the leader has no influence over whatever rewards the organization can provide, followers may be unresponsive to leadership. In such a case, any success achieved will not be a result of leadership.

There may well be a large number of situations in which the ability, experience, training, or knowledge of subordinates guarantee success but render important aspects of leadership redundant. There are a great many tasks which are routine and unambiguous, always done in exactly the same way, or which provide information about how satisfactorily they are being carried out. Their supervision hardly calls for what Bales (1958) called task-oriented leadership.

While on this topic on the limits of leadership's effects it is well to consider the Katz and Kahn idea. They thought of leadership as a form of influence; they called it incremental influence: '... over and above mechanical compliance with routine directives of the organisation...' Ivancevich and Donnelly (1970) operationalized this idea by using the French and Raven (1959) typology of the sources of social power. There are five.

(1) *Reward power* is the power a superior has to provide positive incentives for subordinates.
(2) *Coercive power* is the extent to which a superior is perceived as having power to punish non-compliance in a way which a subordinate wishes to avoid.
(3) *Legitimate power* is that power which rests on the subordinate's acknowledgement that the superior is entitled to expect and he is obliged to give his compliance. As Burke (1972) argues, legitimacy is of crucial importance to the exercise of any leadership. It is, of course, present in abundance in police hierarchies.

Those three bases of power are assigned by the organization. They depend entirely upon the leader's position in the hierarchy. As such they are concerned with authority or command. It is important not to confuse these concepts with leadership. Leadrhip may be effective without either; and an abundance of both need not guarantee its success. Leadership influence is exercised, however, though the incremental possession of the other two categories of social power, viz:

(4) *Referent power* which is the result of one person wanting to identify with another; to perceive, to believe and to behave like he does.
(5) *Expert power* which results from the leader being known to have some knowledge, training, experience which are respected, or from his having displayed some ability convincingly.

In their study in a commercial setting, Ivancevich and Donnelly found strong support for their contention that subordinate performance would relate to referent and expert power of managers. Of course legitimate power was crucial, as it must always be. Coercive power, though, seemed uninfluential in that particular setting. However, for the purposes of the present discussion, and in connection with the Kerr and Jermier proposals, I just want to implant the ideas that leadership behaviour may be justified by virtue of organizational position, but that cannot guarantee its success. Further, as Stogdill (1974) has summarized it, if the person assigned to lead fails to enable the group to achieve its aims then another leader who they believe can will emerge. We might expect that leader to possess referent and expert power.

It has been argued that leadership is, in fact, a quite small part of management's activities. Managers are far too busy to spend much time doing it (see the previous chapter and McCall, 1976). Perhaps so, but it is pervasive. It also excites the imagination. Research, which has taken several directions, has provided us with many facts about leadership, some of which we can put to work.

Born leaders and leaders' characteristics

One of the facts I now possess, school history, politicians' public-relations promoters, journalism, and my own intuitive lay psychology conspired to deny me for a long time. It is that there appears to be no such thing as a born leader. Fiedler, writing in 1977 about some of the fruits of almost twenty years of his research into leadership and the effectiveness of leaders, said that in all that time he had never met a born leader. He had never encountered a leader who would succeed in all situations.

What is more, he reminds us chasteningly of the work of Bavelas and his colleagues (1965). Working with one aspect of leader behaviour they showed how it could be induced by the simple expedient of rewarding somebody for apparently displaying it. The reward was merely the shining of a green light. In one experiment the 'reward' was actually made randomly, regardless of what the target person was doing at the time! Nevertheless the erstwhile follower not only behaved like a leader but also was perceived by the others in his group as its leader. The effect persisted.

The implications, then, are at least two and ought to be encouraging: that nobody is born to lead, and that anybody can learn to lead. We must say more about the latter later.

That the notion of a born or destined leader is mythical I find consoling, frustrating, and challenging. I find consolation in my knowledge about the intentions of those who have created social and educational systems apparently based on the assumption that birth implies, and early experience ensures, leadership. They are wrong. I find it frustrating that that fact has not changed either their beliefs or the ways in which they behave much. More to the point, I find it challenging because the facts make the selection of leaders that much more difficult.

Another fact, which also adds to the difficulties of choosing future leaders, is that there is no characteristic or cluster of characteristics which we can identify and call leadership. Forty years of research, much of it devoted to trying to isolate exactly that—the personal quality or qualities which constitute leadership—failed. No, better than that; the research showed that they do not exist (Stogdill, 1974). Exhaustive study of a variety of acknowledged leaders, of appointed and emergent leaders too, showed that they had virtually no characteristics in common. That applied in the military, in business, and in laboratory groups. To be sure, recent research has revived interest in the trait theory, as it is known (see Stogdill, 1974; House and Baetz, 1979) but the differences found between leaders and followers, between successful and less successful leaders too, are found in differing quantities and do not permit confident predictions to be made. So interviews, paper-and-pencil tests, or any other of the psychologists' stock-in-trade, if used with the intention of measuring or otherwise recognizing the possession of a thing called leadership are used misguidedly. How very convenient it would be were it not so.

Researchers, then, had to adopt new ideas about what leadership might be, and find different ways of measuring it. Two prominent schools arose in the 1940s and 1950s. One decided that leadership was best represented by what leaders actually did when they were leading; how they behaved. The other described leadership in terms of its effectiveness in different situations. Both have been very influential.

Leader behaviour

Psychologists at Ohio State University believed that the greatest understanding of leadership was likely to be brought about by the description and measurement of leader behaviour. They studied industrial behaviour and identified two main dimensions. These they called structure and consideration (Fleishman, 1951; 1953).

Structure includes those behaviours primarily concerned with trying to get the job done. The supervisor makes rules and closely organizes his subordinates' activities, and defines the roles each is expected to play and its relation to his own. He assigns tasks and establishes how best they should be done.

Consideration seems primarily concerned with subordinates' needs, It includes behaviours which indicate respect, trust, and rapport between leader and followers. There is a strong element of a participative approach to decision making and taking, and communications tend to be two-way and open.

Those dimensions are independent of one another. That is to say that because a leader's behaviour is high in one it does not follow that it cannot be high in the other. Behaviour can be characterized by one, the other, both, or neither. Typically, measurements are taken using the Leadership Behaviour Description Questionnaire (Stogdill, 1963). This can be used at any level in an organization providing those who complete it have the chance to observe a person's behaviour as leader of a group to which they belong. In other words, followers complete it about their own leaders. They say how frequently their own leader acts in each of one hundred ways described. They actually cover twelve aspects of leadership including structure and consideration, the subscales for which have been widely used (Cook *et al.*, 1981).

Supervisor' levels of those behaviours have been shown to be associated with the behaviours of their subordinates. Fleishman and Harris (1962) found that leadership low in consideration tended to be accompanied by high rates of grievances and high rates of employee turnover (leaving). Also, once a certain, quite low level of structure is found, any further increase tends to be associated with a sharp rise in the frequency of expressed grievances. A similar effect was observed for structuring and turnover.

Examination of grievances rates and different combinations of the two leader behaviour patterns showed that low levels of consideration were consistently associated with the highest rates of grievances. Matters were improved by even a moderate level of consideration, which was associated with very low levels of grievance, but only when structuring was also low. Grievances increased significantly when higher levels of structures were recorded. The power of consideration, though, is shown by the fact that even the highest rates of structure were accompanied by quite modest rates of grievance when consideration was high too. The relationships were not indentical when employee turnover was the effect measured, but the underlying trends were repeated.

There are indications that the higher in an organization you look the more you may find structuring tolerated, perhaps valued. In the famour International Harvester studies, Fleishman *et al.* (1955) found that during a training programme many supervisors' attitudes changed to show increased consideration. Back on the job, though, much of that altered. The behaviour of some supervisors soon showed less consideration than it had before the training. The main reason appeared to be that the supervisors' own superiors preferred structuring to consideration. It was to that, to their own bosses' styles, that the supervisors responded. The preferences of one's own boss are a powerful enough influence to overcome the effects of successful training.

In a later stage in that research the proficiency ratings of production supervisors were examined. Those highly rated by plant managers had leadership styles high in structure and low in consideration. That probably says something about the pressures managers are under to obtain output, for that pattern of leader behaviour was also found to be associated with high employee turnover, union grievances, absenteeism, and accidents as well as with low levels of worker satisfaction.

Another interesting finding was that foremen whose styles were low in both dimensions were those most often bypassed by subordinates using the informal organization.

It is frequently found that task-oriented leadership is acceptable to subordinates who find their work intrinsically satisfying. This may help to account for the observation by Schrisheim *et al.* (1976) that high ranking employees consistently react favourably to superiors whose style is structuring.

The unsatisfactory application of results from using the Leadership Behaviour Description Questionnaire—or any similarly intended instrument— may actually have contributed to some understanding of two very important aspects of effective leadership behaviour. It had been maintained by theorizers like Schein (1970) that the manager's job as leader is often that of diagnostician. He must be able to recognize and gauge what it is that individuals need and respond to. In turn he must react sensitively and flexibly to these factors; differently to different people. A plausible and intuitively appealing idea, Schein produced no evidence for its effectiveness. In the 1970s, Graen and his colleages (Graen *et al.*, 1972; Dansereau *et al.*, 1973; Graen and Schiemann, 1978) were dissatisfied with conventional measurements of leader style and their shortcomings as predictors of some classes of subordinate behaviour. What had typically happened was that a leader's followers would complete (say) the Leader Behaviour Description Questionnaire, and the average of the scores they assigned would be accepted as that leader's style. Graen saw that more complete accounts of subordinates' different behaviours could be obtained if the averaging procedure was omitted. It was far better to make individual predictions on the basis of the score assigned by each subordinate. And, of course, it is true: a manager does not lead everybody in the same way. He does respond differently to individuals, not always appropriately perhaps, but differently. It is this relationship between leader and each follower which determines much of the consequences of their interaction together. Graen calls this a vertical dyadic linkage; and he distinguishes its measurement from that of what he calls average leadership style.

So it is not only a bright idea for managers to react individually to subordinates but it is also something they do anyway. If he is going to interact differently with different subordinates, though, the manager needs to be able to ensure that the outcomes of the different behaviours that these individual linkages may yield must be fair or, as students of social psychology would say, equitable. It is important that that is so, and that leaders communicate these outcomes clearly (Graen *et al.*, 1972).

And that reinforces another point made by Stogdill (1974) and implicit in the work of Sadler (1966). Sadler found that individual subordinates had clear preferences among the styles they would like their own bosses to exercise. (They experienced it relatively infrequently!) But what appeared to be far more important than that they should experience the style they hoped for was that the style their bosses used they used consistently. They needed to know what to expect. Stogdill found that the one element most reliably related to effective leadership seemed to be the leaders' ability to, as he puts it, structure followers' expectations. Inconsistent leader behaviour obviously prevents subordinates from knowing what to expect.

Situations and personalities

Fiedler (1967; 1972; 1976) agrees that one of the factors which enables a leader to succeed is his characteristic style of leading. But he maintains that an equally important influence on a leader's effectiveness is the situation in which he tries to lead. More specifically he says that situations can be assessed in terms of how favourable or otherwise they are to the leader, and that a style that will succeed when the situation is very favourable or very unfavourable will not when it is only moderately favourable. This view remains controversial since researchers do not invariably achieve results supporting Professor Fiedler's model. Since many do, however, and Fiedler always does (of course), and since he has been doing so for around twenty years, the view remains an influential one.

For the purposes of his model, Fiedler proposes that the favourableness to the leader of the situation be measured along three dimensions. First among these is the quality of the relations existing between the leader and his followers. They may be good or poor. Next in importance is the extent to which what the group have to do is clearly or vaguely defined and how to do it clear or ambiguous. Fiedler calls this 'task structure'. Tasks may be structured or unstructured. Finally, and least important in Fiedler's opinion, comes the power which attaches to the leader's position (not to him personally). For example, can he hire and fire, promote and demote? Position power can be high or low. Those three dichotomies yield eight possible levels of situation favourableness. In descending order of favourableness they are:

Leader–group relations	Task structure	Position power
Good	Structured	High
Good	Structured	Low
Good	Unstructured	High
Good	Unstructured	Low
Poor	Structured	High
Poor	Structured	Low
Poor	Unstructured	High
Poor	Unstructured	Low

Fiedler acknowledges two basic leader styles very similar to those found by the Ohio State researchers and by Bales and his colleagues, he calls them task-motivated and relationship-motivated. It is not clear whether he says, as the others do, that a leader can exercise a style high in both. He seems not to at first sight, but this may be because of his idiosyncratic method of measuring style.

To assess a leader's style using Fiedler's method you invite him to give his opinion about the one person with whom he has ever found it hardest and least enjoyable to work. In fact you ask him to complete a questionnaire called the Least Preferred Coworker (LPC) Scale. From that you derive a LPC score. A low score indicates that the leader is of the type who will try to achieve success on assigned tasks despite any risks to interpersonal relations. A high-LPC leader, on the other hand, is one who wants good interpersonal relations and works for prominence and esteem through them. So, low LPC indicates task relatedness, high LPC means relationship-related.

What Fiedler consistently finds is that when the situation is extremely favourable to the leader or extremely unfavourable to him, low-LPC leaders flourish. In situations intermediate in favourableness to the leader, the high-LPC leaders tend to succeed. The reverse is not found to be the case. Effectiveness is *contingent* upon the interaction of style and situation. Fiedler calls his model the contingency model of leader effectiveness.

The implications of that sort of finding are considerable and radical. It is no longer satisfactory to say that a person is a good or bad leader. It is always necessary to qualify such a remark. We must say the nature of the situation in which a person is an effective or an ineffective leader. Organizations ought to be careful also about their placement of people to positions of leadership. They should want to assess the sort of situations likely to prevail and to know whether their chosen leader can be expected to succeed.

The impact of training and experience

But surely the ability to bridge the differences between the two styles and so become able to succeed in any situation can be instilled by training? That certainly is the impression given by some purveyors of leadership training courses, manuals, whatever. Give them a shot of action-centred leadership (or some such) and it will all come right?

While not ruling out the possibility that somebody will be helped by conventional leadership training, Fiedler is far from hopeful. He reports (1972; 1976) work that he and his associates have carried out in the laboratory and the finding was that trained groups of leaders were no more effective than others without training. Lest the effects be dismissed as mere laboratory results and lacking realism (although care had been taken over the selection of the tasks followers had to carry out) field studies were also conducted. One was on managers and supervisors in US post offices. Another was of police sergeants, and evaluations of their performance by their superiors and by other sergeants were related to the amount of supervisory training they had received. There was no relationship. From laboratory and field studies, the evidence shows that training of leaders does not bring about improved performance by their followers. Fiedler points out that there is nothing unusual in that; careful evaluation of conventional and some less conventional leadership training typically fails to show that it has produced any actual improvement in performance. (I am assuming that we can agree with Fiedler that the single best measure of leader effectiveness is group task performance; and that some improvement in that should come about if leader training is to be of benefit. I do not say it is the only measure).

If training is not going to be effective, surely experience will? Fiedler is right, is he not, to remind us that in seeking to find a senior post, by promotion or selection from outside, we almost always specify amounts of time which we require serious candidates to have spent in prior jobs. We do trust experience.

Fiedler and his colleagues found that experience in an armed service conveyed no advantage there. In one laboratory study new recruits were compared with experienced academy-trained officers and performed just as well as they did. In a host of other studies from a range of occupations, including once again police sergeants, no significant relationship was found showing that subjective or objective measures of performance were greater for more experienced leaders. Evidently automatic trust in experience is misplaced. You can see why Fiedler is controversial.

The reason why experience and training appear to leave matters much as they were is, according to Fiedler, that it improves matters for some but actually makes them worse for others. The contingency model offers an explanation of that. It says, you will recall, that effectiveness depends in part on the favourableness to the leader of the situation. Training and experience improve that favourableness. They may do so by improving relations, by permitting easier structuring of the task, or even perhaps by increasing position power. If they change the situation from one of low favourableness to one of moderate favourableness, the low-LPC leader will become less effective, the high-LPC leader will gain. If the change is from moderate to high favourableness the gain will be the other way round: low-LPC leaders will flourish, the effectiveness of high-LPC leadership will decline. And that is exactly what Fiedler (1972; 1976) reports as taking place, both in the laboratory and in the real work of management, in commerce and in the military.

Things to do

His recommendations? For a start, stop regarding the organization as fixed and humans as infinitely flexible. He regards leader style as a facet of personality; and personality is, after all, a rather constant feature of most people. So do not assume that telling somebody how important it is to be flexible will enable them to change their style at will, and especially not under any kind of pressure. Since we have seen in the previous chapter that managers are pretty well always under pressure of some kind, better assume that they cannot change. So teach them at worst to recognize the favourableness of any situation in which they have to act. Teach them to assess what support they can depend on, how structured the task is, what power their job carries. At best, teach them to engineer situations which increase the probability of their succeeding. If they have subordinates who are themselves leaders, then teach them how to provide those subordinates with situations most conducive to their success. Above all, never assume that all people are the same. Fiedler shows us two influential ways in which people differ.

Summary and comments

Leadership is a real phenomenon, affecting the immediate relation between the person identified as leader and his followers. It determines the effectiveness with which the followers comply with the leader's requirements of them. Some prefer to regard leadership as something attributed to a person by observers after some event. Some doubt the wisdom of retaining the concept at all, so elusive has it proved, and so unhelpful. Masses of research have not yielded any consensus about what it actually is, let alone any great understanding of how it works.

We do know that it is not a thing, a quality which is possessed by some and not by others. We know that nobody is a born leader; we know that leader behaviours can be acquired by pretty well anybody. We know that leader behaviours have proved to be classifiable as task-oriented or relations-oriented, and that emphasis on either or both of these is associated with different behaviours by followers. We are told, however, that some subordinates, some tasks, or some organizational features can render either or both of those behaviours redundant; and that effectiveness may often not come about because of what a leader does at all. Fiedler insists that the behaviours are the outcomes of an aspect of personality. Their effectiveness depends upon the qualities of the situation in which a leader has to operate. Traditional leadership training and experience may be averagely ineffective because of the differential impact the resulting situation has on leadership styles.

There are other aspects of leadership which have not been dealt with. It was judged desirable to spend some time on the broad directions research has taken, rather than exploring expansive theories or fascinating details. The topic is not closed now, however. It is, after all, a pervasive phenomenon. References are sure to be made in subsequent sections and in different contexts.

Motivation

Closely related to leadership is the process we call motivation. Certainly leaders can be said to motivate followers—or to fail to if their leader behaviour does not produce the goods. But motivation is something which the individual can bring to the situation so that more from a leader may even be redundant. Motivation can be provided by the organization, for example by the systems which apply across the board and are not manipulable by immmediate supervisors. Motivation, it is claimed, can also reside in the work itself; and certainly the dedication and effectiveness of some workers in jobs offering relatively little by way of rewards suggests that this must be so. For a long time the deplorably low wages of British policemen did not deter some members of the service from delivering their best efforts. It did not greatly assist recruitment we are told, but those who did join can hardly all have been motivated by factors external to the work. Clearly an individual's values and beliefs can be a powerful source of motivation. To be sure, in this section we shall be most concerned with what people and organizations can do to motivate others: to make them want to do their jobs. Vroom (1964) puts it nicely when he says that motivation is '... a process governing choices made ... among alternative forms of voluntary activity'. Steers and Porter (1979), summarizing several definitions, identify three important themes: what it is that energizes human behaviour; what it is that then directs that behaviour; and how that behaviour can be maintained or sustained.

The process of motivation can be thought of as one by which an individual tries to adjust a state of imbalance. He has some need which is unfulfilled. By behaving in a given way he can achieve some goal or receive an incentive. That may fulfil the need or contribute to its fulfilment. Progress towards fulfilment is the adjustment as the strength of the need is reduced. The trouble for managers is that, as Steers and Porter write, motives have to be inferred. That is especially difficult to do, since one act may be the result of several motives, none of which need be recognizable; nor need the same action represent the same motive on each occasion; and one motive may result in a variety of behaviours. Motives also change and conflict with one another: people are a collection of motives striving for realization. Their orders of priority are different for different people on any one occasion, and probably for any one person on separate occasions. Also, whereas you would expect the realization of some goal to cancel that particular need, it is not always so by any means. The achievement of one ambition often increases the amount of ambition.

This section is not going to solve all your problems of motivating people. What it can do is to describe briefly some of the most popular theories and models, and discuss some of the work associated with them. Do not despair, however. We shall close with a look at a mini-theory which spawns a maxi-technique: something empirically satisfying and practical.

Maslow and needs

It is an astonishing fact that a piece of pure theorizing, not at all intended as a prescription for industry or managers, should have proved one of the most frequently cited and influential papers in management education. I refer to Abraham Maslow's (1943) paper 'A theory of human motivation'. It was intended as a general description of how healthy humans choose what sort of things to do. It has been seized upon by trainers and trainees as though it were some incomparable pearl of wisdom, an insight of blinding brilliance, and a prescription for wise planning. It is not. It is almost certainly mistaken in some very important aspects.

There are, Maslow claimed, five classes of need. These range from the most basic for physiological necessities to the highest order need for what he called self-actualization. In between these, in ascending order, he places safety needs, love needs, and esteem needs. A brief look at each follows.

Physiological needs. These are for food, water, etc. Maslow says these are prepotent. Deprived of food, safety, love, and esteem, a person would, according to Maslow, be driven solely by the need to overcome the lack of food. All faculties would be devoted to satisfying hunger.

Safety. If the physiological needs are comparatively well satisfied, the individual is driven by the need to be secure from threat and danger. This now becomes the energizer, demanding the services of all the abilities. It is, however, only the satisfaction of the physiological needs which permits safety to assume so much importance.

Love. Safe and adequately supplied, then emerges a need to belong, to give and receive affection and love. (Sex may be a purely physiological appetite.) This need now dominates.

Esteem. Basic and relatively basic needs now being satisfied, the individual seeks self-respect. Self-respect comes from self-esteem and the esteem of others. Maslow subdivides these needs. He says that there are, first, the wish to be strong, to achieve, and to be confident, independent, and free. Second he sees the desire for prestige and reputation. Some researchers actually differentiate between self-esteem and autonomy, creating with the latter a sixth need. (See for example, Porter, 1961; 1962; 1963.)

Self-actualization. In Maslow's sense this means realizing your full potential; doing what you have to do; in modern idiom, doing your thing. For these needs to emerge the lower needs must be fulfilled.

Maslow does not insist that a need cannot emerge until all those of lower orders have been completely satisfied. His principle of prepotency predicts that as one group of needs gains fulfilment their importance as energizers of action will diminish. The next higher order needs will then supervene. The emergence can be gradual. It is possible, according to Maslow, to envisage a person with some needs at all levels partially satisfied. But you would expect the lowest levels to be most nearly completely satisfied, and the other progressively less so as you climb the need hierarchy.

From even the simplest of practical points of view all this creates several problems and Maslow's ideas certainly do nothing to diminish the general problems sketched in earlier. How can a manager (or anybody for that matter) hope to recognize the level from which a person's motivation derives at any time? Might not a single set of actions be associated with the fulfilment of needs from several levels? or a variety of actions be intended to satisfy a single class of need? The same actions on consecutive occasions could be made in pursuit of different satisfactions, just as two people behaving similarly at one time may be differently motivated to do so. Problems like these may not be exclusive to Maslow's model; they are the sort of problem this model does nothing to reduce.

More academically there are other serious difficulties. Waters and Roach (1973) examined data obtained by questionnaires intended to sound out the perceptions of managers about the presence of Maslow-type features in their jobs. They used a statistical technique (factor analysis) to discover how many themes there were which accounted for relationship within the data. They found four including one associated with satisfaction of higher order needs and another with satisfaction of lower order needs, but the items did not combine in ways Maslow would predict. Wahba and Bridwell (1973; 1976) report that none of the factor analysis studies they reviewed had showed all of Maslow's five categories as independent factors. Self-actualization did not always show up as a separate factor. Two studies failed to produce any support at all for Maslow.

Some people do not have complete confidence in purely statistical procedures like factor analysis. If they were the only sources of doubt about a theory, then, the doubts might be discounted. In the Maslow case, however, more direct tests only raise more serious objections. Porter (1961; 1962; 1963) using his own Need Satisfaction Questionnaire showed that the importance of different needs depended on the level a manager occupied in an organization, and that that importance did not relate to their satisfaction in the way expected by Maslow. Hall and Nougaim (1968) carried out a study of a group of managers in one organization over a period of years and found virtually no support for Maslow. One of the reflections of Maslow's prepotency principle is the expectation that as a need is satisfied its importance declines. Hall and Nougaim found otherwise: as a need was satisfied it tended to become more important. Wahba and Bridwell, reviewing that and other studies of the gratification–activation principle (a satisfied need will not motivate), observed *at best* only limited support for Maslow's theorizing.

Maslow's notions are evidently not well founded. Assuming as generous researchers have tended to, that the different sorts of needs he has imagined actually exist, their hierarchical organization has not survived close examination. Investigations have shown that the principle of prepotency lacks substance. What is more, when the very assumption of the existence of the need categories is rigorously tested, there is not convincing evidence for its validity. Yet the notions thrive. Why?

I can only assume that a little plausibility is more attractive than verifiability. (Heaven help some of us if our police and court procedures ever become so negligent!) Certainly plausibility is serviceable enough for many useful purposes (see Turk, 1978). Managers are often impatient of erudite theorizing, especially about people, and Maslow's has a pleasing, homely, non-scientistic quality. So managers have taken it to their hearts. And those who have taken it there at all seriously will have sought and given their subordinates the opportunity to develop and exploit their talents, and to exercise the responsibility others might have denied them.

There has been another benefit. The higher order needs, esteem (autonomy), and self-actualization, known collectively as growth needs, have been shown to have a special importance. In general, a process known as job enrichment is that of building into jobs opportunities for the satisfaction of those sort of needs. It is very productive, especially in terms of job satisfaction. But not for everybody (Wanous, 1976). Research has shown that the strength of growth needs can be measured. That strength is the greatest single factor so far identified which determines whether an individual will respond to an enriched job, especially to one enriched by attention to job characteristics (Hackman and Oldam, 1975; 1976).

Herzberg and the two-factor theory

In a great many cases you will find that a phenomenon is measured along a single dimension. There is either a lot of it, none, or some quantity in between those extremes. Personality, for example: by one well known questionnaire, a person is asked to say whether each of a lot of statements applied to him: yes or no. The number of responses representing, say, extraversion are totted up and the more he has given, the more extraverted he has reported himself to be. The fewer responses like that that he makes, the more introverted he appears. Extraversion is a single bipolar dimension, with extraversion at the high end, introversion at the low end.

Job satisfaction is conventionally thought to be like that too. If certain features of work are perceived by a worker to be present in sufficient quantities, he is more satisfied than if they are not. Add a feature—say promotion—and satisfaction increases. Subtract one—say recognition—or fail to increase a quantity—say salary—and dissatisfaction increases. Satisfaction is regarded as a single bipolar dimension, with satisfaction at the high end, dissatisfaction at the low end.

Not all phenomena are unidimensional. Think of health. There is a difference between being well and being healthy. Wellness is simply not being unwell: freedom from defect or disease. Health starts there and requires more, like vigour, some fitness, stamina etc. There are a lot of unhealthy well people around. They are in a sort of neutral state, neither unwell nor healthy. There are two factors at work in this model: the avoidance or escape from ailments and the positive pursuit of health. Herzberg (Herzberg *et al.,* 1959; Hertzberg, 1966) says that that is how job satisfaction—and so motivation—works.

With colleagues Hertzberg published in 1957 a review of studies of motivation, and concluded that there were two basic thrusts. Man strives to avoid pain and discomfort but that after he has accomplished that, further similar striving adds nothing. Separately from that, and in addition to it, man strives to achieve something for himself. In 1959, Hertzberg *et al.* published a theory which was to prove as influential in the world of management as that of Maslow (1943).

They proposed, and in his book (1966) Herzberg developed, an application of those generalities. His research led him to the conclusion that certain features of the working environment, if present sufficiently, could enable workers to avoid being dissatisfied by their jobs. People asked to recall and recount factors at work which were important when things there had not been going altogether satisfactorily had tended to mention aspects like pay, company policies, technical supervision, relations with supervisors and with colleagues, and working conditions. Asked about occasions when work had been satisfying, their accounts tended to emphasize such things as advancement, responsibility, the work itself, recognition, and achievement. The division was not absolutely clear cut: for example, salary was mentioned in both contexts. It is always possible to argue, though, that salary can be a form of recognition (Rosen, 1963). Overall, there remained a quite clear distinction between what dissatisfied people and the factors which led to their satisfaction. Just as in our health analogy, the opposite of dissatisfaction was a lack of dissatisfaction, *not an increase in satisfaction.*

More concretely, the argument is that you may improve work conditions, pensions, canteens, supervision, and pay, and you may make as much allowance as you wish for the expression of social relationships, but you will not increase the satisfaction of members of your organization. However, let any of those fall below a desirable level and you will almost certainly contribute to their being dissatisfied. For that reason those factors are called *dissatisfiers*. They simply ensure that the work environment is not an unhealthy one, they make no positive contribution to fitness and vigour. Indeed, Herzberg's term for the dissatisfiers is *hygienes* or *hygiene factors*.

If you want your people to achieve satisfaction and be motivated, you must provide them with opportunities to experience those other factors, the *satisfiers* or *motivators*: advancement, responsibility, etc. One way in which this can be done is by freeing people from conventional supervision and from being monitored, and by making them accountable for things for which they would otherwise have been answerable to a superior (or a quality checker etc.). This process Herzberg (1968) calls job *enrichment*—to distinguish it from the mere addition of task variety, which he prefers to call job enlargement. Indeed, some experts regard Herzberg's model as something primarily to be applied to jobs and less directly to individuals. Steers and Porter (1979) in their superb book on motivation at work do not include the two-factor approach among contemporary theories, but treat it quite briefly in a chapter on job design. I tend to think that the emphasis may be justified because of the positive influence Herzberg's and similar ideas have had on the revision of jobs, and because of the enormous impact they have had on job satisfaction and its assessment. On the other hand, the brevity of treatment seems a trifle unjust. The two-factor model has generated a huge amount of research and controversy. Bockman (1971) alone summarized nearly fifty pieces of research up to 1970, many of which confirm Herzberg's principles.

It would be too much, though, to hope that all researchers would support Herzberg. Bockman, impressed by the utility of the model, tends to dismiss criticisms as nit-picking. It is not that simple. Opsahl and Dunnette (1966) not only disagree with Herzberg's contention that salary is only a potential dissatisfier but also suggest that Herzberg's own data do not support it. Friedlander (1964) had found that intrinsic job characteristics, which Herzberg would say are satisfiers, acted both as satisfiers and dissatisfiers, while extrinsic factors (i.e. hygienes) had comparatively negligible effects. Dunnette *et al.* (1967) showed that Herzberg's hygienes and motivators do not invariably act in the direction his arguments insist that they will: some act both as satisfiers and dissatisfiers. An extension of that sort of finding had been provided by Ewen *et al.* (1966) who found not only that intrinsic job factors could satisfy and dissatisfy, but also that the amount of satisfaction they provided could determine the effects of pay (extrinsic). They doubted whether satisfiers and dissatisfiers were appropriate concepts for representing how job satisfaction came about. Graen (1966) agreed.

One of the most telling criticisms of Herzberg, however, is that you only get results like his if you use his methods and his categories (not always, though—see Schwab *et al.*, 1971). His method is especially suspect for it relies on people's recollection of what things were like at different times. People's memories are notoriously unreliable. Many reasons have been advanced for why this should be so (see Bass and Barrett, 1981). One which appeals to me is offered by Farr (1977).

Farr reminds us that it is typical of people that, when they observe an event of a state of affairs, they will attempt to satisfy themselves as to its cause. The process is called attribution. Attribution theory has it that you can decide that something you see is caused by characteristics of a person (ability, personality, knowledge, etc.). That would be an *internal* attribution. On the other hand you may conclude that what you see or recall happening came about because of luck, other people, an easy task, etc. (external attributions). It is also typical for people to attribute their own success to internal factors; their relative failures will be attributed externally. And that, says Farr, is what happens when Herzberg or his followers invite people to relate influences on job success or when work was not going so well. The satisfiers are essentially internal factors (achievement, advancement, responsibility ...), dissatisfiers are external (supervisors, policies, conditions ...).

Locke (1975) joins in the general suspicion about details of the model and its associated methods. He reminds us, too, of the very important finding, never satisfactorily catered for by Herzberg, that sources of satisfaction differ for different people. Some are satisfied by the provision of hygienes, others— usually white-collar workers—tend not to be. It is never altogether a straightforward business to predict who will react favourably to job enrichment.

Locke also, however, points out that mistakes in the theory have not led to great difficulties when it comes to applying it. The aim is to increase motivation, satisfaction, and morale by enriching jobs: by adding motivators. It seems to work. It would be nice to be able to say why.

Equity

Equity theory (Adams, 1965) is not one which managers usually sit around and chat about. So, I shall not dwell too long on it. It is important though. It lacks the appeal of Maslow's or of Herzberg's ideas. Yet its basic assumption is one with which most managers would zealously (jealously?) agree ... except when they talk about non-managerial differentials of course. The basic assumption may have been clearly stated for the first time by that idol of every manager, Karl Marx! In the Communist Manifesto (no less!) he wrote that, while a wage economy is the rule, to reward unequal contributions equally would be to practise inequality. What he meant was that it would be to reward inequitably. (Whatever he meant, his basic argument is one conveniently overlooked by some seeking to make cheap debating points from privileged platforms: equity is the aim, not equality.)

The basic ingredients of equity are the inputs a person brings to the situation and the outcomes he derives from it. The mechanism proposed by Adams, and outlined again from an organizational point of view by Mowday (1979), is that a person will compare the ratio of his outputs and inputs to his perception of the similar ratio for whatever is his chosen comparison. Put oversimply, if p is the person and o the other with whom the person compares himself, O is outcome and I input:

$$\frac{Op}{Ip} \text{ is compared with } \frac{Oo}{Io}$$

and if Op/Ip and Oo/Io are perceived as equal ($Op/Ip = Oo/Io$) equity exists. If however,

$$\frac{Op}{Ip} \text{ is less than } \frac{Oo}{Io} \left(\frac{Op}{Ip} < \frac{Oo}{Io} \right)$$

there is a fairly obvious inequity.

Perhaps the person is gaining less than another whose inputs are the same. It may be that the outcomes for both are the same but the other person is contributing less (his inputs are lower). Or maybe some other inequitable combination exists which, it is perceived, favours the other person. It may be helpful at this point to consider what may consitute inputs and outcomes.

In a work organization the most obvious outcome is pay. Others, though, might be time off, perks, status, task assignments, recognition, promotion, responsibility ... or other rewards. Inputs might be education, training, qualifications, experience, skill, seniority, effort, responsibility ... etc. Responsibility is shown in both categories deliberately. It could be either, and which it is depends upon the individual. For some people responsibility is something that they derive from a job. For others it is something which they bring to it. Tornow (1971) showed that whether people perceive such things to be inputs or outcomes is a fairly stable characteristic of individuals, and will strongly influence their personal ideas of equity. Clearly it would be imprudent for a managing officer to assume that his own response to a situation was similar to that of all his subordinates.

The situation envisaged two paragraphs ago ($Op/Ip < Oo/Io$) is known as the underpayment condition. The perception of being relatively underpaid is a perception of inequity. It is fairly obvious that that is uncomfortable. Indeed, it is inequity that energizes a person: he strives to achieve a condition of equity. The form his striving takes will depend upon the basis of his payments.

If the person is on an hourly rate or a salary which he receives regardless of output, then underpayment will induce him either to produce less or reduce the quality of what he produces. A person who is paid by results on a piece-rate scheme, and who feels underpaid will increase the amount he turns out but quality may suffer as a consequence.

So far there is nothing much that intuition would not have told us. But there is another condition of inequity which is a little more surprising, and not always easily perceived by the person. You can be overpaid, or in terms of the model, $Op/Ip > Op/Ip$. Again behavioural predictions are possible and, surprisingly often upheld. They are that in the hourly paid condition the overpaid person will either produce more or improve the quality of what he produces; and in the piece-rate condition the overpaid person will produce less or improve the quality of what he turns out. Goodman and Friedman (1968) found that their overpaid subjects produced more than equitably paid subjects. When experimental instructions made it clear that quality was to be instrumental in resolving inequity, then overpaid subjects improved quality. Pritchard *et al.* (1972) observed both the overpayment and underpayment effects on behaviour. They also recorded that both conditions led to lower satisfaction than an equitably paid situation, especially under a condition of heightened incentive. Carrell (1978) found an interesting situation occurring 'naturally' in which, for reasons not connected with productivity, some clerical workers in departments received a sizeable pay increase while others in the same departments did not. Before the change no inequity was perceived. One month after the change, those who received the raise saw their situation as being *more* equitable; their less fortunate colleagues perceived less equity and the differences are more marked. After nine months there were no perceived differences.

It would appear that the clerks observed by Carrell were using different comparators. Those who received a rise perceived more equity than before, the others less. The lucky ones can hardly have been comparing themselves with the others. That raises the issue of what the possible bases of comparison are. Goodman (1974) suggests that referants fall into three major classes as follows.

Other people. This could be somebody doing a similar job in the same organization. It need not be though. Managers and members of 'craft' trade unions become quite agitated if they feel that their differentials are under attack. British public service employees are not alone in seeking comparability of their rewards with those of other groups. Advertised jobs can enable judgements of equity to be made if the advertisement gives enough information about expected inputs and promised outcomes. I have seen clerical workers incensed at the knowledge that truck drivers could earn as much as they could and have as long holidays. Assuming that working hours (thirty-seven and a half compared to sixty or so), incredibly more favourable pension treatment for virtually the same personal contributions, and some valuable fringe benefits were being taken into account by the affronted clerks, where did their perception of inequity arise?

The system. If you join an organization or accept a posting clearly understanding that, at the end of a term of duty or some other period, you will be promoted and receive an increase in pay, then the system has created a potential referent. Promotion without increase, or increase in reward without advancement in rank, can be perceived as inequitable. The comparison is not with another person; it is with what the system provides.

Yourself. You may compare your condition with what it would be in other jobs, or in some future job. You may compare your actual ability to provide for dependents with your expectations of yourself (they may be reasonable expectations or ideal). We know police officers and their families compare their family lives with those of people in other jobs. You may simply size yourself up in terms of the inputs you can bring to any situation and assess whether the outcomes you obtain now seem equitable for somebody like you.

Whether those proposed categories cover every possible referent is questionable. It is not the intention now to be exhaustive, however. The aim is to illustrate the considerable variety of sources of perceptions of inequity. It might be rash for a manager to assume that behaviour by a subordinate which suggested that he was aggrieved by some inequity would be easily changed by attention to the most obviously likely source.

For the behaviour of the aggrieved person may not be confined to the sort of adjustments to productivity mentioned earlier and that experimentalists like to study. Apart from changing inputs and outcomes, people may deny the existence of differences, or distort them in their own minds so as to minimize their effects. Denying reality is all too often like papering over cracks but neglecting defective foundations. Another tactic which may be employed is what Adams calls leaving the field. At work, if inequity is sharp enough and cannot be resolved by less drastic methods, the victim may just leave. The astute manager may become aware of the intention to do so and avoid the loss by redressing the inequity.

There are obviously difficulties in applying equity theory in organizational settings. Mowday (1979) discusses this issue, but unlike Lawler (1968) is not yet convinced that the theory can simply be regarded as an important component of the larger expectancy theory (to which we shall turn next). Certainly there must be merit in trying to ensure that conditions for people at work are equitable, or that the opportunities to achieve equity are not counterproductive. Managers will be well advised, then, to bear the concept and its implications in mind when organizing work.

Expectancy theory

Vroom (1964) made a fairly simple statement when he argued that an individual's motivation is the result of combining:

(1) his expectation that working hard will increase the probability that he will receive some outcome;
(2) the value of that outcome to the individual;
(3) the likelihood that that outcome will lead to the accomplishment of some other outcome that he desires.

The expectation element Vroom called *expectancy* (E). The value to the person of an outcome he named *valence* (V). The association of one outcome with another is its *instrumentality* (I). You may see expectancy models referred to as VIE models of motivation. The relationship which Vroom saw existing among the three components of the motivating force is multiplicative. Applied experimental psychologists assign values to the elements and test the model. Valence can have any value, negative or positive (obviously some outcomes can be undesirable, e.g. work hard and you will work yourself out of a job). Expectancy is a probability that something will happen if the person does work hard, and probabilities always take on values from 0 to 1. Instrumentality, according to this version, is a correlation—a statement of how closely associated two events are—and they take on values of from −1 (the more you find of one outcome, the less you find of the other) through 0 (no prediction is possible), to +1 (achievement of the second outcome is invariably associated with achievement of the first).

The theory offered possible explanations of much of the observations made by researchers into motivation at work. It also introduced important themes of psychological reality into study of the topic. Previously, little if any allowance had been made for the facts that people are individuals and individuals are different. Not everybody will be energized by the prospect of self-actualization; job enrichment ought not to be assumed universally efficacious. Maslow and Herzberg seem to overlook such facts. VIE allows for the attractiveness of outcomes to *individuals*. It *requires* some accounting for *subjective* probability, which Cohen (1958) repeatedly showed is not only often quite different from rational probability but also usually dictates human decisions and choices. It also, especially in its later elaborations, demands that allowance be made for environmental influences rather than placing sole reliance on factors within the individual to account for what the individual does.

Like a great many theories it has had to undergo revision and extension as successive forms fail to account for this or that observed phenomenon or effect. In its bare $F = V \times I \times E$ form, the model takes no account of a person's experience. Yet expectancy will be altered if, for example, effort on previous occasions has failed to achieve an anticipated outcome. A feedback loop is required. Similarly, a single effort can affect a number of outcomes, some more desirable than others, some perhaps very undesirable. Some way needs to be found of expressing that. Individual differences among workers, organizational features and procedures, all have been seen to affect the motivation which people bring to bear on their work. The model has become progressively elaborated. Careful research, trying to take account of as many as possible of the influences and their interactions, frequently fails to find the relationships which the chosen version of the theory predicts (see for example Lawler and Suttle, 1973). Nevertheless, the model makes some valuable claims, and has some interesting implications for managers' and organizations' behaviours. Before looking more closely at some of these, however, a brief return to the nature of expectancy is in order.

It is now seen that there are two basic expectancies which influence work behaviour. The first is simply that if he exerts himself a person can expect to achieve some required performance or level of performance. This is usually written $E \rightarrow P$. The second is that that level of performance will yield the desired (or instrumental) outcome. In its simplest form this would be written P→O. We could then express motivation as (E→P) × (P→O). But it cannot be that simple. Outcomes have valences. Performance is associated with a number of outcomes. The second expectancy becomes Σ (P→O) × V, which means the sum of all the associations of perceived possible outcomes with levels of performance and with each outcome's valence for the individual. That has to be combined with the various expectancies about effort and performance. In the Lawler (1971) version this becomes:

$$\Sigma \{(E{\rightarrow}P) \times \Sigma \,[(P{\rightarrow}O) \times V]\,\} {\rightarrow} Effort {\rightarrow} Performance {\rightarrow} Outcomes$$

which is not as complicated as the notation makes it look, but as Lawler and Suttle (1973) demonstrate, is very difficult indeed to test.

My purpose in recording that elaborate form here is to try to help relate some of the individual, historical, and environmental influences which, it is thought, can affect motivation by having an impact on either or both of those expectancies. It may also help managing officers to envisage aspects of their situations through which they can understand or influence performance there.

Take for instance the historical aspect: the experience to affect both expectancies. A person can judge whether effort of a certain kind is likely to produce a required level of performance. A managing officer can help in two ways: by assuring a subordinate that that is in fact so; but probably far more importantly by indicating the nature of the effort which is required. As regards the second expectancy, that performance leads to outcomes, the individual's expectancy will be affected by his own experience and his knowledge of that of others. The managing officer has a crucial role to play here, though, in making clear the level of performance which is necessary if desired outcomes are to be achieved. In other words he must clarify for his subordinates the relationship between performance and outcome. If he cannot do it, the organization must.

Harking back to leadership again (I said it would happen), there is a theory similar to expectancy theory dedicated to explaining and predicting the outcomes of leaders' behaviours. It is called the path–goal theory (House, 1971). It says that a leader's effectiveness depends on his ability to make clear for his followers the path to work goals. He does this both by making it easily recognized and by making it easier to follow—by removing obstacles etc. The other crucial function for the leader is that of influencing the satisfactions and other rewards to subordinates according to the extent to which they attain the work goals. In short, it is the application of expectancy theory to individual immediate subordinates.

One of the complications for managers of working on the second expectancy, be it as general motivators or as immediate superiors (leaders), is this notion of valence. Lawler and Suttle (1973) in their own study of managers found that weighting expectancy items by valence did not increase the predictability of behaviour. This is not always the case, as Porter and Lawler (1968) show. But it is found disappointingly often. It may be the idea of valence which is wrong, the predicted relationship may not be true, or the way in which it is measured may give misleading data. It is probably still prudent to anticipate that different outcomes will have different values to individuals, and that behaviour in pursuit of them will vary in some related fashion. To the manager who would motivate according to the principles of this theory falls the testing task of discovering those valencies, and relating desired behaviour to valued outcomes.

Two important individual differences are noted by Lawler as influencing expectancies. A person's characteristic self-esteem will impact on the first and help determine whether he will believe that his own efforts will yield a satisfactory level of performance. And a person's locus of control—an indication of whether he believes what happens to him happens because of what he does or because of outside agencies—will affect the second: the extent to which he believes that performance by him is enough to guarantee an outcome. Giles (1977) confirms the importance of this personality variable, in particular in its relationship to the satisfaction of higher order needs, another important influence on the P→O expectancy.

The final influence on expectancies mentioned by Lawler and one we have already considered the importance of is the equity of the outcome. If a person believes that his performance will yield him an outcome which he judges inequitable, then we have seen some of the unanticipated effects that may have on his behaviour.

There are some environmental factors over which a manager may expect to have only limited control, if any. One which James and his colleagues (1977) showed to be important in this context is the psychological climate of the organization. It affects individuals' perceptions of expectancy and of instrumentality—for example, that achievement of goals will lead to secondary outcomes. The aspects of climate which they investigated were leadership facilitation and support, job variety and autonomy, job importance and challenge, job pressure and conflict, workgroup identification, cooperation, friendliness, and warmth, and organizational concern for the individual. Their importance to aspects of expectancy theory were, in general, confirmed; and their importance to motivating employees was re-emphasized. An individual's perception of the organization's climate is clearly an influential feature of his work environment.

Research intended to test details of the elaborated theory typically yields disappointing results. Campbell and Pritchard (1976) summarize many of these studies and the difficulties besetting them. They conclude that the VIE model may look simple, but what it is intended to define is a very complicated system of poorly understood factors. Nadler and Lawler (1977) are, however, more encouraged by the mass of studies which support some important predictions. They make some recommendations, a few of which have been mentioned here already, but all of which will bear some consideration. First, what ought managers to do?

They should discover what outcomes are valued by each employee. Then they should decide what levels of performance they require and ensure that the levels are realistic, that they can be attained. The all important task for managers then is directly, explicitly, and clearly to link the desired goals to the levels. This ought to be done not simply by statements of intent but, more importantly, by public displays of the working connection. And Nadler and Lawler remind us of an absolutely crucial point, one which pops up in various guises throughout this book. It is a subordinate's *perception* of the situation which matters, not its reality.

There are one or two other recommendations made by Nadler and Lawler. Managers need to be sure that no other expectancies, informal or otherwise, conflict with these they set out to establish. They must also ensure that any increases in rewards associated with desired behaviour are large enough to make the behaviour possible. Finally, as has already been said, they must attend to the equity. *Equality* of treatment is held to be unlikely to motivate.

Many of the recommendations made to organizations are probably difficult to apply in an organization like a police service, where pay systems are not noted for their flexibility. Wherever there are some rewards which are not fixed, it would make good motivational sense, according to expectancy theory, to leave their distribution to managing officers who are relied on to motivate individuals. The service should then help these officers make clear to their subordinates the direct link between these rewards and performance levels. The service would be well advised also to develop and apply methods of measuring motivation. Levels ought really to be monitored. Do not risk assuming that they will be those wishfully perceived by seniors.

Summary and comments

We have looked at some of the models which have been offered to explain, predict, or influence people's motivation at work. There are plenty more, but I have chosen some which represent those which are typically dealt with during management training, or which are thought to bear acceptable, if challenging, implications for the practice of management. All are to a greater or lesser extent unsatisfactory. *Maslow's* ideas do not even attain an acceptable level of plausibility, but leave a residue of good intentions. Herzberg's ideas gain significantly more support, but his claim for motivational influence may be exaggerated. Job enrichment may be more closely related to job satisfaction than to motivation (Umstot *et al.,* 1976), and the connection between these two is far from clear (Gruneberg, 1979). Nevertheless it is readily applicable. *Equity theory* is a rather special case which allows some counter-intuitive predictions to be made. Many people, however, think it unnecessary to invoke the theory to understand the effects it tries to explain. Others see equity as a special component of the more general *expectancy theory*. At present this theory is too general and not capable of encompassing the great complexity of the situations it is intended to describe and prescribe. It has the great merit, however, of directing attention to individuals, and to the great variety of factors which affect their responses to motivational efforts. Several valuable themes of action or intention follow, not the least of which, it seems to me, is the desirability of entrusting as much as possible of the motivational efforts to immediate superiors. This will tie together as closely as possible a manager officer's leadership and motivational roles.

Hopeful and helpful though they are, the theories presented do not seem to me to offer the manager anything much more nourishing than food for thought; interesting problems to solve. Now, if there is one thing managers already have in abundance it is problems to solve. So, grateful though they may be for the intellectual stimulation, and valuable though the ideas and discoveries undoubtedly are, I cannot help thinking that they would be even more delighted if somebody were to offer the occasional solution. The 'that's-all-very-well-but-what-can-I-do' response is one often on the tip of a manager's tongue; even more often it is a demand they make.

Goal setting

Locke (1968) does not claim that his ideas on goal setting constitute anything so grand as a theory. Rather he prefers to think of them as a technique. He commends it as a soundly based, effective technique for obtaining desired performance from subordinates ... or from anybody for that matter. Accounts of the technique in action suggest that quite fine tuning of performance is available. Effort can be directed to particular tasks or other aspects of a job (Locke and Bryan, 1969). Desired amounts, qualities, or types of results can be obtained (Steers, 1977). Goals serve other useful purposes too, but for now I want to attend to this direct purpose of motivating others.

The premise on which the argument in favour of goals is based is that our behaviour is, for the most part, intentional. That is to say, when we take some action we have decided to do it because we value whatever change it will bring about. Ryan (1970) points out that intentional behaviour tends to persist until the intention is achieved. He concludes that a level of performance will be closely related to the goals somebody sets for himself or those which he accepts from another. We shall see that that latter source of goals is of great importance.

Locke (1968 and since) maintains that people inevitably set goals for themselves. Indeed he has found statistically, and it has been for all practical purposes confirmed by Carroll and Tosi (1970), that none but the largest incentives has any motivating effect independent of the goals. All of which means that incentives are only effective to the extent that, as a result of them, people change their goals.

The effectiveness of goals as motivators of behaviour is now known to depend upon their being specific, difficult to attain, and accepted. Also it is often asserted that goals which are participatively set will be more effective than those which are assigned.

Steers and Porter (1974) report that the specifity of goals is consistently related to performance. This was so in real life situations and in the laboratory. Latham and Yukl (1975) reviewed eleven studies of the effects of setting specific goals in organizations. Overwhelmingly the evidence supported Locke's contention that specific goals are superior as a motivator to general goals. Later, Dossett *et al.* (1979) also found specific goals induced performance superior to that obtained by general goals. In case it is not entirely clear, a specific goal is one which describes exactly what is to be achieved, usually (and best) expressed in terms of quantity. General goals are vague and expressions of intentions or aims. An example of the former might be: ensure that no vehicles stop within two hundred yards of (name) school's gates between 0830 and 0930 on weekdays during term time. General goals with the same situation in mind might be: keep traffic moving along (name) road; or improve road safety figures in (name) road. General goals are sometimes caricatured as 'do you best' goals. It is frequently the plea from people in what they like to consider professional groups, that goals, especially specific goals, cannot be set for them. Teachers are notorious for this. They really appear to believe that no aspect of their work can be prescribed or evaluated. I have heard police plead similarly, although not so defensively. I have no doubt that all who make claims like those, given time, encouragement and, perhaps, help, could come up with some really useful goals for themselves. Of course they would also need some commitment to the mission ... probably gained by accepting a specific goal!

One of the reasons why accepting that particular specific goal would make success more likely is that the task is truly quite a hard one. Locke has no doubt that the more difficult a goal is the more energizing it will be. Latham *et al.* (1978) confirmed findings to this effect, and Garland (1982) in a successful replication of one of Locke's original experiments again found a highly significant relationship between goal difficulty and performance. That rule is tested by a minority of findings (e.g. Becker, 1978); and in a recent laboratory study, Mowen *et al.* (1981) found a connection between response to role difficulty and method of incentive payment. There is little doubt, though, that the general rule is the more difficult the goal the better the performance.

The third prerequisite for a successful goal is that it should be accepted by the person who is being expected to work towards it. In the Umstot *et al.* (1976) experiment, acceptance of goals was seen as the variable which determined whether individuals challenged by specific, difficult goals responded to them with productive effort. In fact in the Mento *et al.* (1980) study, goal acceptance was not strongly related to effort; but as is so often found to be the case, it was associated with the valence of the goal. In any case, rejection of a goal does not necessarily imply acceptance of no goal. There is a very practical reason why acceptance of a goal is desirable. If a rejected goal proved impossible to achieve, the failure is too easily rationalized by an I-did-not-say-I-could-do-it, -you-said-I-could response.

A way to achieve acceptance should be to have subordinates participate in the goal setting. The values of many in our society do suggest that participation is virtuous. By many psychologists it is reckoned an effective action. The evidence on the effectiveness of participation in goal setting, as with participation in decision making, is, however, far from convincing. Latham and Yukl (1975) find that the results of studies in organizations do not permit a clear conclusion to be drawn. (So at least we can conclude that participation is not inevitably beneficial.) Latham *et al.* (1978) confirm that a participation in goal setting is no more effective than assigning goals when it comes to gaining their acceptance. In another study the same researchers found that it did not produce significantly better performance either. Both these effects were confirmed by Dossett *et al.* (1979). When goal difficulty was held constant, participation was not superior to assigned goals, either in terms of performance or goal acceptance. In the one study in which participation was more effective, Latham and Saari (1979) explain that as the task was unusually ambiguous, perhaps the participation actually helped structure the task. Reviewing participation in decision making, including goal setting, Locke and Schweiger (1979) found no convincing evidence that it improves productivity. They did detect some support for its enhancing effect on employee satisfaction. Wall and Lischeron (1977) conclude that satisfaction was not consistently shown to have increased. They did find some benefits, similar to improvements in psychological climate; but not those traditionally claimed. So, in short, participation in goal setting is neither necessary nor particularly of help in realizing the motivating effect of the goals.

One other effect of goal setting deserves special mention; its influence on the effectiveness of feedback or knowledge of results. Contrary to what intuition probably suggests, knowledge of results by itself does not lead to improvements in performance. This was quite clearly demonstrated by Locke and Bryan (1969). It has been confirmed, certainly by Latham *et al.* (1978), who found that knowledge of results affects performance *only if it is used to set specific goals*. Field studies reviewed by Latham and Yukl (1975) do not include any in which feedback and goal setting are studied separately, but do tend to support the view that knowledge of results depends for any effectiveness it might have as a motivator on being used in conjunction with or as a source of goal setting. Kim and Hammer (1976) were able to show that goal setting is effective, but that feedback can actually increase that effectiveness when the two are used together.

In summary then it seems fair to claim that goal setting is a technique for planning and improving subordinated performance. It is tried and tested in a variety of situations. Although it may improve relationships and work climate, participative goal setting seems to offer no advantages in terms of resulting effort. (It is not unreasonable to suppose that it will be less efficient that assigning goals too.) For the greatest benefit to be gained, goals need to be specific, difficult to attain *but attainable*, and accepted. Goal setting can confer motivational influence on knowledge of results; and feedback can improve the effectiveness of goal setting. One last point, in part confirmation of the possibility mentioned earlier that the ability to set goals may be increased with help, Ivancevich and Smith (1981) show how improvement in goal setting and in the resulting performance can be accomplished by training managers in the conduct of goal-setting interviews. (The goals were assigned, not participatively decided.)

Set goals.

Further reading

Suggestions for further reading for Chapters 8–10 appear at the end of Chapter 10.

Management 3—Performance Evaluation

The evaluation of performance

This is often called appraisal. The terms are to all intents and purposes inter-changeable. They both mean to determine the amount of something or to fix its value. *The Shorter Oxford English Dictionary* (1965) also allows evaluation the meanings 'to find a numerical expression for' and 'to express in terms of the known'. The former is something many appraisal procedures attempt, the latter is something which some I have met do not attempt, but should.

Evaluation in some form goes on all the time. If you decide that a colleague is a dependable partner on patrol you have probably evaluated his performance. If your superior decides to delegate some important task to you, then you can bet he has evaluated your performance. Of course either of these two evalua-tions might to a greater or lesser extent have been one of a person and not of his performance. Trustworthiness might have been a characteristic involved. But to make the assessment on the basis of appearance or some general impression would have been a riskier practice. Far better to reflect on what has actually been observed on previous similar occasions and use that behavioural informa-tion. That is a fairly general rule: evaluate performance in behavioural terms. But if you prefer or are obliged to do it in terms of *traits,* be sure that the rela-tionship between the traits and behaviour at work is clearly defined and understood. (A trait is an inherited or acquired individual characteristic.)

Why do it?

In a great many organizations, including police forces, this process of evalua-tion has been formalized and channelled so as to try to make it usefully serve one or more organizational purposes. Kane and Lawler (1979) note four of these: as a source of information on which to base decisions about where a person will work most effectively and whether he should be promoted; as the basis on which to allocate rewards; to enable selection methods and training programmes to be evaluated; and to enable managers to tell subordinates how well they are performing, usually with the intention of helping them improve. Bass and Barrett (1981) elaborate a little on those, but the essence is the same. They do, however, remind us that in these relatively enlightened days when many employees are entitled to non-arbitrary treatment, employers may feel that they should maintain accurate records of performance with which to confront underperformers and to support decisions to discipline or dismiss those who persist. Some managers do evaluate for that reason. Another, more benign purpose often claimed for performance evaluation, is that of providing objectives for training programmes (Cummings, 1973). It is very questionable whether a performance evaluation procedure can do all that is piously hoped for from it (Savage, 1982). I know from my experience and that of associates, that most schemes achieve precious little. One colleague, on entering a large organization as a senior personnel manager found a hideously complicated appraisal system had been imposed by personnel experts. Challenged to justify it they trotted out all the old reasons and the many purposes it was expected to serve. Challenged again to demonstrate its effectiveness in achieving these purposes they could not do it. Finally the experts agreed that the sole probable benefit from a ritual annual review of performance was the opportunity it gave busy people to show that they were interested in one another. All the other claimed purposes could be achieved more easily and more effectively in other ways. The residual scheme in that organization is now very much simpler and much much less pretentious.

There is a dubious reason sometimes given by managers, and in my experience always given as a reason of last resort by personnel administrators, for writing down performance evaluation. That is to have a record in case it is ever needed ... part of what Douglas McGregor (1960) called a JIC system (just in case). I have already noted that modern social legislation has to some exent legitimized that reason. (Mind you, there are more efficient ways of protecting yourself if that is your concern; and a formal evaluation system complete with annual form-filling ritual is by no means essential for that purpose.) The danger can be the bureaucrat or designer/purveyor of systems who wants to introduce one because it may be useful, or because it is a good thing. (The designer may add that other successful companies have them, implying that his systems have made the success possible.) Soon the bureaucrat will be running the show. Fulfilling the requirements of the system will become an end in itself. Do not have an appraisal system only because it seems a good idea to.

Some police forces may be among those who do that. Two junior-rank policemen I have spoken to very recently have been scornful of the systems to which they must submit. The ritualistic nature in their cases is taken to extremes. It is not at all obvious (to me) that it is the most appropriate superior who is most involved. The review is conducted at a prescribed time irrespective of how long either party has been in the particular part of the force. The form used requires assessment largely of personal characteristics with no obvious attempt to link them to work behaviour, and without clear anchors (more about them later). The feedback interview in one of the cases has degenerated to the point where the subordinate quickly leads it around to an unrelated topic he knows is of particular interest to the (otherwise bored?) superior.

I am going to risk a speculation. My guess would be that the system and, on that occasion, that supervisor, are virtually powerless to influence most of the outcomes for which performance evaluation is thought to be important. Issues of assignment and postings can be and probably are handled effectively without it. Pay rates are determined elsewhere. Training probably goes on according to separately determined principles, with special educational and training items dealt with individually. Such feedback as is given may be less-than-well-informed, and in any case may be seen as irrelevant since it comes from a distance. Such agency feedback as may be effective will have been given long ago and by somebody closer to the actions under review. Now I am uncomfortably aware that I have no scientific justification for generalizing these misgivings to the extent I have done. But it is a broad stroke I am wanting to paint here. Suppose I am to any significant extent right. In such circumstances, what point is there in having an evaluation system, however imaginatively documented? In at least one of those two cases we know that not even a benign assurance was given of genuine interest.

An appraisal system is a possible help in solving one or more practical problems. Before rushing into accepting some package system or whatever, would it not be quite a bright idea to identify your problem? Then see what information *you* need to solve that problem? If, after doing that, you seriously think that formally evaluating employee performance will give you that information, fine: design your evaluation instruments so that they stand a fair chance of delivering what *you* want. Also do it so that you can use them comfortably and accurately; there need be no special virtue in uniformity. If you subsequently find that the system is not serving your purposes, ditch it. Do not let it become an empty ritual, or you risk frustrating yourself and your subordinates. They may attribute to you cynicism. You will not structure some important expectations—one of the few things, you may recall, that we do know that successful leaders do.

It is by the effectiveness of the different methods of evaluation, by the difficulties of the judgmental processes themselves, and by how different approaches try to help overcome these difficulties, that psychologists are largely intrigued.

Some problems

It you say 'criterion' to an occupational psychologist, chances are his eyes will light up ... unless they glaze over. The first response is that of the psychologist who believes that evaluation of performance is a serious attempt at measurement of something clearly conceptualized. The second is probably that of the person for whom evaluation implies an earnest discussion dedicated to the mysteries of something he calls personal growth—which evidently need not be as unpleasant as at first sight it may appear. I jest (I think); I caricature extremes (I think); in the space bounded by those two dimensions there lies a host of preferred approaches. Many of them may successfully combine the two. My preference, however, tends to the former: my eyes brighten somewhat.

If I want to evaluate performance I must have a clear idea of what successful performance will be. I must be able to define or describe it. If I cannot, how shall I be sure consistently to recognize it when I see it? How shall I know whether a performance I can see is unsuccessful, not very successful, quite successful, entirely successful, or even better? I could have a hunch about it of course. Or I could assume that somebody I like, or whose company is somehow satisfying, is doing a good job. But formal performance evaluation is intended to overcome guessing, favouritism, or attitude effects. I could deal in characteristics: simply say how loyal, intelligent, adaptable, flexible, leaderlike, industrious, dependable, etc., my subordinate is. I would then have to make a lot of assumptions: that these characteristics are important, uniformly important perhaps; that they can easily be measured, regularly observed; and that opportunities to display them where I can see them are frequent and generously distributed. It often seems that completing an evaluation report in those terms says more about the person making the evaluation than it does about the person being evaluated. The reason seems likely to be that that sort of evaluation allows too many of our own attitudes to intrude and sway our judgements (Smith, 1973). What we are supposed to be evaluating is somebody's *performance*.

So, it will usually be more satisfactory to evaluate performance by comparing the performance you see against a description of successful performance. That description is known as the *criteria*. One of the problems which delights and perplexes psychologists is that of deciding on the nature of the criteria. For instance, should we use a single composite criterion or multiple criteria?

Criteria

A single composite criterion is one which somehow encapsulates overall performance. At its best this will be achieved by identifying the separate important components of performance, deciding how important each should be (attaching a weighting to each) and combining them accordingly. The observed performance can be assessed in the same terms, and the assessed performance of individuals can be simply compared. This sort of criterion has its uses. It is probably necessary if pay awards depend on merit, if layoffs are decided on grounds of operational effectiveness, or for promotions.

On the other hand, composite evaluations can be very difficult to interpret. Two equal values may not imply the same sorts of effectiveness. It is probably the tendency of some people to overinterpret the evaluation (Landy and Trumbo, 1976) which contributes to some psychologists' dislike of composite criteria. After all, why should anybody be entitled to look at an assessment based upon a limited number of even the most influential job elements and from it infer that there is something called overall job performance?

The alternative is to maintain the separateness of the individual job elements and express the criteria in terms of each: multiple criteria. The managing officer who wants to influence a subordinate's performance will need information about the latter's performance on individual aspects of his job. Feedback will have to be couched in these terms. If the organization is trying to use the evaluation to establish training objectives, any of the multiple criteria may separately contribute.

The nature of this particular controversy helps emphasize the importance of the *purpose* of the evaluation. Both types of criteria have their uses, and one could not easily substitute for the other. They are not, however, mutually exclusive. If anything they are complementary. Indeed, Schmidt and Kaplan (1971) argue that the development of multiple criteria must precede the derivation of a single composite criterion; and then each is put to work to do what the organization requires of it.

Criteria are complex. They are samples of behaviour, and sampling is not guaranteed to be accurate. For instance you may not choose the best kind of behaviour to measure. Suppose that you regarded relations with the community as an important dimension of a police officer's performance. You may decide that the best way to measure this is to count the number of allegations made against an officer that he has falsely arrested people. In fact, what might prove a more effective measure could be the number of times it was alleged that he used physical force or, conceivably, the number of allegations of his discourtesy (performance indices from the list used by Cascio and Valenzi, 1978).

There again, if you sample an individual's behaviour at one time or for a particular period, can you feel confident that what you see is representative of his behaviour on a criterion? If you sample different people's at different times or over different periods, can you reasonably compare them? This is a version of what Bass and Barrett (1981) call opportunity bias. They offer the example of evaluating a police officer's performance according to the number of arrests he makes. That would not be satisfactory unless other factors were taken into account. The district that he had to patrol would probably exert quite an influence on that criterion behaviour.

A variation on the first possible source of sampling error is that which arises between people. Is it inconceivable that an officer who makes several false arrests cautiously ought to be assessed differently to he who makes none but whose characteristic surliness provokes a lot of complaints? It does not matter whether the example is realistic; the point is that criteria may need flexible application.

Those three dimensions of samples which may explain errors are called by Landy and Trumbo (1980) the *variables* dimensions, the *time* dimension, and the *people* dimension.

A character of some criteria which adds to the difficulty of choosing and using them is that they are dynamic. They change. An officer straight out of police college, having done well in training, may perform very well. After a year, though, assuming he is still doing well, the way in which he is successful will have changed. It would not be appropriate to apply the same criterion to his performance. Later still, yet other criteria may be appropriate. Given that fact, it might well be the case that using the same evaluation system on all three occasions would be less than satisfactory. Certainly using it in the same way would not do.

Not all criteria are dynamic; some are relatively stable. Bass and Barrett (1981) remind us of the Gordon and Cohen (1973) finding that the speed at which trainees complete the first four tasks in a training programme reflected the speed with which they completed the others and the whole programme. Speed of completion was a stable criterion; and would therefore be a fair class evaluation dimension *in the situation studied*.

We would go on considering individual difficulties over the criterion. Let us be positive instead. Landy and Trumbo suggest that the development of criteria and criterion-related measurement can benefit if we strive to fulfil three requirements: make criteria—

(1) reliable
(2) valid, and
(3) practical.

A digression is necessary. Reliability and validity are so important that a simple explanation of their technical sense is obligatory.

Reliability. Reliability is consistency. For any measurement to be useful it must be consistent. For any measuring instrument to be useful it too must be consistent. Imagine trying to measure your waist with an elastic tape. Or imagine a clock running at randomly varying speeds. They are useless tools because they do not measure consistently: in our sense, they are not reliable. The problems with criteria which were outlined earlier are all sources of unreliability: they introduce errors into our measurements.

Validity. This takes many forms, but essentially in this context it means that our sample of performance is truly representative of performance in some important aspect of the work. The popular definition of validity, when the concept is applied to a psychological test, for example, is that it represents the extent to which the test actually measures what we are using it to measure. The form of validity which Dunnette (1963) recommends as the most appropriate in our context is *construct* validity. This is often the most important form for psychologists, since it is the one which is concerned with what our measures actually mean (Cronbach, 1970).

Practicality. This hardly needs comment. Among the desirable characteristics of a criterion offered by Blum and Naylor (1968) and repeated by Landy and

Trumbo (1980), the latter isolate four which contribute to the practicality of criteria. These are that they should be *realistic, predictable, inexpensive,* and *measurable.*

Problems with measurement

There are at least three kinds of data used in evaluating performance: *objective, personnel,* and *judgemental.* Objective data are unambiguous items like number of parts made, number of pages proofed, number of arrests leading to prosecution ... etc. For many jobs it is probably very difficult to obtain or use those, not least because of some of the obstacles already discussed (e.g. opportunity bias). These can produce differences between individuals which are nothing to do with their ability. In other words they are often not reliable (but see Cascio and Valenzi, 1978). Personnel data, like absences, sickness rate of advancement, are also difficult to use, and for similar reasons: they do not affect individuals consistently or for controllable reasons. In general we are left with judgemental data. Superiors register judgements about the performance of their subordinates. Judging brings a special set of problems—those associated with rating errors made by the evaluators. Several well established sources of error are studied.

Accuracy. Managers do not judge accurately. It is difficult to provide objective benchmarks against which to assess the accuracy of judgements. Gordon (1970) achieved an accepted standard and observed differences in the accuracy of managers. Borman (1979) found that inaccuracy was resistant to training. He also observed that raters were able to rate more accurately on some dimensions than on others. This effect was consistent and is thought by Borman to be a reflection of the ambiguity and consistency of the performances, which determine the clarity with which these dimensions are perceived and understood. In addition to the basic fact of inaccuracy, there is differential accuracy to contend with. Gordon (1970) observed that managers rated good performances more accurately than the poorer performances. Arvey and Hoyle (1974) also found that raters made more rating errors when judging the poorest performances.

A possible contributory factor to differential ratings of poor performers is the experience supervisors have of working on the same task. Mitchell and Kalb (1981) found in a laboratory study of a proof-reading task, that experienced supervisors tended to attribute poor performance to the environment more than the inexperienced supervisors did. A subsequent field study found that army officers who had experience in jobs in which they had observed others performing badly, tended to attribute that bad performance to factors like the difficulty of the task, working conditions, the amount of support given, that is to say to external factors. As Mitchell and Kalb observe, it is typical for supervisors to blame subordinates for their poor performances; experience in the subordinated jobs, though, may enable the supervisors to take environmental factors into account.

Severity. This is an error sometimes found. It is committed by those raters who consistently rate subordinates low. This may be a result of the standards set by the rater; it may just be his predisposition. This affords us a nice example of a *reliable* judgement which is not *valid*. Of consistency there is plenty; accuracy is very questionable.

Leniency. This is severity's opposite. This is the consistent tendency to assign generous ratings. McGregor (1960) observed that when a superior knew that his evaluation would be used for administrative pruposes he rated more highly than he would otherwise. It is also found that a superior who will have to feed back to the subordinate his performance rating will rate generously, and that the worst performers will be most generously treated. Bass and Barrett (1981) list these and other reasons, usually associated with the rater's perception of himself, why lenient assessments are made.

Ivancevich (1979) found that intensive training can reduce leniency errors, and that the improvement was maintained twelve months after the training. A more conventional training method, using discussion groups, lectures, case analyses, and reviewing the evaluation method wrought no change.

Central tendency. Some people are reluctant to use the ends of scales; they do not care to say that performance is either exceptionally good or exceptionally poor. The resulting evaluations cluster around the average rating and so fail to discriminate among performers. This is particularly damaging if the ratings are intended for use in validating a selection procedure.

Halo. Halo is an effect which pervades a great many judgements and decisions if care is not taken or if the danger is not well understood. People do form a generally favourable or a generally unfavourable impression of others. A general impression may be induced by one favourable assessment. The Asch (1946) study of the effect of a single word on overall impressions is a splendid example of that mechanism. The one impression influenced all the others. Closer still to the mark is the study by Nisbett and Wilson (1977) in which it was shown that separate objective factors were judged according to a similar halo, warm or cold. Halo also is influenced when some diffuse general impression may simply affect every separate judgement about an individual. Landy and Trumbo (1976) show another way in which halo can infect judgements. A supervisor who attaches particular importance to one aspect of performance may record evaluations on others which support that on his favourite.

Attempts to reduce halo effects by training raters have met with mixed success. Warmke and Billings (1979) had one group of trainees construct a new graphic rating scale. This proved effective in reducing halo in training but the improvement was not maintained in the real-life work situation. Rather like the influences on leader style noted in the previous chapter, training is less potent than the context in which the trainee subsequently carries out evaluation.

Borman (1979) trained raters who then achieved significant reductions in halo. The successful scheme comprised three hours of training on observational error and rating biases. However, in the light of the Warmke and Billings finding, Borman is cautious about the probability of the improvement carrying over to the work situation where real administrative decisions are called for.

Recently an attempt has been made to tackle the problem from the other end, as it were. Landy *et al.* (1980) proposed that, if you cannot stop managers being influenced by halo, you can let them get on with it, then detect and correct for the influence of halo statistically. They showed how it might be done. Their reasoning, methods, and conclusions have been severely criticized (Harvey, 1982; Hulin, 1982; Murphy, 1982). The attempt, then, has not exactly succeeded. Nevertheless, Landy *et al.* (1982) do not despair of the approach altogether. They remind us that they never did suggest that their 'purified' scores were necessarily representative of a true state of affairs, but were probably the means by which a truer relationship between item assessments could be made clear. As such they may be a very useful adjunct to the rater's original scores.

Rating scales

The way in which psychologists have traditionally tried to reduce rater errors is by carefully designing rating forms and scales. If by the wording of scales or some other methodological device you can edge a person towards a discriminating way of thinking, then perhaps you can overcome halo, for example.

The simplest rating scale is one with a high end and a low end and steps in between. The rater simply indicates the point on the scale which he thinks best represents his evaluation of the performance in terms of the aspect (or trait) being considered (see figure 10.1).

Other words are possible of course. In figure 10.1 the low end could be Unacceptable, the other Outstanding. Further help can be given to raters by numbering the intervening steps. The aim is to implant the idea of an equal-interval scale between the extremes, and so encourage the rater to discriminate among performances ... or performers.

The descriptive terms at the ends of those scales are known as *anchors*. They fix the scale's position in some kind of conceptual space. In the example given the anchors are simple and qualitative. We shall see that anchors can be more elaborate and more constraining.

The type of scale illustrated in figure 10.1 has one advantage: it is simplicity itself to use. Its great disadvantage is that it is almost impossible to interpret; I cannot tell what you may have had in mind when you put your mark. That, of

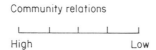

Figure 10.1 A simple form of rating scale

course, is because of another disadvantage: you have been given no structure by which to assign the values implied by the scale points. In an attempt to overcome that, some scales have labels attached to all or some intermediate points as well as to the end (and sometimes midpoint) anchors (see figure 10.2).

If a numerical value is assigned to each scale point, and if there are to be several scales, the likelihood is that an overall evaluation will be achieved by summing all the values chosen. In that case some care should be taken over the value each scale is given. Spector (1976) has tabulated scale values for some frequently used responses.

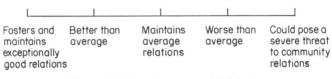

Figure 10.2 A rating scale with labels

In the example in figure 10.2 the designers have introduced the notion of average and helped fix the meaning of all the scale points. That makes it easier to use, but you will probably agree that it is really no easier to interpret than the earlier example. A very clear idea is needed of behaviour which represents the maintenance of average community relations—or the average of whatever you are setting out to evaluate—if such a scale is to be useful. Average is an awful word, nearly always best avoided where any ambiguity is possible. A management teacher whose lectures I once attended referred to words like average, satisfactory, reasonable, when used alone, as weasel words. Precision may not be possible, but approximate (which is not a weasel word when it is used properly) descriptions are desirable.

What is sought, then, is some sort of scale with anchors and labels which help its user to say what he means and its reader to be able to infer what the user meant when he used it (see figure 10.3). (I do not know how genuinely useful those terms in figure 10.3 are. I am concerned only to illustrate the method.)

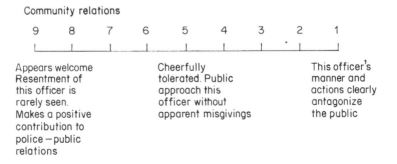

Figure 10.3 A rating scale with anchors and labels

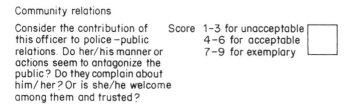

Community relations

Consider the contribution of   Score   1–3 for unacceptable
this officer to police –public   4–6 for acceptable
relations. Do her/his manner or   7–9 for exemplary
actions seem to antagonize the
public? Do they complain about
him/her? Or is she/he welcome
among them and trusted?

Figure 10.4 Another method of rating people

Another method, a version of one shown by Guion (1965) is shown in figure 10.4.

Scales of this type have recently been developed and applied with some success to the evaluation of police performance by Lee *et al.* (1981).

It is not clear how many points it is best to have on a scale. Bass and Barrett (1981) cite evidence that there seems little point in having more than five anchors. They also allow the possibility of advantage using seven points or even nine points. Beyond that they feel it is unlikely that judges can make fine enough discriminations.

Ranking

Most such rating scales—they are generally known as graphic rating scales—are norm-referenced. That is to say that the performance of one person is being compared with that of others doing the same job. A very explicit case of the form is that in which the people doing a particular job in an organization are directly compared with one another. This may be carried out by ranking them all from best to worst, or by making paired comparisons. The latter means comparing every person with every other one at a time. By scoring 2 for the better in each pair, 0 for the worse, and 1 each if they are judged equal, a league table is easily established. It then remains to describe the performance of the first and last, and some evaluation of all is achieved.

Of course that has the advantage of forcing some kind of discrimination; it does not, however, ensure that the discrimination is valid (Bass and Barrett, 1981).

Forced distribution

One technique which has been suggested to overcome inappropriate discriminations is that which obliges raters to follow a given distribution. The forced-distribution method, as it is known, relies on the truth of the assumption that employees' performances will be distributed in a known way. That is to say that there will be a known percentage performing exceptionally; another, larger, group will not perform that well, but will achieve better than standard performance; a third, probably rather large, category will include all those who perform at or close to standard performance; and so on. The rater's job is to put into each category the names of the people whose performance justifies it. It is fair to say, unfortunately, that forcing people to distribute their evaluations in a predetermined manner is not often altogether satisfactory; and Bass and Barrett warn of undesirable rivalries resulting. While hardly daring to offer it as evidence, I can say that I have worked with such a system and my impression was that it disaffected managers without noticeably motivating those they managed, although not all of the effect may have been attributable to the forced distribution process. What many managers did do though was to resent, resist, and refuse the obligation. It was also amusing to note that the distribution tended not to change when, with relatively little employee turnover, it ought to have as employee performances generally improved. That, after all, was the aim of the evaluation: to motivate people to perform better.

More to the point here, perhaps, is the work done with the Michigan State Police by King *et al.* (1980) over a three year period. They used forced-choice performance evaluation in an attempt to overcome halo. The scales proved reliable enough, but the halo effect was not diminished.

Checklists

An alternative to a norm-referenced scheme is one which is criterion referenced: performance is compared with a performance standard. A step towards this is the checklist approach. In this, a collection is made of statements of recognizable job behaviours. These might be items like: produces clear comprehensive written reports: impresses well in court; is frequently in error on essential points of law. These are all assigned values by a group of judges and the average of the most useful items is retained as the values for those. The rater's job is then to judge which statements apply to each individual whose performance he is evaluating. The final evaluation is the total of those statements' values—which, of course, the rater does not know. The problem is that the overall judgement which this method yields tends only to satisfy those concerned with a composite criterion, unless the superior is content to allow some third party to derive multiple-criteria-related judgements from his choice of statements.

A new variation on the summated checklist method is the mixed standard rating scale (Blanz and Ghiselli, 1972). It is intended to overcome some usual rating errors, particularly halo. As usual, dimensions are chosen: carefully selected component behaviours of a job. For each dimension three norm-referenced (but they could be criterion-referenced) statements are devised, one each to represent superior, typical, and inferior performance. Then a small deception is practised. The statements are all presented in random order. The rater is then asked to say whether the subordinate being rated performs better than, about the same as, or worse than the performance described by each statement.

There is a coding system, now revised by Saal (1979) for his study of the method's applications in Kansas police departments. This assigns numerical values to the possible response combinations. These are the evaluations.

There are not many data yet from using the method. Those that are published do not yield consistent results about its effectiveness in limiting leniency and halo effects. However, Finley *et al.* (1977) found that the system, when used to evaluate the performance of retail store managers, lessened halo but not leniency errors. More encouraging, particularly in the context of this book, is the Saal and Landy (1977) finding of reduction in leniency and halo errors in the evaluation of police officers' performance.

The method is still being developed. It is interesting and reckoned to be promising. It remains to be seen whether the promise will be fulfilled.

Critical incidents

It is extraordinarily difficult to get some people to describe effective or ineffective performance. Even if you explain that you want an example of good practice, many supervisors, especially in the 'professions', will dismiss your request with an 'I-know-it-when-I-see-it-but-it-cannot-be-described' kind of response. In fact it usually can be described; described quite closely, and in terms which other practitioners can recognize. A method whereby the impossibility may be accomplished is by using Flanagan's technique of critical incidents (1954).

Typically a supervisor is invited to record recollections of separate acts by subordinates which have affected the performance of the team, department, organization ... whatever. The acts may be examples of extremely effective or extremely ineffective behaviours. The supervisor is required to say what the circumstances were in which each act took place, exactly what the act was, and what its actual observed effects were. In this way a picture can be compiled of the sorts of actions which are valued or deplored, and of the categories of behaviours or functions which are the components of actual performance, *as it is actually observed and actually expressed by the person evaluating it.* To put it another way, the supervisor is making statements of useful criteria. The potential applications in training, goal setting, or performance evaluation contexts are fairly evident (see, for example, Kirchner and Dunnette, 1957).

Behaviourally anchored rating scales (BARS)

It was that potential which helped Smith and Kendall (1963) on their painstaking pursuit of anchors for rating scales. In particular they were concerned to evaluate the performance of nurses. They wanted to do this not just for the sake of monitoring (it is worth noting) but as one means of improving nursing performance. By the end of the study they were persuaded that their method held promise for the construction of scales suitable for evaluating other complex tasks, when performances are comparable. Certainly others have fulfilled their hope that their procedure would prove useful in industrial, educational, and social areas of research (e.g. Fogli *et al.,* 1971).

They used groups of judges, all of them head nurses, either at conferences or through the mail. Their first task was to find the qualities or characteristics to be evaluated. Those most frequently included by judges in the lists they prepared were retained, *as was the nurses' own language.* (It is as defeating as it is infuriating to be asked to use the jargon of another specialism on such tasks. It is also thoughtlessly rude to impose yours on another's scheme.) Also, to ensure that the important aspects of the job were covered, they collected and classified critical incidents.

Groups then decided on general statements which defined high, acceptable, and low levels of performance on each of the qualities which the first stages produced. More examples of behaviour in each quality were then sought and these were expressed as expectations—that is, instead of stating how a person has behaved, they are couched in terms of how he or she could be expected to behave. This was intended to encourage conscientious rating which of course should minimize the common rating errors. Verification is also relatively easy. It is, perhaps, as well to note here that the police samples employed by Landy *et al.* (1976) objected strongly to the use of 'could be expected to' in the anchor terms. They argued that evaluation is made of past performance not that which might happen in the future. In fact Smith and Kendall provided for that, since their system required raters to give examples of the actual behaviour from which they inferred the expectations they recorded. The issue invoked here—that of justifying a rating—is of such general importance that I shall return to it.

The examples of behaviour, in their revised forms, were judged independently and assigned to the qualities each judge perceived that they represented. If there was not enough agreement about an example's allocation, then it was eliminated. Similarly, if examples originally designed to represent a quality were not consistently reassigned to that quality, then the quality was not retained. A further step, in which actual nurses whose performances were known were described using the examples, tested the ability of the examples to discriminate adequately among performances.

Only after all these careful precautions were taken and still further judges called upon to assign numerical values to the examples on each quality and between 0 (low), 1 (average), and 2 (high). If on an item such judgements were widely dispersed, or the value to be derived could have been one of several then that item was eliminated. Only then was a mean (average) value calculated for each item which remained, and the example placed appropriately on the scale for its quality.

The scales which remained were very reliable scales and provided a frame of reference within which different behaviours might be compared and evaluated. Even so, as Smith and Kendall are scrupulous to point out, it cannot be supposed that all ambiguity is avoided; nor should it be expected that these carefully constructed scales can of themselves overcome such tendencies among raters as leniency. The method is, however, acknowledged as a significant steps forward along the path towards an objective, easily used, behaviourally based, readily interpreted evaluation of performance. Great hopes were raised. Inevitably some were to be dashed.

Cascio and Valenzi (1977) found that halo and leniency were not eradicated by using BARS. Friedman and Cornelius (1976) in testing the effects of the participation of raters in the construction of scales (BARS and graphic rating scales) point to the huge part in the variance of ratings played by what they call undesirable components. These include any attributable to the rater or to the occasion and which, when raters had not participated in developing the scales, accounted for ninety-five per cent of the total variance. Bass and Barrett (1981) point out that, despite the care taken to employ the scale users' own language, there is no guarantee that the original compilers' successors will attach exactly the same meanings to anchors. Similarly the anchors themselves can become out of date and no longer truly represent the performance levels they once did. This is not always so with other formats.

It is evident that care needs to be taken over where and by whom BARS will be used. It is by no means clear that those constructed for use in one situation or organization apply equally in another (Borman and Vallon, 1974). This has two effects: scales are not transferable and performance evaluations may well not be comparable. The Landy *et al.* (1976) study already referred to gives some hope in this regard. They found that scales developed in one police setting could very well be used in others: raters from agencies not involved in constructing the scales were able to use the scales effectively enough. Klimoski and London (1974) showed that superiors and peers (among nurses) are able to use different qualities when making evaluations. This applied also to self-assessments, which were effectively made on qualities different to those that superiors could use; an important point.

A particularly disappointing finding is that BARS may not produce results superior to those obtained by using other, more conventional graphic rating scales. Friedman and Cornelius (1976) showed that errors were generally lower using graphic rating scales. Bernadin *et al.* (1976), comparing BARS and summated scales, were distinctly discouraged, but like so many investigators, display a touching faith in BARS. Clearly people feel that they ought to be superior to other methods. Yet Borman (1979), studying the effects of scale format and training, observed that BARS was far from being the least prone to rater error, nor was it the most accurate method. Dickinson and Zellinger (1980) were able to demonstrate that the mixed standard scale (see page 198) may be more effective than BARS. If BARS cannot be shown to have any practical advantage over other scales, then plainly it is difficult to justify committing to their construction the resources needed. (Smith and Kendall employed over six hundred judges. The more economical Landy *et al.* (1976) used one hundred and sixty-eight on constructing supervisory scales and two hundred and forty on the peer scales.)

But if the psychometric advantages confidently expected by psychologists have not yet been realized, there are some gains. Dickinson and Zellinger (1980) found that users of the different formats in their study clearly felt that BARS was the form most likely to meet the goals of assessment. It was also expected to provide the best feedback to those whose performance was being evaluated—an issue of great importance and of which more will be said shortly. Although the instructions provided for using the BARS in this study were less readily understandable than those for the mixed standards scales, the BARS was judged easier to use; and it was the form most preferred by the users. These benefits may outweigh the psychometric shortcomings which BARS have yet to overcome.

Ivancevich (1980) certainly indicates that this may be so. In a longitudinal study (one using the same subjects over a period) he observed the effects of using behavioural expectation scales (BES) and a trait evaluation system regularly used by a firm of engineers. Over a period of twenty months the results were distinctly encouraging, although as Ivancevich acknowledges it may be premature to attribute them entirely to the rating format. Nevertheless the BES-rated engineers did report attitudes which were more favourable to performance evaluation and less job-related tension. They also showed a markedly greater improvement in one objective aspect of performance (scheduling) than their counterparts who were rated more traditionally. The BES evaluation method was considered fairer, more accurate, clearer, more comprehensive, and as providing more meaningful feedback. Ivancevich was encouraged by the fact that these effects were achieved even though the supervisors had not been trained to use the system. Clearly, qualitative advantages can accrue from the use of BARS. Bernadin and Smith (1981) acknowledge this, but still insist that careful construction of scales with scrupulous attention to methodology should overcome the psychometric shortcomings which tend to bedevil performance evaluation regardless of the system employed (so far). The persistence of these shortcomings in the BARS method is frankly disappointing.

Distributional measurement

A problem arises with the typical appraisal, no matter which system or instrument you use in your evaluation, when it is done on some regular basis and relatively infrequently—e.g. annually. Usually a superior (despite the fact that peers *must* know some things better) assigns a score or value to a subordinate's performance, be it overall or on several scales, as it is recalled during the period which has elapsed since the ritual was last completed. What does that score or value represent? Is it average performance? Probably. Let us imagine that you take a test of some ability. You score 150. A psychologist will then be able to tell you the range within which your 'true' score probably lies. He will not be saying that 150 is not your score, he is simply admitting that he cannot be certain. Statisticians have provided him with a way of hedging his bets. If you take the test more than once then the average of your scores will indicate your true score. The more tries you have the closer the mean will approximate your true score. The variations on either side of the mean are regarded as errors of measurement. Is that reasonable? Suppose your 'true' score appears to be 120. Should we forget that 150? Why should we be allowed to? You showed that you *can* perform that well. It might be very helpful to know how often. The same goes for performance at work. Would it not be fairer and more helpful to use a method which records our exceptional performances, and their frequency?

Yes, say Kane and Lawler (1979). They say that we need to forget about trying to design better rating scales and concentrate on what we ought to be measuring. This, they suggest, is not a person's typical performance level, but is the distribution of the rates at which that person performs at different levels. This is called distributional measurement, and the system by which they hope to operationalize the principle Kane and Lawler call Behavioural Discrimination Scales (BDS). The process by which it is envisaged these scales will be constructed is complex and beyond the scope of this chapter. Suffice it now to say that a modified critical incidents method would yield scalable *performance specimens*, which are statements of classes of performance behaviours. After scaling and establishing the items' ability to discriminate consistently between satisfactory and unsatisfactory performances, an appraisal form is laid out which enables reasonable expectations and actual observations to be reported and compared in a valid manner.

At present, BDS is an idea. It remains to be seen whether its originators' hopes of it, and of lesser methods of distributional measurement, can live up to their expectations. Those expectations are certainly high. Many psychometric difficulties of evaluation will be avoided. Relevance is ensured and accurate feedback will also be very useful to its recipient. Evaluation relates entirely to past performance, and so avoids the hazards of having people infer capabilities.

How often should performance be evaluated?

Frequently during this chapter reference has been made to annual, regular, or ritual evaluations. There have also been plenty of illustrations of why they are less than satisfactory. Indeed they are not particularly useful in a great many cases.

At the simplest level, the needs of employees differ. Starters probably need more frequent feedback about their performance than do more experienced job holders. Some jobs take longer to complete than others, and the sooner performance there can be evaluated the more likely (presumably) is performance on the next similar job likely to benefit. Kane and Lawler speculate about the value of Eliot Jaques's (1961) concept of the time span of discretion in this context. The time span of discretion, to put it crudely, is the period which must elapse between somebody doing a job and his errors becoming apparent. Kane and Lawler are just floating ideas. Every managing officer will know that his day-to-day coaching role requires him to consider subordinates' progress towards completion of tasks, let alone waiting for their consequences to feed through. So, frequent evaluation is the message: not necessarily regular, but as frequent as individual assignments and personal needs dictate.

This was a major conclusion of a very influential study by Meyer *et al.* (1965). They observed the process and effects of a carefully designed annual appraisal system carried out by properly trained managers. The evaluation was used to decide pay increases as well as for other administrative purposes. It was also intended to fulfil the one function generally recognized as the most important for an appraisal interview: to help subordinates improve their performances.

Conventional widom has it that praise, or positive feedback, reinforces desired behaviour, makes frequent repetition more likely, and so should improve performance. Negative feedback, on the other hand, is expected to spur the receiver into action so as to avoid the criticism, in future. The poor performance is removed and there is an overall improvement.

Meyer *et al.* found that those, like many pious hopes, were misplaced. Praise, it transpired, produced little or no effect. Adverse criticism actually led to decrements in performance. The more criticism an individual received, the more defensive he was seen to become, and in extreme cases people could be seen to withdraw altogether psychologically from the interview. In many cases the feedback interview seemed to constitute a real threat to the subordinates' self-esteem.

Meyer and his colleagues recommended the separation of appraisal for improving performance from that for determining pay levels. For one thing the system was not working as intended. Although those who received most criticism also received lower overall assessments (suitable for determining pay awards, you will recall) they did not receive proportionately reduced increases in money. But more importantly, it was Meyer's intention to separate the extreme examples of what he saw as the two quite disparate roles of the appraising manager: the *counsellor* helping towards improving performance and the *judge* determining reward levels.

I do not think this distinction is drawn finely enough. It is sometimes suggested that managers might with advantage employ sophisticated interviewing techniques claimed by some as the skills of counselling. Providing nobody is deceived, it should do little harm. But there is an important outcome sought by most users of these techniques: they try to establish an open, trusting relationship in which their abilities to help the other person can best be used. Trust, you will recall, is a prerequisite of accurate upward communication in organizations, so on the face of it it seems a bright idea.

I am grateful to my colleague, Ruth Sage, herself engaged in occupational psychology and counselling, for pointing out to me her misgivings and so what seems a very real problem which arises if a manager uses these techniques successfully but carelessly or manipulatively. (In other words if he abuses them.) If a subordinate is convinced by his superior's adept use of the techniques that he can trust him and can disclose his opinions, feelings, shortcomings—whatever—freely to somebody who obviously values him and seems concerned only to support and help him, the chances are he is deceived. The superior's first duty is to the organization. A prominent task in his discharge of that duty is evaluating a subordinate's performance: *judging* him. If a disclosure is made, the substance of which indicates less than full compatibility with the organization's best interests, can the superior overlook it and devote himself to his subordinate's needs? He *must* judge. The question then arises: if a manager deliberately uses these techniques and engages his subordinate's (misplaced) trust is he not behaving unethically?

Perhaps it will be better to forget the idea of counselling in this context. Stick to giving feedback considerately and trying to ensure that it is accurate and accurately perceived. Ilgen *et al.* (1979) argue that the skilful interviewer has a very important advantage in that he can help his interviewee achieve an accurate perception of the feedback he is delivering. Perception of feedback poses a major problem, together with its acceptance and the recipient's responsiveness to it. So skilful interviewing is an important ingredient of successful appraisal.

Fletcher and Williams (1976) studied effects of appraisal interviews evidently less punishing than some witnessed by the Meyer team. They found that half of those interviewed did not expect to improve their performances as a result of the interviews—but then we know that feedback by itself does not change behaviour. Most of them, however, approved of the process and held attitudes towards it and beliefs about it which were generally favourable. Even allowing for the fact that ninety per cent of them perceived that their interviewers rated their performances as good, very good, or outstanding, we can agree with Fletcher and Williams that people want feedback. They welcome information about how they stand and how well they are doing their jobs.

That still leaves us with the problem of how to use appraisal to improve performance. Fletcher and Williams clearly believe they have shown that feedback interviews solve this, but their evidence is singularly unconvincing, at it consists merely of the numbers of people who think they have done better or who expect to do better as a result of their interviews. The Meyer data, moreover, showed as has been repeatedly written here, that feedback alone did not produce an improvement in performance. Goal setting, however, did. What is more, although participation in setting goals was beneficial for those accustomed to a participative environment, it was not a necessary ingredient. The important thing was to set goals which subordinates accept. So, said Meyer and his colleagues, make the appraisal interview a meeting at which goals are set and progress is reviewed.

This led them to their very radical proposal that regular annual sessions should be abandoned. Goal setting and review is really an extension of every manager's day-by-day coaching role, and so should appraisal be. It should be carried out frequently, as frequently as tasks or individuals make it advisable. They called their method work planning and review (WPR).

There were many interesting and valuable effects of carrying out WPR. One was the new role in which many managers found themselves during interviews: that of problem solver. One reason for this was that, in discussing progress, it was very often the subordinate who took the initiative by presenting his account of events. This shift released the interviewer from his role as judge, and—although Meyer *et al.* do not express it in quite this way—he was no longer what we would now think of as a counsellor–adviser. Of course, problem solving is something typical of a manager's work, so the method takes best advantage of some of his expertise.

A fear expressed by some managers was that, since the work planning and review (WPR) approach was essentially, indeed importantly, a short term one, no account would be taken of long term or broader objectives. Happily this proved not to be the case. Meyer *et al.* report that, in the course of the discussion of very specific targets there was a natural progression to the consideration of longer range plans, including quite often the career aspirations and plans of subordinates.

The scheme is also a forerunning version of the Kane and Lawler concept of distributional measurement, and it can provide a very ready approach to the description of required behaviours and their frequencies. Indeed, it seems to me that a combination of the two may well afford its users a valuable and, what is most important, thoroughly practical system of performance evaluation, meeting many of the requirements which are notably missed by existing schemes. Another step which might be considered is that of restoring some attention to objective measures of performance. At the outset the difficulties of doing this were acknowledged, but Cascio and Valenzi (1978) have found that supervisory BARS reports on the performance of police officers can be predicted from frequency counts of objective variables like the number of personnel complaints, the number of reports of the use of force, or the number of commendations and awards.

The need to observe and record

Whatever the method you choose or are obliged to use to evaluate and report your evaluation of a subordinate's performance there are two preparatory steps you must take. You must observe the subordinate's behaviours closely and accurately. And you must record them carefully throughout the period on which your evaluation will be based. Both of these steps are obviously closely related to the concept of the criterion (or criteria) against which you will judge performances. What is also very important is that the records you make are probably your best guarantee that your evaluation will be both reliable and valid. Or put it another way: you can bet that if you do not take these precautions then your evaluation is unlikely to be accurate. You cannot do it from unassisted memory. Bernadin and Smith (1981) write: '... asking a person to do a summary rating after 6 to 12 months of performance without any record of observation invites virtually every type of rating error possible.'

Let us take this a step further. Suppose you are convinced of a suspect's guilt. Could your conviction obtain his? No: the system does not permit it. You have to produce evidence and allow others to assess that to determine the issue of guilt. Phantasize for a moment. Suppose we had a system which did permit one person to collect evidence and decide the outcome. Would it be satisfactory for that person privately to weigh the evidence, pronounce a verdict, but only publish the latter? Of course not. How could such a verdict be challenged? An unscrupulous agent of such a system could do unimaginable harm. So could a careless one. The matter is far more important than one of mere law or legality (gasp!): surely it is one of ethics. To label anybody or their behaviour in any way which significantly affects them or attitudes towards them is a very serious business. To do so without making explicit to them and others the characteristic or behaviour which justifies that label is unethical.

Performance evaluation is a system in which one person forms impressions, gathers facts ... whatever, and effectively pronounces judgement on another. Happily recent trends have opened the process up, made challenge possible, discussion likely. But deciding what is recorded is still, usually, the prerogative of the judge. That being so I want to agree with Marion Kellogg (1965): that to record any summary assessment of a subordinate's performance without also recording the behaviour which leads you to that assessment (i.e. the evidence) would be unethical.

Quite apart from the most serious aspect (the ethics of evaluation), recording evidence makes abundantly clear to whoever reads your appraisal exactly what you meant when you made it and precisely what can be inferred from the label you have stuck on the subordinate. Two of the basic difficulties of graphic rating scales, and probably of all evaluation records, are lessened by that valuable safeguard.

Needless to say managers hate the very idea of doing it. I have known some show uncharacteristic creativity in their invention of reasons why it will be impossible. All of them, though, prove on inspection to be nothing more than elaborations of the assertion that they should not have to do it; their word on the matter should be enough. I fear they are wrong; they should have to; their word alone is not enough.

It is hard to do if you have to rely on memory; especially when the demands on your attention are as many and as frequently changing as those on anybody in a supervisory job. The only way to ease the difficulty, as well as to improve the reliability of your evaluation and its validity, is to keep records. Learn to observe objectively and to record accurately. If psychology has a part to play in training managers to appraise performance, it is more likely to be in helping them achieve objectivity and accuracy than in coaching them in the unbridled subjectivity (Smith, 1973) of the face-to-face or, worse, the heart-to-heart conversation.

Summary and comments

The psychology of appraisal has, you might say, been given the treatment. That is because, of all the topics touched on in discussions with some serving officers, it seemed to generate the greatest response. Concern for deserving subordinates led to anxiety to have a tool which could be used to their fair advantage. Reactions to the systems they were obliged to use ranged from resigned acceptance to angry dissatisfaction. It became an important topic. So it should. It also exemplifies several of the other issues written about in the two previous chapters. It can be seen as an integral part of a managing officer's hectic job—especially when WPR is the process chosen—and it is that same pace and variety of activity which undoubtedly contributes to the difficulty of evaluating accurately. Delivery of feedback, and whatever other discussion may be a part of a procedure, is a fine example of a difficult communication task, difficult for both parties. Clearly evaluation is an act of leadership, most obviously to the extent that expectations are clarified by it. And its most obvious purpose is one of motivating subordinates and improving their performances.

Performance evaluation is not an end in itself, so it ought never to be carried out for its own sake or in the interests of convention or experts. It is unlikely to fulfil all the usual expectations of it. It should only be used for clearly defined purposes which its format is designed to serve. Those purposes are represented by the criterion, and they will decide when a single composite criterion or multiple criteria will be employed. Without a criterion evaluation is impossible. A criterion had better be in terms of behaviour or clearly related to actual performance.

Increasingly sophisticated graphic rating scales have not altogether overcome the problems associated with ambiguity. Nor have they, or any widely used method, succeeded in eliminating errors of response set, severity, leniency, or halo. Some progress has been made and more promise remains to be tested. Much faith continues to be shown in behaviourally anchored rating scales (BARS), although they have yet to be found consistently superior to some other methods. That fact raises questions about the economy of constructing the scales. Participation in scale construction appears to be an effective training for using them accurately.

Perhaps psychometric methods are not the best to use in performance evaluation. Distributional measurement may offer more satisfactory instruments which do not lose sight of performances at all levels.

The interview has become an important stage in appraisal, not least as a means of motivating a subordinate and of delivering feedback. Feedback alone does not motivate and may have an effect opposite to that desired and conventionally claimed for it. Translating feedback into goals is effective and a fruitful means of doing this is through work planning and review. This process can also realize many of the aims of conventional appraisal while casting superiors in a role which suits them.

The goal setting and review method recommended requires frequent interviews. Regularity of evaluation is not important. The distributional measurement device outlined also calls for frequent measurement and does not require regularity. If, for sound reasons, like contributing to promotion decisions, a recorded system of assessment is held to be desirable, and can be shown to be really useful, then consideration might be given to combining these two methods. They should be able to support and gain from one another.

If it is your duty to evaluate the performance of subordinates and you are not satisfied that what you are required to do serves your organization's purpose or that of subordinates, then dare I suggest you ask some questions? Find out what the deviser of your system wants or expects it to do, and how. Test all assumptions. Check that everybody is trying to solve the same problems, and that they are the right ones. If not, perhaps the scheme should be junked and a fresh start made. That would probably be better than allowing a given system to slide into disrepute—which is where some seem to be heading.

I am only too aware that in an organization where uniforms are worn, military-style salutes exchanged, and some people are addressed as sir, challenging authority or questioning its wisdom head-on is uncomfortable, even to contemplate. It is far easier to let it go, to chat for the obligatory time about something that interests you (astronomy, my junior policeman acquaintance told me was effective in his case—or was it astrology?). Well, you have to ask yourself how much it matters. The officers on our course thought it mattered a lot.

It is just possible that it really does not matter! The decisions which are said to depend on appraisal, like pay, promotion, placement, training, and development and so on, may be being taken quite decently elsewhere. After all, police pay scales are nationally determined, placements are decided somewhere, and it is quite likely that training is quite effectively planned quite routinely. Promotion is a special issue, and it is not clear how much current practice contributes to these decisions. It seems likely that it identifies who is qualified for it, but not who is best qualified. If that is satisfactory, so be it. It follows that if important decisions can be taken without the ritual and additional load of an evaluation system, then you might as well not have one.

But it ought to matter. Appraisal is a potentially useful tool. There are, or there ought to be, some purposes to which it is well suited, for which it may be the best approach. I doubt whether any 'expert' can tell you what they are and deliver you a system and say use it. You must say what they are, because they have to be your purposes. Whatever they turn out to be, it seems likely that they will continue to be best served by processes rather like those we use for evaluation now. The effectiveness of these processes, though, will be enhanced if their users strive for objectivity, accuracy, civility, sincerity, and *flexibility*.

All but the last of these are characteristics of content or substance, not of form. Form is mere ritual; a display of going through motions; transparent. Some rely on ritual to remind the rest of us of how important we ought to think they are. Real people do not. What is more, managers cannot afford to; they are too busy. In any case the manager who only observes form will soon be seen through. The communicator whose prime concern is form risks (or succeeds in?) transmitting and receiving nothing. Superiors who go through motions neither lead nor motivate, even though they may command and direct. Evaluating or appraising performance gives you a rare chance to realize all these failures at once—but you do not have to.

Suggestions for further reading for chapters 8, 9, and 10

Books of readings comprising chapters by a number of authors collected or commissioned by the books' editors, represent the best value. There are so many good ones it is almost invidious to choose. Nevertheless, with apologies to many omitted, I must name some.

So try:

Perspectives on Behaviour in Organisations, edited by Hackman, Lawler and Porter and published by McGraw-Hill in 1977 (new edition planned).

From the same publishers, Fred Luthans and Kenneth Thompson produced a revised edition of *Contemporary Readings in Organisational Behaviour (1981).* I enjoy the faintly iconoclastic and reconstructive purposefulness of these chapters.

Psychology at Work edited for Penguin by Peter Warr is now in its second edition and represents fantastic value. It is worth having even for the editor's introductory chapter with his analysis of the distinction between applied psychology and 'pure' psychological research—simple as a paper clip, and just as ingenious.

Textbooks abound too, and the number in second or subsequent editions testifies to their merit. I like, and recommend many, but if I had to choose three I'd go for:

Psychology and Work by Peter Ribeaux and Steve Poppleton, published by MacMillan (1978). Slender but brisk, and thorough.

People, Work and Organisation by Bass and Barrett for Allyn and Bacon covers a lot of ground. It is in its second edition.

Psychology of Work Behaviour by Landy and Trumbo, published by Dorsey, is my favourite general textbook. It is firm but fair, easily read and crystal clear, and addressed directly to the reader. The revised edition was published in 1980. Unfortunately there does not seem to be a paperback edition.

Finally, some specialist books:

The Nature of Managerial Work by Henry Mintzberg published in 1973 by Harper and Row, New York.

Communication in Organisations, by Gary Hunt published in 1980 by Prentice Hall, New York.

Handbook of Leadership by Ralph Stogdill published in 1974 by Free Press, New York.

Motivation and Work Behaviour edited by Richard Steers and Lyman Porter published in 1979 by McGraw-Hill, New York. Superb.

Performance in Organisations: Determinants and Appraisal by Cummings and Schwab published in 1973 by Scott Foresman.

References

Adams, J.S. (1965). 'Inequity in social exchange', in *Advances in Experimental Social Psychology* (Ed. L. Berkowitz), Academic Press, New York.

Apter, M. (1982). *The Experience of Motivation*, Academic Press, London.

Arvey, R.D., and Hoyle, J.C. (1974). 'A Guttman approach to the development of behaviourally based rating scales for systems analysts and programmer analysts', *Journal of Applied Psychology*, **6**, 61–58.

Asch, S.E. (1946). 'Forming impressions of personality', *Journal of Abnormal and Social Psychology*, **41**, 258–290.

Asch, S.E. (1958). 'Effects of group pressure upon modification and distortion of judgements'. In *Readings in social psychology* (Eds. E.E. Maccoby, T.M. Newcomb, & E.L. Hartley), (3rd ed.), Holt, Rinehart & Winston, New York.

Bales, R. (1958). 'Task roles and social roles in problem-solving group', in *Readings in Social Psychology*, 3rd Edition (Eds. E. Maccoby, T. Newcomb, and E.L. Hartley), Methuen, London.

Baron, R., Byrne, D., and Griffit, W. (1974). *Social Psychology: Understanding Human Interaction*, Allyn and Bacon, Boston.

Bartlett, F.C. (1932). *Remembering*, Cambridge University Press.

Bass, B.M., and Barrett, G.V. (1981). *People, Work and Organisations*, 2nd Edition, Allyn and Bacon, Boston.

Bass, B.M., and Ryterband, E.C. (1979). *Organisational Psychology*, 2nd Edition, Allyn and Bacon, Boston.

Bavelas, A., and Barrett, D. (1951). 'An experimental approach to organisational communication', *Personnel*, **27**, 366–371.

Bavelas, A., Hastorf, A.H., Gross, A.E., and Kite, W.R. (1965). 'Experiments on the alteration of group structure', *Journal of Experimental and Social Psychology*, **1**, 55–70.

Becker, L.J. (1978). 'Joint effect of feedback and goal setting on performance: a field study of residential energy conservation', *Journal of Applied Psychology*, **63**, 428–433.

Benson, H., Beary, J., and Carol, M.P. (1974). 'The relaxation response', *Psychiatry*, **37**, 37–46.

Berkowitz, N.H., and Bennis, W.G. (1961). 'Interaction patterns in formal service-oriented organisations', *Administrative Science Quarterly*, **6**, 25–50.

Bernadin, H.J., Alvares, K.M., and Cranny, C.J. (1976). 'A recomparison of behavioural expectation scales to summated scales', *Journal of Applied Psychology*, **5**, 564–570.

211

Bernadin, H.J., and Smith, P.C. (1981). 'A clarification of some issues regarding the development and use of behaviourally anchored rating scales (BARS)', *Journal of Applied Psychology*, **66**, 458–463.

Biddle, B.J. (1979). *Role Theory, Expectations, Identities and Behaviours*. Academic Press, New York.

Blanz, F., and Ghiselli, E.E. (1972). 'The mixed standard scale: a new rating system', *Personnel Psychology*, **25**, 185–199.

Block, E. (1975). *Voiceprinting*, McKay, New York.

Blum, M.L. and Naylor, J.C. (1968). *Industrial Psychology: its theoretical and social foundations*. Harper & Row, New York.

Bockman, V.M. (1971). 'The Herzberg controversy', *Personnel Psychology*, **24**, 155–189.

Borman, W.C. (1979). 'Format and training effects on rating accuracy and rater errors', *Journal of Applied Psychology*, **64**, 410–421.

Borman, W.C., and Vallon, W.R. (1974). 'A view of what can happen when behavioural expectation scales are developed in one setting and used in another', *Journal of Applied Psychology*, **59**, 197–201.

Brown, G.W. (1979). 'The social etiology of depression', in *Psychobiology of Depressive Disorder* (Ed. R.A. Depugh), Academic Press, New York.

Brown, J.A.C. (1954). *The Social Psychology of Industry*, Penguin, Harmondsworth.

Bull, R., and Clifford, B.R. (1976). 'Identification: the Devlin Report', *New Scientist*, **70**, 307–308.

Bull, R., and Clifford, B.R. (1983). 'Earwitness voice recognition accuracy', in *Eyewitness Testimony: Psychological Perspectives* (Eds. G.L. Wells and E.F. Loftus), Cambridge University Press, New York.

Bull, R. and Green, J. (1980). 'The relationship between physical appearance and criminality', *Medicine, Science and the Law*, **20**, 79–83.

Bull, R., Rathborn, H., and Clifford, B.R. (1983). 'The voice recognition accuracy of blind listeners', *Perception*, in press.

Bull, R. and Reid, R.L. (1975). 'Police Officers' recall of information', *Journal of Occupational Psychology*, **48**, 73–78.

Burke, P.J. (1972). 'Leadership role differentiation', in *Experimental Social Psychology* (Ed. C.G. McLintock), Holt Rinehart and Winston, New York.

Burns, T. (1954). 'The directions of activity and communication in a departmental executive group', *Human Relations*, **7**, 73–97.

Burns, T., and Stalker, G.M. (1961). *The Management of Innovation*, Tavistock, London.

Butler, R.P., and Jaffe, C.L. (1974). 'Effects of incentive, feedback and manner of presenting the feedback on leader behaviour', *Journal of Applied Psychology*, **59**, 332–336.

Calder, I. (1977). 'An attribution theory of leadership', in *New Directions in Organisational Behaviour* (Eds. B. Staw and G. Salanckik), St. Clair Press, Chicago.

Campbell, J.P., and Pritchard, R.D. (1976). 'Motivation theory in industrial and organisational psychology', in *Handbook of Industrial and Organisational Psychology* (Ed. M.D. Dunnette), Rand McNally, Chicago.

Carkhuff, R.R. (1969). *Helping and Human Relations*, Holt Rinehart and Winston, New York.

Carlson, S. (1951). *Executive Behaviour*, Strombergs, Stockholm.

Carmichael, L., Hogan, H.P. and Walter, A.A. (1932). 'An experimental study of the effect of language on the reproduction of visually perceived form', *Journal of Experimental Psychology*, **15**, 73–86.

Carrell, M.R. (1978). 'A longitudinal field assessment of employee perceptions of equitable treatment', *Organisational Behaviour and Human Performance*, **21**, 108–118.

Carrington, P. (1978). *Freeman in Meditation*, Anchor Press/Doubleday, Gander City, New York.

Carroll, S.J., and Tosi, H.L. (1970). 'Goal characteristics and personality factors in a management-by-objectives program', *Administrative Science Quarterly*, **15**, 295–305.

Carver, C.S., Coleman, A.E., and Glass, D.C. (1976). 'The coronary-prone behaviour pattern and the suppression of fatigue on a treadmill test', *Journal of Personality and Social Psychology*, **33**, 460–466.

Cascio, W.F., and Valenzi, E.R. (1977). 'Behaviourally anchored rating scales: effects of education and job experience of raters and ratees', *Journal of Applied Psychology*, **62**, 278–282.

Cascio, W.F., and Valenzi, E.R. (1978). 'Relations among criteria of police performance', *Journal of Applied Psychology*, **63**, 22–28.

Chesney, M.A., and Rosenman, R. (1980). 'Type A behaviour in the work setting', in *Current Concerns in Occupational Stress* (Eds. C.L. Cooper and R. Payne), Wiley, Chichester.

Clifford, B.R., and Bull, R. (1978). *The Psychology of Person Identification*, Routledge and Kegan Paul, London.

Cohen, A.R. (1958). 'Upward communication in experimentally created hierarchies', *Human Relations*, **11**, 41–53.

Cole, P., and Pringle, P. (1974). *Can You Positively Identify This Man? George Ince and the Barn Murder*, Deutsch, London.

Collaros, P.A. and Anderson, L.R. (1969). 'Effect of perceived expertness upon the creativity of members of brainstorming groups', *Journal of Applied Psychology*, **53**, 159–163.

Cook, T.D., Hepworth, S.J., Wall, T.D., and Warr, P.B. (1981). *The Experience of Work*, Wiley, Chichester.

Cooper, C.L., and Marshall, J. (1976). 'Occupational sources of stress: a review of the literature relating to coronary heart disease and mental ill health', *Journal of Occupational Psychology*, **49**, 11–28.

Cooper, C.L., and Marshall, J. (1978). *Understanding Executive Stress*, Wiley, Chichester.

Corcoran, D.W.J. (1962). 'Noise and loss of sleep', *Quarterly Journal of Experimental Psychology*, **14**, 178–182.

Cottrell, N.B. Social facilitation. In C.G. McClintock (Ed.), *Experimental social psychology*. New York: Holt, 1972, pp. 185–236.

Cox, T. (1978). *Stress*, MacMillan, London.

Cronbach, L. (1970). *Essentials of Psychological Testing*, 3rd Edition, Harper and Row, New York.

Cummings, L.L. (1973). 'A field experimental study of the effects of two performance appraisal systems', *Personnel Psychology*, **26**, 489–502.

Dansereau, F., Cashman, J., and Graen, G. (1973). 'Instumentality theory and equity theory as complementary approaches in predicting the relationship of leadership and turnover among managers', *Organisational Behaviour and Human Performance*, **10**, 184–200.

Davidson, M., and Veno, A. (1980). 'Stress and the policeman', in *White Collar and Professional Stress* (Eds. C.L. Cooper and J. Marshall), Wiley, Chichester.

Davis, T.R.V., and Luthans, F. (1979). 'Leadership reexamined: a behavioural approach', *Academy of Management Review*, **2**, 237–248.

Deffenbacher, K.A. (1980). 'Eyewitness accuracy and confidence', *Law and Human Behavior*, **4**, 243–260.

Dent, H. and Gray, F. (1975). 'Identification on parade', *New Behaviour*, **1**, 366–369.

Devlin Report (1976). *Report to the Secretary of State for the Home Department of the*

Departmental Committee on Evidence of Identification in Criminal Cases, HMSO, London.

Dickinson, T.L., and Zellinger, P.M. (1980). 'A comparison of the behaviourally anchored rating and mixed standard scale formats', *Journal of Applied Psychology,* **64**, 147–154.

Dohrenwend, B.S., and Dohrenwend, B.P. (1973). *Stressful Life Events: Their Nature and Effects*, Wiley, New York.

Dossett, D.L., Latham, G.P., and Mitchell, T.R. (1979). 'Effects of assigned versus participatively set goals, knowledge of results and individual differences on employee behaviour when goal difficulty is held constant', *Journal of Applied Psychology,* **64**, 291–298.

Dunnette, M.D. (1963). 'A note on the criterion', *Journal of Applied Psychology,* **47**, 251–254.

Dunnette, M.D., Campbell, J.P., and Hakel, M.D. (1967). 'Factors contributing to job satisfaction and job dissatisfaction in six occupational groups', *Organisational Behaviour and Human Performance,* **2**, 143–174.

Dunnette, M.D., Campbell, J., and Jaastad, K. (1963). 'The effect of group participation on brainstorming effectiveness for two industrial samples', *Journal of Applied Psychology,* **47**, 30–47.

Edwards, J. (1973). 'The status of voiceprints as admissible evidence', *Syracuse Law Review,* **24**, 1261–1278.

Egan, B. (1975). *The Skilled Helper*, Brooks/Cole, Monteray, California.

Eisenberg, T. (1975). 'Labor-management relations and psychological stress—view from the bottom', *The Police Chief,* **42**, 54–58.

Ellis, A. (1978). 'What people can do for themselves to cope with stress', in *Stress at Work* (Eds. C.L. Cooper and R. Payne), Wiley, Chichester.

Ellis, H.D. and Davies, G., with Shepherd, J. (1977). *An Investigation of the Photo-fit System for Recalling Faces*. Report to the Social Science Research Council.

Ewen, R.B., Smith, C., Hulin, C., and Locke, E. (1966). 'An empirical test of the Herzberg two-factor theory', *Journal of Applied Psychology,* **50**, 544–550.

Eysenck, H.J. (1964). *The Psychology of Fear and Stress*, Weidenfeld and Nicholson, London.

Eysenck, H.J., and Rachman, S. (1965). *The Causes and Cures of Neurosis*, Routledge and Kegan Paul, London.

Farr, R.M. (1977). 'On the nature of attributional artefacts in qualitative research. Herzberg's two-factor theory of work motivation', *Journal of Occupational Psychology,* **50**, 3–14.

Fayol, H. (1916, 1950). *Administration industrielle et générale*, Dunod, Paris.

Fenz, W.D. (1975). 'Strategies for coping with stress', in *Stress and Anxiety*, Vol.2 (Eds. G. Sarason and C.D. Spielberger), Hemisphere, Washington.

Fiedler, F.E. (1967). *A Theory of Leadership Effectiveness*. McGraw-Hill, New York.

Fiedler, F.E. (1972). 'How do you make leaders more effective? New answers to an old puzzle', *Organisational Dynamics*, Autumn 1972, 3–18.

Fiedler, F.E. (1976). 'The leadership game: matching the man to the situation', *Organisational Dynamics*, Winter 1976, 6–16.

Fiedler, F.E. (1977). 'Style or circumstance: the leadership enigma', in *Organisational Design, Development and Behaviour* (Ed. K.O. Magnusen), Scott, Foresman and Co, Glenview, Illinois.

Finley, D.M., Osburn, H.G., Dublin, J.A., and Jenneret, P.R. (1977). 'Behaviourally based rating scales: effects of specific anchors and disguised scale continua', *Personnel Psychology,* **30**, 659–669.

Fisher, D. (1981). *Communication in Organisations*, West Publishing Company, St. Paul, Minnesota.

Flanagan, J.C. (1954). 'The critical incident technique', *Psychological Bulletin,* **51**. 327–358.

Fleishman, E.A. (1951). 'Leadership climate and supervisory behaviour', *Columbus Ohio Personnel Research Books*, Ohio State University, Columbus.

Fleishman, E.A. (1953). 'The description of supervisory behaviour', *Journal of Applied Psychology,* **37**, 153–158.

Fleishman, E.A., and Harris, E.F. (1962). 'Patterns of leadership behaviour related to employee grievances and turnover', *Personnel Psychology,* **15**, 43–56.

Fleishman, E.A., Harris, E.F., and Burtt, H.E. (1955). *Leadership and Supervision in Industry*, Ohio State University Bureau of Educational Research, Columbus.

Fletcher, C., and Williams, R. (1976). The influence of performance feedback in appraisal interviews, *Journal of Occupational Psychology,* **49**, 75–83

Fodor, E.M. (1974). 'Disparagement by a subordinate as an influence in the case of power', *Journal of Applied Psychology,* **59**, 652–655.

Fogli, L., Hulin, C.L., and Blood, M.R. (1971). 'Development of first-level behavioural job criteria, *Journal of Applied Psychology,* **55**, 3–8.

Fox, A. (1968). 'Industrial sociology and industrial relations', *Research Paper No. 3*, Royal Commission on Trade Unions and Employers' Associations, H.M. Stationery Office, London.

French, J.R.P., and Caplan, R.D. (1972). 'Organisational stress and individual strain', in *The Failure of Success* (Ed. A.J. Marrow), Amacom, New York.

French, J.R.P., and Raven, B.H. (1959). 'The basis of social power', in *Studies in Social Power* (Ed. D. Cartwright), University of Michigan Institute for Social Research, Ann Arbor.

Friedlander, F. (1964). 'Job characteristics as satisfiers and dissatisfiers', *Journal of Applied Psychology,* **48**, 388–392.

Friedman, B.A., and Cornelius, E.T. (1976). 'Effect of rater participation in scale construction on the psychometric characteristics of two rating scale formats', *Journal of Applied Psychology,* **61**, 210–216.

Friedman, M.D., and Rosenman, R.H. (1974). *Type A Behaviour and Your Heart,* Knopf, New York.

Garland, H. (1982). 'Goal levels and task performance: a compelling replication of some compelling results.' *Journal of Applied Psychology,* **67**, 245–248.

Gibson, H.B. (1982). 'The use of hypnosis in police investigations', *Bulletin of the British Psychological Society,* **35**, 138–142.

Giles, W.F. (1977). 'Volunteering for job enrichment; a test of expectancy theory predictions', *Personnel Psychology,* **30**, 427–435.

Goffman, E. (1964). *Stigma*, Prentice-Hall, Englewood Cliffs.

Goodman, P.S. (1974). 'An examination of referents used in the evaluation of pay', *Organisational Behaviour and Human Performance,* **12**, 170–195.

Goodman, P.S., and Friedman, A. (1968). 'An examination of the effect of wage inequity in the hourly condition', *Organisational Behaviour and Human Performance,* **3**, 340–352.

Gordon, M.E. (1970). 'The effect of the correctness of behaviour observed on the accuracy of ratings', *Organisational Behaviour and Human Performance,* **5**, 366–377.

Gordon, M.E., and Cohen, F.L. (1973). 'Training behaviour as a predictor of trainability', *Personnel Psychology,* **26**, 261–272.

Gowler, D., and Legge, K. (1980). 'Evaluative practices as stressors in occupational settings', in *Current Concerns in Occupational Stress* (Eds. C.L. Cooper and R. Payne), Wiley, Chichester.

Graen, G.B. (1966). 'Addendum to 'an empirical test of the Herzberg two factor theory'', *Journal of Applied Psychology,* **50**, 551–555.

Graen, G., Dansereau, F., and Minarni, T. (1972). 'Dysfunctional leadership styles', *Organisational Behaviour and Human Performance,* **7**, 216–236.

216

Graen, G., and Schiemann, W. (1978). 'Leader member agreement: a vertical dyadic linkage approach', *Journal of Applied Psychology*, **63**, 206–212.

Gray, J.A. (1971). *The Psychology of Fear and Stress*, Weidenfeld and Nicolson, London.

Greene, H. (1975). 'Voiceprint identification: the case in favour of admissibility', *American Criminal Law Review*, **13**, 171–200.

Gruneberg, N.M. (1979). *Understanding Job Satisfaction*, MacMillan, London.

Guest, R.H. (1956). 'Of time and the foreman', *Personnel*, **32**, 478–486.

Guion, R.M. (1965). *Personnel Testing*, McGraw-Hill, New York.

Gupta, N., and Beehr, T. (1979). 'Job stress and employee behaviours', *Organisational Behaviour and Human Performance*, **23**, 373–387.

Hackman, J.R., and Oldham, G.R. (1975). 'Development of the job diagnostic survey', *Journal of Applied Psychology*, **60**, 159–170.

Hackman, J.R., and Oldham G.R. (1976). 'Motivation through the design of work: test of a theory', *Organisational Behaviour and Human Performance*, **16**, 250–279.

Hall, D.T., and Nougaim, K.E. (1968). 'An examination of Maslow's need hierarchy in an organisational setting', *Organisational Behaviour and Human Performance*, **3**, 12–35.

Hall, M. (1974). 'The current status of speaker identification by use of speech spectrograms', *Canadian Journal of Forensic Science*, **7**, 152–176.

Harvey, R.J. (1982). 'The future of partial correlation as a means to reduce halo in performance ratings', *Journal of Applied Psychology*, **67**, 171–176.

Hecker, M. (1971). 'Speaker recognition', *American Speech and Hearing Association*, monograph no. 16.

Helson, H. (1964). *Adaptation Level Theory*, Harper and Row, New York.

Herzberg, F. (1966). *Work and the Nature of Men*, World, Cleveland.

Herzberg, F. (1968). 'One more time: How do you motivate employees?', *Harvard Business Review*, **46**, 53–62.

Herzberg, F., Mausner, B., Peterson, R.O., and Capwell, D.F. (1957). *Job attitudes: Review of Research and Opinion*, Psychological Services of Pittsburgh.

Herzberg, F., Mausner, B., and Synderman, B. (1959). *The Motivation to Work*, Wiley, New York.

Holmes, T.H., and Rahe, R.H. (1967). 'Social readjustment rating scale', *Journal of Psychosomatic Research*, **11**, 213.

House, R.L. (1971). 'A path-goal theory of leader-effectiveness', *Administrative Science Quarterly*, **16**, 221–238.

House, R.J., and Baetz, M.L. (1979). 'Leadership: some empirical generalisation and new research directions', in *Research and Organisational Behaviour* (Ed. B. Staw), JAI Press Inc, Greenwich, Connecticut.

Housel, T.J., and Davis, W.E. (1977). 'The reduction of upward communication distortion', *Journal of Business Communication*, **14**, 49–65.

Hulin, C.L. (1982). 'Some reflections on general performance dimensions and halo rating error', *Journal of Applied Psychology*, **67**, 165–170.

Ilgen, D.R., Fisher, C.D., and Taylor, M.S. (1979). 'Consequences of individual feedback on performance in organisations', *Journal of Applied Psychology*, **64**, 349–371.

Ivancevich, J.M. (1979). 'Longitudinal study of the effects of rater training on psychometric error in ratings', *Journal of Applied Psychology*, **64**, 502–508.

Ivancevich, J.M. (1980). 'A longitudinal study of behavioural expectation scales: attitudes and performance', *Journal of Applied Psychology*, **65**, 139–146.

Ivancevich, J.M., and Donnelly, J.H. (1970). 'Leader influence and performance', *Personnel Psychology*, **23**, 539–549.

Ivancevich, J.M., and Smith, S.V. (1981). 'Goal-setting interview skills training. Simulated and on-the-job analyses', *Journal of Applied Psychology*, **66**, 697–705.

Jablin, F.M. (1979). 'Superior-subordinate communication: the state of the art', *Psychological Bulletin,* **6**, 1201–1222.

James, L.R., Hartman, A., Stebbins, M.W., and Jones, A.P. (1977). 'Relationships between psychological climate and a VIE model for work motivation', *Personnel Psychology,* **30**, 229–254.

Jaques, E. (1961). *Equitable Payment,* Wiley, New York.

Johnson, T.W., and Stinson, J.E (1975). 'Role ambiguity, role conflict and satisfaction: moderating effects of individual differences', *Journal of Applied Psychology,* **60**, 329–333.

Jones, S. (1969). 'The design of instructions', *Training Information Paper No. 1,* HMSO, London.

Kahn, R.L. (1973). 'Conflict, ambiguity and overload: three elements in job stress', *Occupational Mental Health,* **3**, 1.

Kane, J.S., and Lawler, E.E. (1979). 'Performance appraisal effectiveness: its assessment and determinants', in *Research in Organisational Effectiveness* (Ed. B. Staw), JAI Press Inc. Greenwich, Connecticut.

Kasl, S.V. (1978). 'Epidemiological contributions to the study of work stress', in *Stress at Work* (Eds. C.L. Cooper and R. Payne), Wiley, Chichester.

Katz, D., and Kahn, R.L. (1966). *The Social Psychology of Organisations,* Wiley, Chichester.

Kelley, H.H. (1951). 'Communication in experimentally created hierarchies', *Human Relations,* **4**, 39–56.

Kellogg, M. (1965). *What to do about Performance Appraisal,* American Management Association.

Kerr, S., and Jermier, J.M. (1978). 'Substitutes for leadership: their meaning and measurement', *Organisational Behaviour and Human Performance,* **22**, 375–403.

Kersta, L. (1962). 'Voiceprint identification', *Nature,* **196**, 1253–1257.

Kessler, R.C. (1979). 'Stress social status and psychological distress', *Journal of Health and Social Behaviour,* **20**, 259–272.

Kim, J.S., and Hammer, W.C. (1976). 'Effect of performance feedback and goal setting on productivity and satisfaction in an organisational setting', *Journal of Applied Psychology,* **61**, 48–57.

King, L.M., Hunter, J.E., and Schmidt, F.L. (1980). 'Halo in a multidimensional forced-choice performance evaluation scale', *Journal of Applied Psychology,* **65**, 507–516.

Kirchner, W.K., and Dunnette, M.D. (1957). 'Identifying the critical factors in salesmanship', *Personnel,* **34**, 54–59.

Kirkham, G. (1974). 'From professor to patrolman: a fresh perspective on the police', *Journal of Police Science and Administration,* **2**, 127–137.

Klimoski, R.J., and London, M. (1974). 'Role of the rater in performance appraisal', *Journal of Applied Psychology,* **58**, 445–451.

Kroes, W.H. (1976). *Society's victim—the Policeman—an Analysis of Job Stress in Policing,* Thomas, New York.

Kyriacou, C., and Sutcliffe, J. (1978). 'A model of teacher stress', *Educational Studies,* **4**, 1–6.

Landy, J.F., Farr, J.L., Saal, F.E., and Freytag, W.R. (1976). 'Behaviourally-anchored rating scales for rating the performance of police officers', *Journal of Applied Psychology,* **61**, 750–758.

Landy, F.J., and Trumbo, D.A. (1976). *Psychology of Work Behaviour,* The Dorsey Press, Homewood, Illinois.

Landy, F.J., and Trumbo, D.A. (1980). *Psychology of Work Behaviour—Revised Edition,* The Dorsey Press, Homewood, Illinois.

Landy, F.J., Vance, R.J., and Barnes-Farrell, J.L. (1982). 'Statistical control of halo—a response', *Journal of Applied Psychology,* **67**, 177–180.

Landy, F.J., Vance, R.J., Barnes-Farrell, J.L., and Steele, J. (1980). 'Statistical control of halo error in performance ratings', *Journal of Applied Psychology*, **65**, 501–506.

La Rocco, J.M., House, J.S., and French, J.R. (1980). 'Social support, occupational stress and health', *Journal of Health and Social Behaviour*, **21**, 202–218.

Latham, G.P., Mitchell, T.R., and Dossett, D.L. (1978). 'Importance of participative goal setting and anticipated rewards in goal difficulty and job performance'. *Journal of Applied Psychology*, **63**, 163–171.

Latham, G.P., and Saari, L.M. (1979). 'Importance of supportive relationships in goal setting', *Journal of Applied Psychology*, **64**, 151–156.

Latham, G.P., and Yukl, G.A. (1975). 'A review of research on the application of goal setting in organisations', *Academy of Management Journal*, **18**, 824–845.

Lawler, E.E. (1968). 'Equity theory as a predictor of productivity and work quality', *Psychological Bulletin*, **70**, 596–610.

Lawler, E.E. (1971). *Pay and Organisational Effectiveness: a Psychological View*, McGraw-Hill, New York.

Lawler, E.E., Porter, L.W., and Tannenbaum, A. (1968). 'Managers' attitudes towards interactive episodes', *Journal of Applied Psychology*, **52**, 432–439.

Lawler, E.E., and Suttle, J.L. (1973). 'Expectancy theory and job behaviour', *Organisational Behaviour and Human Performance*, **9**, 482–503.

Leavitt, H.J. (1958). *Managerial Psychology*, University of Chicago Press.

Leavitt, H.J., and Mueller, R.A.H. (1951). 'Some effects of feedback on communication', *Human Relations*, **4**, 401–410.

Lee, R., Malone, M. and Greco, S. (1981). 'Multitrait—multimethod—multirater analysis of performance ratings for law enforcement personnel. *Journal of Applied Psychology.'* **66**, 625–632.

Lester, D., and Gallagher, J. (1980). 'Stress in police officers and department store managers', *Psychological Reports*, **46**, 882.

Lester, D., and Mink, S.R. (1979). 'Is stress higher in police officers? An exploratory study', *Psychological Reports*, **45**, 554.

Likert, R. (1961). *New Patterns of Management*, McGraw-Hill, New York.

Lin, N., Simeone, R.S., Ensel, W.M., and Kuo, W. (1979). 'Social support, stressful life events and illness a model and an empirical test', *Journal of Health and Social Behaviour*, **20**, 108–119.

Locke, E.A. (1968). 'Toward a theory of task performance and incentives', *Organisational Behaviour and Human Performance*, **3**, 157–189.

Locke, E.A. (1975). 'Personnel attitudes and motivation', *Annual Review of Psychology*, **26**, 457–479.

Locke, E.A., and Bryan, J.F. (1969). 'The directing function of goals in task performance', *Organisational Behaviour and Human Performance*, **4**, 35–42.

Locke, E.A., and Schweiger, D.M. (1979). 'Participation in decision-making one more look', in *Research in Organisational Behaviour* (Ed. B. Staw), JAI Press Inc, Greenwich, Connecticut.

Loftus, E., and Palmer, J. (1974). 'Reconstruction of automobile destruction an example of the interaction between language and memory', *Journal of Verbal Learning and Verbal Behaviour*, **13**, 585–589.

Maginn, B.K., and Harris, R.J. (1980). 'Effects of anticipated evaluation on individual brainstorming performance', *Journal of Applied Psychology*, **65**, 219–225.

Maier, N.R.F., Hoffman, L.R. and Read, W.H. (1963). 'Superior—subordinate communication: The relative effectiveness of managers who held their subordinates' positions.' *Personnel Psychology*, **16**, 1–11.

Margolis, B.L., Kroes, W., and Quinn, R. (1974). 'Job stress, an unlisted occupational hazard'. *Journal of Occupational Medicine*, **1**, 659–661.

Marshall, J. (1969). 'The evidence: Do we see and hear what is? Or do our senses lie?', *Psychology Today*, **2**, 49–52.

Martin, T. (1974). 'Application of limited vocabularly recognition systems, in *Speech Recognition* (Ed. D. Redd), Academic Press, New York and London.

Maslow, A.H. (1943). 'A theory of human motivation', *Psychological Bulletin*, 50, 370–396.

McCall, M.W. (1976). 'Leaders and leadership: of substance and shadow', in *Perspectives on Behavour in Organisations* (Eds. J.R. Hackman, E.E. Lawler, and L.W. Poster), McGraw-Hill, New York.

McGrath, J. (1970). *Social and Psychological Factors in Stress*, Holt, Rinehart and Winston, New York.

McGregor, D. (1960). *The Human Side of Enterprise*, McGraw-Hill, New York.

McKelvie, S. (1976). 'The effect of verbal labelling on recognition memory for schematic faces', *Quarterly Journal of Experimental Psychology*, 28, 459–474.

McLean, A. (1979). *Work Stress*, Addison-Wesley, Reading, Massachusetts.

Mellinger, G.D. (1956). 'Interpersonal trust as a factor in communication', *Journal of Abnormal and Social Psychology*, 52, 304–309.

Mento, A.J., Cartledge, N.D., and Locke, E.A. (1980). 'Maryland vs Michigan vs Minnesota another look at the relationship of expectancy and goal difficulty to task performance, *Organisational Behaviour and Human Performance*, 25, 419–440.

Meyer, H.H., Kay, E., and French, R.P. (1965). 'Split roles in performance appraisal', *Harvard Business Review*, 43, 123–129.

Miles, R.H. (1980). 'Organisation boundary roles', in *Current Concerns in Occupational Stress* (Eds. C.L. Cooper and R. Payne), Wiley, Chichester.

Milgram, S. (1974). *Obedience to authority*. Harper & Row, New York.

Miner, J.B. (1977). 'Twenty years of research on role-motivation theory of managerial effectiveness', *Personnel Psychology*, 31, 739–760.

Mintzberg, H. (1971). 'Managerial work: analysis from observation', *Management Service*, 18, 97–110.

Mintzberg, H. (1973). *The Nature of Managerial Work*, Harper and Row, New York.

Mintzberg, H. (1975). 'The manager's job: folklore and fact', *Harvard Business Review*, 53, 49–61.

Mitchell, T.R. and Kalb, L.S. (1981). 'Effects of outcome knowledge and outcome valence on supervisors' evaluations.' *Journal of Applied Psychology*, 66, 604–612.

Morris, J.N., Heady, J.A., and Raffle, A.B. (1956). 'Physique of London busmen', *Lancet, ii*, 569–578.

Mowday, R.T. (1979). 'Equity theory predictions of behaviour in organisations', in *Motivation and Work Behaviour* (Eds. R.M. Steers and L.W. Porter), McGraw-Hill, New York.

Mowen, J.C., Middlemist, R.D., and Luther, D. (1981). 'Joint effects of assigned goal level and incentive structure on task performance: a laboratory study', *Journal of Applied Psychology*, 66, 598–603.

Murphy, K.R. (1982). 'Difficulties in the statistical control of halo', *Journal of Applied Psychology*, 67, 161–164.

Nadler, D.A., and Lawler, E.E. (1977). 'Motivation: a diagnostic approach', in *Perspectives on Behaviour in Organisations* (Eds. J.R. Hackman, E.E. Lawler, and L.W. Porter), McGraw-Hill, New York.

Nichols, R.G. (1962). 'Listening is good business.' *Management of Personnel Quarterly*, (Winter 1962), 4.

Nisbett, R.E., and Wilson, T.D. (1977). 'The halo effect: evidence for unconscious alteration of judgments', *Journal of Personality and Social Psychology*, 35, 250–256.

Opsahl, R.L., and Dunnette, M.D. (1966). 'The role of financial compensation in industrial motivation', *Psychological Bulletin*, 66, 94–118.

O'Reilly, C.A., and Roberts, K.H. (1974). 'Information filtration in organisations: three experiments', *Organisational Behaviour and Human Performance*, 15, 66–86.

220

Osborn, A.F. (1953). *Applied Imagination: Principles and Procedures of Creative Thinking*, Schriber, New York.
Osgood, C.E., Suci, G.J. and Tannenbaum, P.H. (1957). *The Measurement of Meaning*, University of Illinois Press, Urbana.
Patterson, K. (1978). Face recognition: more than a pretty face. In *Practical Aspects of Memory* (M.M. Gruneberg, P.E. Morris and R.N. Sykes, Eds.), Academic Press; London.
Payne, R. (1979). 'Demands, supports, constraints and psychological health', in *Response to Stress: Occupational Aspects* (Eds. C.J. McKay and T. Cox), International Publishing Corporation, London.
Payne, R. (1980). 'Organisational stress and social support', in *Current Concerns in Occupational Stress* (Eds. C.L. Cooper and R. Payne), Wiley, Chichester.
Penfield, R.V. (1974). 'Time allocation patterns and effectiveness of managers', *Personnel Psychology*, 27, 245–255.
Pfeffer, J. (1977). 'The ambiguity of leadership', *Academy of Management Journal*, 2, 104–112.
Piliavin, I., and Briar, S. (1964). 'Police encounters with juveniles', *American Journal of Sociology*, 70, 206–214.
Porter, L.W. (1961). 'A study of perceived need satisfactions in bottom and middle management jobs', *Journal of Applied Psychology*, 45, 1–10.
Porter, L.W. (1962). 'Job attitudes in management: I. Perceived deficiencies in need fulfillment as a function of job level', *Journal of Applied Psychology*, 46, 375–384.
Porter, L.W. (1963). 'Job attitudes in management: II. Perceived importance of needs as a function of job level', *Journal of Applied Psychology*, 47, 141–148.
Porter, L.W., and Lawler, E.E. (1968). *Managerial Attitudes and Performance*, Dorsey Press, Homewood, Illinois.
Pritchard, R.D., Dunnette, M.D., and Jorgenson, D.O. (1972). 'Effects of perceptions of equity and inequity on worker performance and satisfaction', *Journal of Applied Psychology*, 56, 75–94.
Quinlan, D.M., and Blatt, S.J. (1972). 'Field articulation and performance under stress: differential predictions in surgical and psychiatric nursing training', *Journal of Consulting and Clinical Psychology*, 39, 517.
Rackham, N. (1971). *Developing Interactive Skills*, Wellens Publishing, Northampton.
Read, W.H. (1962). 'Upward communication in industrial hierarchies', *Human Relations*, 15, 3–15.
Reid, R.L., and Bull, R. (1973). 'Arrests attributed to briefings', *The Police Journal* (Oct.–Dec.).
Rogers, C.R., and Roethlisberger, F.J. (1952). 'Barriers and gateways to communication', *Harvard Business Review*, July/August.
Rosen, H. (1963). 'Occupational motivation of research and development personnel', *Personnel Administration*, 26, 37–43.
Rotter, J.B. (1966). 'Generalised expectancies for internal versus external control of reinforcement', *Psychological Monographs*, 80, Whole No. 609.
Rubin, I.M., and Goldman, M. (1968). 'An open system model of leadership performance', *Organisational Behaviour and Human Performance*, 3. 143–156.
Russell, J. (1976). Cited in Zillman, D. (1979), *Hostility and Aggression*, Erlbaum, Hillsdale, New Jersey.
Ryan, T.A. (1970). *Intentional Behaviour*, Ronald Press, New York.
Saal, F.E. (1979). 'Mixed standard rating scale a consistent system for numerically coding inconsistent response combinations', *Journal of Applied Psychology*, 64, 422–428.
Saal, F.E., and Landy, F.J. (1977). 'The mixed standard rating scale: an evaluation', *Organisational Behaviour and Human Performance*, 18, 19–38.
Sadler, P.J. (1966). *Leadership style, Confidence in Management and Job Satisfaction*, Ashridge Management College.

Sargent, S.S. (1939). 'Emotional stereotypes in the Chicago Tribune', in *Sociometry*, Vol. 2, (Ed. J.L. Moreno), Beacon House, New York.

Savage, A. (1982). 'Reconciling your appraisal system with company reality', *Personnel Management*, May 1982.

Sayles, L.R. (1964). *Managerial Behaviour: Administration in Complex Enterprises*, McGraw-Hill, New York.

Scarman, L.G. (1981). *The Brixton disorders 10–12 April 1981*, CMND 8427, HMSO, London.

Schein, E. (1970). *Organisational Psychology*, Prentice-Hall, Englewood Cliffs, N.J.

Schmidt, F.L., and Kaplan, L.B. (1971). 'Composite vs multiple criteria: a review and revolution of the controversy', *Personnel Psychology*, 24, 415–434.

Schrisheim, C.A., House, R.J., and Kerr, S. (1976). 'Leader initiating structure: a reconciliation of discrepant research results and some empirical tests', *Organisational Behaviour and Human Performance*, 15.

Schuler, R.S. (1979). 'Effective use of communication to minimise stress', *The Personnel Administrator*, June, 40–44.

Schuler, R.S. (1980). 'Definition and conceptualisation of stress in organisations', *Organisational Behaviour and Human Performance*, 25, 184–215.

Schwab, D.P., DeVitt, and Cummings, L.L. (1971). 'A test of the adequacy of the two-factor as a predictor of self-report performance effects', *Personnel Psychology*, 24, 293–303.

Shapira, Z., and Dunbar, R.L.M. (1980). 'Testing Mintzberg's managerial roles classification using an in-basket simulation', *Journal of Applied Psychology*, 65, 87–95.

Shepherd, J., Ellis, H.D., and Davies, G.M. (1982). *Identification Evidence: A Psychological Evaluation*, Aberdeen University Press, Aberdeen.

Sherif, M. A study of some social factors in perception. *Archives of Psychology*, No. 187.

Shoemaker, D., South, D., and Lowe, J. (1973). 'Facial stereotypes of deviants and judgements of guilt or innocence.' *Social Forces*, 51, 427–433.

Simpkins, L., and West, J. (1966). Reinforcement of duration of talking in trial groups', *Psychological Reports*, 18, 231–236.

Smith, H.C. (1973). *Sensitivity Training*, McGraw-Hill, New York.

Smith, P.C., and Kendall, L.M. (1963). 'Retranslation of expectations: an approach to the construction of ambiguous anchors for rating scales', *Journal of Applied Psychology*, 47, 149–155.

Spector, P.E. (1976). 'Choosing response categories for summated rating scales', *Journal of Applied Psychology*, 63, 374–375.

Steers, R.M. (1977). *Organisational Effectiveness: a behavioural view*. Goodyear, Santa Monica, California.

Steers, R.M., and Porter, L.W. (1974). 'The role of task-goal attributes in employee performance, *Psychological Bulletin*, 81, 434–452.

Steers, R.M., and Porter, L.W. (1979). *Motivation and Work Behaviour*, 2nd Edition, McGraw-Hill, New York.

Stewart, R. (1963). *The Reality of Management*, Heineman, London.

Stewart, R. (1967). *Managers and Their Jobs*, MacMillan, London.

Stewart, R. (1976). *Contrasts in Management*, McGraw-Hill, London.

Stogdill, R.M. (1974). *Handbook of leadership*. The Free Press, New York.

Stuhr, A.W. (1962). 'Some outcomes of the New York employee survey. Social science research reports, IV. Surveys and inventories', in *Organisational Psychology* (Eds. B.M. Bass and E.C. Ryterband), Allyn and Bacon, Boston.

Taylor, D., Block, C., and Berry, P. (1958). 'Does group participation when using brainstorming facilitate or inhibit creative thinking?', *Administrative Science Quarterly*, 3, 23–47.

Tornow, W.N. (1971). 'The development and application of an input–outcome moderator test on the perception and reduction of inequity', *Organisational Behaviour and Human Performance*, 6, 614–638.

222

Tosi, O., Oyer, W., Lashbrook, C., Pedrey, J., and Nash, E. (1972). 'Experiment on voice identification', *Journal of the Acoustical Society of America*, **51**, 2030–2043.
Turk, D.C. (1978). 'Application of coping-skills training to the treatment of pain', in *Stress and Anxiety*, Vol. 5, (Eds. C.D. Spielberger and I.G. Sarason), Hemisphere, Washington.
Umstot, D.D., Bell, C.H., and Mitchell, T.R. (1976). 'Effects of job enrichment and task goals on satisfaction and productivity: implications for job design', *Journal of Applied Psychology*, **61**, 379–394.
Van Harrison, R. (1978). 'Person–environment fit and job stress', in *Stress at Work*, (Eds. C.L. Cooper and R. Payne), Wiley, Chichester.
Vroom, V.H. (1964). *Work and Motivation*, Wiley, New York.
Wahba, M.A., and Bridwell, L.G. (1973). 'Maslow reconsidered: a review of research on the need hierarchy theory', in *Motivation and Work Behaviour*, 2nd Edition (Eds. R. Steers and L.W. Porter), McGraw-Hill, New York.
Wahba, M.A., and Bridwell, L.G. (1976). 'Maslow reconsidered: a review of research on the need hierarchy theory', *Organisational Behaviour and Human Performance*, **15**, 212–240.
Wall, T.D., and Lischeron, J.A. (1977). *Worker Participation*, McGraw-Hill, New York.
Walter, J.D. (1981). 'Police in the middle: a study of small city police intervention in domestic disputes', *Journal of Police Science and Administration*, **9**, 243–260.
Wanous, J.P. (1976). 'Who wants job enrichment?', in *Perspectives on Behaviour in Organisations* (Eds. J.R. Hackman, E.E. Lawler, and L.W. Porter), McGraw-Hill, New York.
Warmke, D.L., and Billings, R.S. (1979). 'Comparison of training methods for improving the psychometric quality of experimental and administrative performance ratings', *Journal of Applied Psychology*, **64**, 124–131.
Warr, P., and Knapper, C. (1968). *The Perception of People and Events*, Wiley, Chichester.
Wason, P.C., and Johnson-Laird, P.N. (1972). *The Psychology of Reasoning: Structure and Content*, Batsford, London.
Waters, L.K., and Roach, D. (1973). 'A factor analysis of need-fulfillment items designed to measure Maslow need categories', *Personnel Psychology*, **26**, 185–190.
Weick, K.E. (1974). 'Review essay: the nature of managerial work', *Administrative Science Quarterly*, **19**, 111–118.
Weidner, G., and Matthews, K.A. (1978). 'Reported physical symptoms elicited by unpredictable events and the Type A coronary-prone behaviour pattern', *Journal of Personality and Social Psychology*, **36**, 1213–1220.
Weinshall, T.D. (ed) (1979). *Managerial Communication: Concepts Approaches and Techniques*. Academic Press, London.
Willits, R.D. (1967). 'Company performance and interpersonal relations', *Industrial Management Review*, **7**, 91–107.
Yarmey, D. (1979). *The Psychology of Eyewitness Testimony*, The Free Press, New York.
Yarmey, A.D., and Tressillian Jones, H. (1982). 'Police awareness of the fallibility of eyewitness identifications', *Canadian Police College Journal*, **6**, 113–124.
Young, J.W. (1978). 'The subordinate's exposure of organisational vulnerability to the superior: sex and organisational effects.' *Academy of Management Journal*, **21**, 113–122.
Zajonc, R.B. (1965). Social facilitation. *Science*, **149**, 269–274.
Zillman, D. (1979). *Hostility and Aggression*, Erlbaum, Hillsdale, New Jersey.
Zimbardo, P.G. (1970). The human choice: individuation, reason, and order versus deindividuation, impulse and chaos. In *Nebraska Symposium on Motivation*, (Eds. W.J. Arnold and D. Levine). University of Nebraska Press, Lincoln.

Index

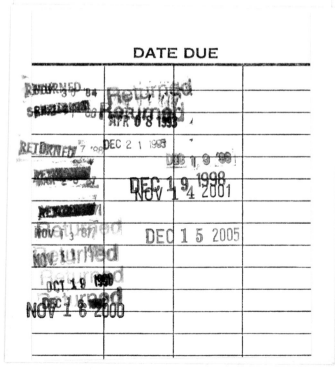